Abusive Endings

1. *The Trouble with Marriage: Feminists Confront Law and Violence in India*, by Srimati Basu

2. *Caught Up: Girls, Surveillance, and Wraparound Incarceration*, by Jerry Flores

3. *In Search of Safety: Confronting Inequality in Women's Imprisonment*, by Barbara Owen, James Wells, and Joycelyn Pollock

4. *Abusive Endings: Separation and Divorce Violence against Women*, by Walter S. DeKeseredy, Molly Dragiewicz, and Martin D. Schwartz

Abusive Endings

Separation and Divorce Violence against Women

WALTER S. DEKESEREDY,
MOLLY DRAGIEWICZ, AND
MARTIN D. SCHWARTZ

UNIVERSITY OF CALIFORNIA PRESS

University of California Press, one of the most distinguished university presses in the United States, enriches lives around the world by advancing scholarship in the humanities, social sciences, and natural sciences. Its activities are supported by the UC Press Foundation and by philanthropic contributions from individuals and institutions. For more information, visit www.ucpress.edu.

University of California Press
Oakland, California

© 2017 by The Regents of the University of California

Library of Congress Cataloging-in-Publication Data

Names: DeKeseredy, Walter S., 1959- author. |
  Dragiewicz, Molly, author. | Schwartz, Martin D.,
  author.
Title: Abusive endings : separation and divorce
  violence against women / Walter S. DeKeseredy,
  Molly Dragiewicz, and Martin D. Schwartz.
Description: Oakland, California : University of
  California Press, [2017] | Includes bibliographical
  references and index.
Identifiers: LCCN 2017005896 (print) |
  LCCN 2017011355 (ebook) | ISBN 9780520285743
  (cloth : alk. paper) | ISBN 9780520285750 (pbk. :
  alk. paper) | ISBN 9780520961159 (epub and ePDF)
Subjects: LCSH: Family violence—United States.
Classification: LCC HV6626.2 .D44 2017 (print) |
  LCC HV6626.2 (ebook) | DDC 362.82/920973—dc23
LC record available at
  https://lccn.loc.gov/2017005896

Manufactured in the United States of America

25 24 23 22 21 20 19 18 17
10 9 8 7 6 5 4 3 2 1

*To the female survivors of separation/divorce violence
and the front-line workers who help them*

CONTENTS

Preface ix

Acknowledgments xi

1. Conceptualizing Separation/Divorce Violence against Women   1

2. The Extent and Distribution of Separation/Divorce Assault   29

3. New Technologies and Separation/Divorce Violence against Women   65

4. Explaining Separation/Divorce Violence against Women   86

5. Children as Collateral Victims of Separation/Divorce Woman Abuse   115

6. What Is to Be Done about Separation/Divorce Violence against Women?   141

Notes 175

References 181

Index 221

This book examines violence committed, mostly against women, by partners after they begin to leave, while they leave, or after they leave an intimate relationship. The U.S. Department of Justice's National Crime Victimization Survey (NCVS), the largest American survey of victimization, provides information on this crime. Figure 1 was created by Martin D. Schwartz from combined data from the years 2003 through 2012, and it shows the rates of victimization for each marital status, per 1,000 persons in the population aged 12 or more. Offenders in this chart include current or former spouses, boyfriends, or girlfriends (Truman and Morgan 2014, 11).

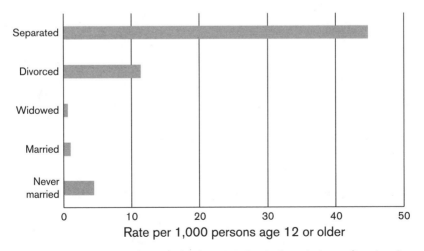

Figure 1. The risk, by marital status, of violent victimization by an intimate. (Developed by Martin D. Schwartz from government records and documents.)

ACKNOWLEDGMENTS

This book is a collective effort. Not only is it coauthored but it is also heavily informed by loved ones, caring friends, and inspiring colleagues. We must first thank Claire Renzetti for encouraging us to take on this project and for the countless other things she has done for us over the past thirty years. Special thanks also go to Maura Roessner, senior acquisitions editor at the University of California Press. Her keen insight made this book much better than it otherwise would have been. We were also greatly aided by Jack Collins, Molly Yeager, and Rachel Fairchild, who did yeoman work trying to keep up with all of our changes, updates, and fixes.

Over the years, we have greatly benefited from the comments, criticisms, lessons, emotional support, and influences of many people. They include (while hoping we have not left too many out): Rowland Atkinson, Bernie Auchter, Karen Bachar, Ronet Bachman, Gregg Barak, Ola Barnett, Raquel Bergen, Helene Berman, Rebecca Block, Jan Breckenridge, Anne Brewster, Avi Brisman, Henry Brownstein, Liqun Cao, Steve Cake, Gail Caputo, Gary Cassagnol, Susan Caringella, Pat Carlen, Kerry Carrington, Bill Chambliss, Meda Chesney-Lind, Ann Coker, Kimberly Cook, Terry Cox, Wesley Crichlow, Francis T. Cullen, Elliott Currie, Kathleen Daly, Juergen Dankwort, Jodie Death, Joseph F. Donnermeyer, Desmond Ellis, Rachel Fairchild, Jeff Ferrell, Bonnie Fisher, William F. Flack Jr., Diane Follingstad, David O. Friedrichs, Rus Funk, Alberto Godenzi, Edward Gondolf, Carol Gregory, Steve Hall, Amanda Hall-Sanchez, Barbara Hart, Ronald Hinch, Kate Hoffman, Sandra Huntzinger, Mark Israel, Rita Kanarek, Peter Kraska,

David Kauzlarich, Dorie Klein, Clifford Jansen, Victor Kappeler, Mary Koss, Salley Laskey, Julian Lo, Michael J. Lynch, Brian MacLean, Louise McOrmond-Plummer, Daniel Martinez, Anne Menard, James Messerschmidt, Raymond Michalowski, Bill Miller, Jody Miller, Susan L. Miller, Dragan Milovanovic, Jayne Mooney, Warren S. E. Morgan, Louise Moyer, Christopher Mullins, Kyle Mulrooney, Darlene Murphy, Stephen Muzzatti, Heather Nancarrow, Nancy Neylon, James Nolan, Patrik Olsson, Sue Osthoff, Reiko Ozaki, Sandy Ortman, Barbara Owen, Ellen Pence, Ruth Peterson, Lori Post, Gary Potter, Mike Presdee, James Ptacek, Callie Rennison, Robin Robinson, Jeffrey Ian Ross, Dawn Rothe, Michale Salter, Linda Saltzman, Daniel Saunders, Donna Selman, Aysan Sev'er, Susan Sharp, Michael D. Smith, Natalie Sokoloff, Betsy Stanko, Cris Sullivan, Thomas Sutton, Kenneth Tunnell, Ron Weitzer, David Wiesenthal, Simon Winlow, Jock Young, Julia Zafferano, and Joan Zorza. Since many of these people disagree with one another, we accept full responsibility for the information presented in this book.

Over the years, we have greatly benefited from the assistance of many practitioners heavily involved in the constant struggle to end woman abuse. People affiliated with Luke's Place, the Ontario Women's Directorate, the Ohio Attorney General's Office, the Ohio Domestic Violence Network, the Athens County Coalition Against Sexual Assault, My Sister's Place of Athens, various social services based in Athens and other parts of Ohio, the California Coalition Against Sexual Assault, and other organizations contributed to our empirical, theoretical, and political efforts.

Abusive Endings could not have been completed without the ongoing support of our loved ones. Carol Blum has been a rock of support and a helpful critic for more than thirty years.

Pat and Andrea DeKeseredy were always there when we needed them. Walter's "fur children" Bennie, Captain, Higgins, Jinksie, Noodle, and Pheobe were also key sources of social support. Snicker helped Marty by eating all the bacon. Hershey was of no help whatsoever.

Molly Dragiewicz would like to thank Matt Benner, Lucy Brenner, Kay Dragiewicz, Judy Dragiewicz, Larry Dragiewicz, and Marc Dragiewicz for their ongoing love and support. She would also like to thank her lovely colleagues in the School of Justice and Faculty of Law at QUT for making it such a positive work environment. She is grateful for the inspiration and advice that she gets in real life and online from her involvement with the American Society of Criminology Division on Women and Crime and all of her DV friends and colleagues.

The cover for this book was adapted from *A Survivor's Journey: The Domestic Violence Awareness Mural*, which was painted in 2010 in Washington, D.C., by artist and educator Joel Bergner, who is the codirector of the organization Artolution. For this project, he partnered with the organization DASH (District Alliance for Safe Housing). The mural was designed based on interviews with survivors of domestic violence and depicts their experiences overcoming past trauma and looking toward a brighter future. Joel's work can be seen at www.joelartista.com and www.artolution.org. We thank Joel for letting us use his beautiful mural as the cover art for this book. His work makes a positive contribution to neighborhoods around the world.

CHAPTER ONE

Conceptualizing Separation/Divorce Violence against Women

[M]ale partners believe they, and not their wives or third parties such as judges and lawyers, are primarily responsible for deciding when they are truly separated or even divorced from the female partners who left them.

Ellis, Stuckless, and Smith 2015, 2

The argument above applies not only to patriarchal married men but also to many sexist males in cohabiting and more casual relationships. As we have repeatedly stated elsewhere (e.g., DeKeseredy and Schwartz 2009), numerous men, regardless of the type of intimate union they want to maintain, have a "fanatical determination" to prevent their partners from exiting a relationship. They use a variety of means to try "to keep them in their place" (Russell 1990). Sometimes these methods turn out to be lethal, and the motivation may be mixed with some notion of "If I can't have you then no one can." Researchers have termed the killing of females by male partners *intimate femicide* (Adams 2007; Dobash and Dobash 2015).

Jody Lee Hunt has provided a recent example. On December 1, 2014, he murdered his former girlfriend Sharon Kay Berkshire, two of her lovers (Michael Frum and Jody Taylor), and Doug Brady, a business competitor, before killing himself. These were not Hunt's first violent acts nor his first act of violence against women. He had committed a number of the acts that many researchers claim are risk factors associated with intimate femicide, and, in fact, Berkshire herself had filed restraining orders against him in late 2013 and October 2014. For example, in 1999, Hunt had abducted and held his pregnant girlfriend at gunpoint for several hours in a Winchester, Virginia, auto-parts factory before surrendering to police. He was sentenced to three years in prison for this, though Virginia allowed him to serve his time concurrently with a five-year term in West Virginia for wanton endangerment (Licata, Fehrens, and Hoff 2014). With an earlier Pennsylvania conviction, this gave Hunt criminal convictions in three states. In 2006, he was court ordered to pay more than $12,000 in back child support (Stroud and Mattise 2014).

Mass murderers tend to be greeted with outrage in the media. In Hunt's case, however, his prior hurtful conduct received short shrift from the local mainstream media when compared to the journalistic attention focused on suggestions from friends and family that he was not, in fact, a violent man. After he killed four people, the press reported such reactions as "I just think the man had a total breakdown. Overwhelmed from the grief of a love lost and money problems" (cited in Mayo 2014, 1). One of Hunt's friends was quoted in a local newspaper as saying, "Our Jody wasn't that man." Hunt's second cousin said that he "was the type of person that wanted to help everybody out" (cited in DPost.com 2014, 1). And Brian Nicholson, one of Hunt's employees, said, "But he wasn't (enraged). He held it in. But a body can only take so much, I guess" (cited in Goldstein 2014, 1). After being sure to portray Hunt as basically a good man who suddenly "lost it," a local newspaper, the *Dominion Post*, published a lead story two days after the killings about a candlelight vigil held for Hunt at J&J Towing and Repair.

What compels a man such as Jody Hunt to commit murder? Certainly it is easy to dismiss him as a man who is sick or "mentally disturbed," as Monongalia County Sheriff Al Kisner did. However, one aim of this book is to debunk the myth that men who kill intimate partners are all mentally disturbed. Of course, some killers do have serious mental health problems (just as there are such people in all walks of everyday life), but the truth is that most men who engage in lethal and nonlethal violence against women are "less pathological than expected" (Gondolf 1999, 1). Men with serious mental disorders account for only about 10 percent of all incidents of intimate violence (DeKeseredy 2011). Much more will be said about intimate femicide in relationships and why men kill the women who want to, are trying to, or who actually leave them, in Chapters 2 and 4. Our concern in this book is with violence against these women (and the peripheral damage visited on people nearby, as seen in the Hunt case).

An important definitional problem faces us immediately, however. What *is* separation/divorce violence? Sometimes it is easy to define. Violence after a formal court ordered declaration of divorce can usually be simple to categorize. People who have court orders of formal separation can also be delineated. However, sometimes people are effectively separated without meeting the technical requirements for legal separation. Others, we argue, are effectively separated even without living apart. Thus, one of the objectives of this first chapter is to challenge the "common sense" notion that it is essential for a couple to be living apart to be considered separated or divorced. We will make the case for a broad, gender-specific definition of separation/divorce violence.

DEFINITION OF SEPARATION AND DIVORCE

New studies on the topics covered in this book are being conducted, and some new theories are being constructed, but one thing the social scientific community has not agreed on is a firm definition of separation/divorce (DeKeseredy and Schwartz 2011).[1] Among those who study intimate relationships, the problem of defining violence against women[2] has led to scholarly debates that are "old, fierce, and unlikely to be resolved in the near future" (Kilpatrick 2004, 1218). This debate has been duplicated in this newer and more narrow field of conceptualizing separation/divorce violence. Although researchers here tend to admire each other's work, they remain divided into two camps (DeKeseredy and Rennison, 2013b) over the question of whether there must be physical separation to be included in this category. This is hardly a trivial concern, because how relationships and behaviors are defined can have major effects on the lives of people. Definitions are used as tools in social struggles. For example, one powerful political tool has been the rate of unemployment in a society, but little attention is paid by the general public to how these figures are derived. Is a graduate research engineer who works twenty hours a week for minimum wage at an ice cream stand over the summer fully employed? Is someone who has spent years looking for a new job but has now given up and sits at home awaiting word of some new opportunity an unemployed person? Usually, the answer is that the first is fully employed, and the second is no longer unemployed because she has stopped actively applying for jobs. Similarly, the definition of the poverty line is both a political tool and a practical one. Setting the line low, or not changing it with inflation, means that fewer people are "living in poverty," although they are as poor as ever. If the poverty line determines things such as who qualifies for shelter or subsidized housing or food aid, it can have major health consequences also. Violence against women is another politicized topic, and the definitions we devise and the way we use concepts turn back on us and reflect a particular reality (DeKeseredy and Schwartz 2011). Just as we can reduce the number of people living in "poverty" by changing the definition of poverty, we can devise definitions in the violence against women arena that ignore and abandon many women.

Thus, to define separation/divorce violence, we must first decide what constitutes "separation." One way to do this is to look at the legal definition. Jody Hunt and Sharon Berkshire had lived together, but she had moved out. However, West Virginia law defines legal separation only in terms of a temporary status for married couples preparatory to divorce (HG.org 2015). In fact, Berkshire had completely severed the relationship with Hunt and had begun a new relationship with Michael Frum, and later moved in with him. Hunt had no legal ties to her of any sort. Does this mean that they were not "separated" and that his crime was not one of separation/divorce violence?

But that is not the major problem here. Most social scientific studies of separation/divorce assault are willing to assume that any couple formerly living together and now separated physically can be considered to be separated or divorced.[3] For example, Brownridge (2009) restricts his analysis to "post-separation violence," which he defines as "any type of violence perpetrated by a former married or cohabiting male partner or boyfriend subsequent to the moment of physical separation" (56). Although this definition would cover Hunt/Berkshire, we would disagree with both his conceptualization and with state laws as being too narrow. Separation and divorce are not functions only of proximity and physical space. We agree with Brownridge that a woman does not have to be legally related to a man to experience separation/divorce abuse. The problem is that many women remain in the same households as their male partners but are emotionally separated from them. One definition of emotional separation, a major predictor of a permanent end to a relationship, is a woman's denial or restriction of sexual relations and other intimate exchanges (Ellis and DeKeseredy 1997). Of course, it may involve a variety of activities to disentangle oneself emotionally from a partner, even if a strategic decision is made to continue to engage in sexual relations. This distancing, indeed, may not involve any outward behavior changes in the woman. However, recognizably emotionally exiting a relationship can be just as dangerous as physically or legally exiting one because it, too, increases the likelihood of male violence and other types of abuse, including stalking and sexual assault (Block and DeKeseredy 2007; DeKeseredy and Schwartz 2009; McFarlane and Malecha 2005). Of course, many women emotionally exit a relationship before ending it with physical separation and are not subjected to violence, just as many women physically separate and divorce men without later physical violence. The issue here is that, by defining separation as requiring physical separation, one defines away the great many cases where women who are not yet ready economically or emotionally (or are too frightened to leave) are subjected to physical, psychological, or economic violence—or even lethal violence.

Female emotional exits are common, especially if women are in abusive relationships and have difficulties leaving. This may not be a linear process, where emotional separation builds until the day that she moves out or begins a discussion of why he needs to move out. All too often it is unplanned, precipitated or propelled forward by unexpected events or playing out in unplanned-for directions. A difficulty in moving forward might be financial, in that she may not be able to set up a new household, especially if she has children. Sometimes the difficulty is fear, when she believes his claims that he will kill her if she leaves. She may leave, only to have him track her down and force her to return. Often the problem is that she has no support from her family, her friends, the police, or the clergy, who all may tell her that her place is with her husband (R. Klein 2012). Of course, there are other reasons and stories. None of this is new or unknown to workers in the field. These are not the women who, according to a popular belief, are "unable to make decisions in their own interest" (Davies, Lyon, and Monti-Catania 1998, 14). Rather, Okun (1986) found that women left their abusers an average of five times before permanently successfully ending the relationship. Horton and Johnson (1993) reported in their study that it took women who were leaving abusive men an average of eight years to permanently exit.

What is often not discussed in the field is that large numbers of women emotionally exit their relationship but remain physically "based on whether they have the resources and social support necessary to leave an abusive relationship, the assailants' expected responses, and the fact that the assailants' behavior is not within their control unless society cooperates" (Goodkind et al. 2003, 350). Resources and social support are vital if a woman is to safely exit a dangerous relationship. This may involve neighbors providing a safe place to sleep, supportive relatives, community social service agencies willing to help her set up a new home, or finding the fairly large amount of money that it takes in many cities to get an apartment and make down payments on utilities, in addition to obtaining furniture and clothes. If she has children, the financial and emotional toll expands dramatically (R. Klein 2012), and many options may be legally closed off to her.

If a survivor's neighbors, relatives, or community members adhere to "nonintervention norms" (Browning 2002), she may have no options but to stay and instead to engage in emotional exiting. A survivor of separation/divorce assault interviewed by DeKeseredy and Schwartz (2009) provides a powerful example:

> There was too many of them that stood out of their homes and it was really aggravating, really aggravating when, I mean, it took my son to beg for my life. But here is our neighbors out here, seeing this man beat this female off the swing set, beating her with his fist, kicking her with his feet, grabbing her by the hair of her head, smearing her face and what, . . . you're gonna stand up there and aren't gonna call the law? Or you are gonna stand up there and you aren't gonna come down? . . . But they could clearly see us. And they was outside standing and he was just thumping me so hard, so hard. And nobody called the law. Nobody did. Nobody came down to yank him off me. Nobody did anything. (11)

Although social scientists have long studied events where witnesses fail to help someone being attacked, it is unclear whether nonintervention norms are more prominent in rural than in urban areas. Recently, online bulletin boards lit up across the country debating the wisdom of intervention after the July 4, 2015, stabbing up to forty times of a young man being robbed on a busy MetroRail (subway) train in Washington, D.C. (CBS News 2015). There is no guarantee that neighbors or the public will intervene in any attack, and there are plenty of people and police to argue that it is always a bad idea for untrained members of the public to intervene, because they too can then get hurt (Dvorak 2015).

As will be made more explicit in Chapter 4, many women can only emotionally exit because they have a well-founded fear of physically leaving their partners due to these men's extremely jealous and possessive behaviors. We could provide readers with numerous examples of women terrified to "flee the house of horrors" because they have routinely heard their partners say "If I can't have you, nobody can," "You have no right to leave me," and "I own you" (Adams 2007, 166; Sev'er 2002). Such fear is not at all irrational. These threats are all too often real: the risk of lethal and nonlethal assaults peaks in the first two months following separation and when women attempt permanent separation through legal or other means (DeKeseredy and Schwartz 2009; Ellis, Stuckless, and Smith 2015). It is thus not surprising to hear that many of Stark's (2007) female clients told him that "they were never more frightened than in the days, weeks, or months after they moved out" (116).

The above relatively short time frame is referred to by Ellis, Stuckless, and Smith (2015) as the *proximal* phase of separation: the two- to "six-month period immediately following the female partner's move to a separate residence and the initiation of formal separation proceedings" (9–10). More specifically, Ellis and his colleagues identify two other phases, covering the period before the man finds out that she plans to leave (acute), and the period more than six months after separation (distal). They found that the risk of male-to-female violence varied in each phase, with the risk highest in the proximal phase. Although these categories are quite helpful and do underline the great danger in the period immediately following the physical separation, there is another phase that these researchers left out: the period between the time that the man realizes that the woman is going to separate, and the time that she actually does. This would include the time when she is actually in the process of moving out. Although this area has not been well studied, we would argue that this is, in fact, the most dangerous phase of all. One important piece of evidence came in DeKeseredy and Schwartz's (2009) qualitative study of separation/divorce sexual assault in rural southeast Ohio. There, thirty-two (74 percent) of the forty-three victimized women interviewed were sexually assaulted when they expressed a desire to leave a relationship but before they actually took the physical step of separation. Twenty-one (49 percent) were sexually abused when they were trying to leave or while they were leaving, and fourteen (33 percent) were victimized after they left. Sexual assault may or may not have a slightly different dynamic than the physical assault that we are talking about in this chapter, but it does give us reason to believe that physical assault would follow the same pattern. Much more difficult to measure might be lethal assault (Dobash and Dobash 2015), which we also suggest would peak right after the woman announces a decision to leave.

There are other problems with legal definitions of separation/divorce and the one offered by Brownridge (2009). Overall, outside of the violence literature, there has been extensive discussion of the fact that separation and divorce is a process, and one that might go forward and backward in fits and starts. It may begin long before anyone moves out or initiates legal proceedings, and it may continue long after the divorce is final. However, researchers actively gathering data find that they must develop a working definition of concepts like separation, such as defining its beginning to be when someone moves out. A major point here is that researchers must be careful to provide and follow definitions of what they are studying, as it can affect the findings. Noting the limitations of any particular definition or research decision would also be helpful. As mentioned earlier, defining separation as beginning at physical parting would have the effect of ignoring the large number of beatings, rapes, and other attacks that occur when a woman emotionally exits a relationship but remains in the home, when she decides to leave her partner, or when she makes an unsuccessful escape from a "dangerous domain" (DeKeseredy 2014; Johnson 1996; Ptacek 1999). With various studies using different definitions of separation/divorce, there is an obvious concern for accuracy and the ability to generalize. Our preference is to include all victimized women into such surveys, rather than to define many of them out of the sample. Again, these are not esoteric academic disputes but can have real consequences in many arenas. Activists have long known that there are many calls for limiting the amount of money for social services, and that the struggle for effective social support services can be hindered by definitions that exclude many victimized women. Restrictive definitions result in lower estimates of abuse, which can ultimately decrease the probability of scarce resources being mobilized to curb separation/divorce assault and other variants of female victimization in intimate contexts (DeKeseredy 1995; DeKeseredy and Rennison 2013b; Smith 1994).

For many years, researchers of violence against women have known that the decision to permanently leave a relationship may be long and complex, taking difficult and challenging turns (Kirkwood 1993; Goetting 1999). It is, as mentioned above, a process rather than a decision. A woman may simultaneously feel oppressed and trapped by an inability to leave a relationship. This incapacity may stem from a fear of being killed, financial or economic reasons, a lack of adequate arrangements to care for her children, or a variety of other reasons (Davies 2011; Renzetti 2011). Generally, exiting a relationship takes place over time (DeKeseredy and Rennison 2013b; Mahoney 1991). Definitions that arbitrarily require the woman to have physically left the home can only result in underreporting the extent of violence against separating women.

Many definitions also fail to mention cohabitation. This is problematic because, though "a marriage license is a hitting license" (Straus, Gelles, and Steinmetz 1981), "a marriage license probably does not change the dynamic of . . . abuse within an ongoing intimate relationship" (Campbell 1989, 336). As a matter of fact, a metastudy of various studies that compared married to cohabiting men found that cohabiting men are at least twice as likely to beat female intimates as are married men, with some studies suggesting that the cohabiting rate is four times the married rate (Brownridge and Halli 2001).

Looking at sexual abuse, Canadian national survey data show that many women are sexually abused by their common-law partners, and male cohabitors are more likely to sexually abuse their partners than are men in casual or serious dating relationships (DeKeseredy and Schwartz 1998). More relevant to this book is Finkelhor and Yllo's (1985) finding that 20 percent of the women in their sample who had separated from cohabitors experienced forced sex, along with 23 percent of currently cohabiting women, compared to 3 percent of married women. Fully 25 percent of all of the women who were legally separated or divorced reported experiencing forced sex. This was a study of what many call marital rape, so physical, economic, or emotional violence was not included. The difficulty is that this survey did not specify when the violence occurred—whether it was before the separation, during, or after. However, one study that underscored the danger of terminating a cohabiting relationship was DeKeseredy and Schwartz's (2009). There, of the eighteen cohabiting women in this qualitative series of interviews about sexual assault, twelve (67 percent) stated that they were sexually assaulted when they expressed their desire to leave their relationship. More research on the violent outcomes of ending a common-law union is much needed, but the limited work done so far strongly suggests that definitions of separation and divorce should include people who fall under this intimate relationship status category.

Based on an in-depth review of the extant literature, "separation and divorce" here means physically, legally, or emotionally exiting a marital or cohabiting relationship (DeKeseredy and Schwartz 2009). Consistent with our previous work on this topic, we focus on women-initiated exits because "they are the decisions that challenge male hegemony the most" (Se'ver 1997, 567). Our definition is broad, since legal and other complexities complicate the picture when trying for a narrow definition. A woman might emotionally initiate the separation, but the man may be the one who files for a divorce or moves out. Even in these situations, she might continue to consider herself the one who left (Hopper 1993).

SUGGESTIONS FOR FUTURE EFFORTS TO CONCEPTUALIZE SEPARATION/DIVORCE

Our definition does not cover all possible situations of separation and divorce violence.[4] Brownridge's (2009) definition, which is more narrow than ours, has an element missing from other feminist conceptualizations. His definition was "any type of violence perpetrated by a former married or cohabiting male partner or boyfriend subsequent to the moment of physical separation" (56). This recognizes that dating breakups may also be dangerous. Most separation/divorce assault studies have overlooked this possibility (Brogan 2013). However, some researchers have gathered data on the stalking of ex-girlfriends and male "minor aggression," such as making threats (Edwards and Gidycz 2014; Fisher, Daigle, and Cullen 2010; Williams and Frieze 2005), but not in the broader context of examining separation assault. It is logical to assume that researchers would uncover a high rate of victimization during and after the process of leaving a dating relationship given the alarmingly high rates of various types of male-to-female abuse in teen and adult dating relationships.[5]

There are also other important relationships and victimized people who have been left out of a literature heavily marked by heteronormativity. As Ball (2013) puts it, "The existence of intimate partner violence within non-heterosexual and/or non-cisgendered relationships is gaining greater recognition" (186). Of course, similar omissions mark the bulk of the empirical, theoretical, and policy work on any type of intimate partner violence. There is, to be sure, much violence in same-sex relationships. Roughly one-third of lesbian, gay, and bisexual people experience physical violence of this type in their lifetime, and it is estimated that intimate sexual violence is experienced by 5 percent of LGB people during the same time frame (Messinger 2014). Nonetheless, we know little about the abuse that occurs during and after exiting same-sex unions. Block and DeKeseredy (2007) seem to be the only researchers thus far to conduct a separation/divorce assault study that reports data on harms done both to heterosexual women and to women trying to leave or who have left same-sex relationships. Messinger's (2014) comprehensive review of thirty-five years of research on what he refers to as "same-sex intimate partner violence" makes no mention of abuse that occurs during and after the process of relationship dissolution. Violence that occurs as part of exiting a relationship is certainly not purely a heterosexual phenomenon, and new conceptualizations should broaden to account for this reality.

The separation/divorce assault research community has responded faster to critiques of narrow definitions of violence or abuse than it has to narrow definitions of exiting. Perhaps it is because debates about defining abuse have a longer history, are more intense, and involve more researchers (DeKeseredy and Rennison 2013b) that the published materials on definitions are more numerous. Because this question is very important, we turn to a discussion of this issue next.

DEFINING VIOLENCE AGAINST WOMEN

Male separation/divorce assaults on women are social problems that challenge all of us to look at how we understand relationships, gender differences, power, and how to define male-to-female violence in intimate contexts.[6] But what, exactly, is violence against women, and why do we not offer the now commonly used term *intimate partner violence?* Before answering these questions, it is necessary to state that our conceptualization of violence against women is heavily informed by definitions provided by women who have been abused by men or are still being abused, as well as by people working on the front line (e.g., staff in battered women shelters) to help women and children who are living with abuse. Our definition is also informed by qualitative and quantitative research conducted by us and our colleagues in Canada, the United States, and Australia, but it is essential to prioritize experiential knowledge because it

> Challenges the usual tendency of social scientists to theorize *about* other people, rather than *with* them;
> Gives voice to at least some women who have been abused;
> Opens the doors to self-help and peer support programs in which women can share their experiences; and
> Helps those responding to violence against women to identify the need for change as different women with different experiences challenge what is accepted as "fact" or "truth" about woman abuse. (DeKeseredy and MacLeod 1997, 46)

When most people think of violence, they think of physical brutality. Many people also automatically think of cases of forced sexual penetration they may have heard about. But people who have experienced any type of physical violence often say that it is the psychological, verbal, and spiritual violence that hurts the most and longest (Walker 1979). NiCarthy (1986) developed some of the first descriptions of emotional abuse, but Kirkwood (1993) carefully worked out that there are different types of emotional violence. Some come from a reaction to the physical abuse, but another major component is the nonphysical acts aimed directly at causing an emotional reaction. Unlike conceptions such as the battered woman syndrome, which leaves one thinking of these women as pathologically damaged, this began the process of thinking of battered women, and particularly those who remain in a relationship for a time, as normal people caught in an abnormal and horrible set of circumstances, doing the best that they can.

For instance, all of the forty-three survivors of separation/divorce sexual assault interviewed by DeKeseredy and Schwartz (2009) developed adverse post-assault psychological conditions, such as depression, sexual aversion, and fear. This is not surprising, because, in addition to being sexually abused in a variety of ways, 88 percent were psychologically abused, 70 percent were economically abused, 12 percent had pets who were harmed by their abusers, 37 percent were stalked, and 51 percent experienced the destruction of prized possessions.

Rita, one of DeKeseredy and Schwartz's interviewees, is a prime example of a woman who has experienced considerable trauma related to nonphysical forms of separation/divorce assault:

> I could care less if I ever have sex again in my life. I could care less if I ever had another relationship with a man again in my life. Oh, it's scarred me for life. I think it's physically, mentally—well, maybe not so much physically—but emotionally has scarred me for life. You know, and that's the reason why I don't socialize myself with people. I isolate myself from people because if I don't, I get panic attacks. And the dreams, they, they're never gone. They're never gone. I mean, I don't care how much you try to put it out of your head, the dreams always bring it back, always. I've been in a sleep clinic where they would videotape me sleeping, being in and out of bed, crawling into a corner screaming. "Please don't hurt me, don't hurt me, don't shoot me, don't" whatever. (83)

Laureen is another interviewee who shared her traumatic psychological abuse experiences:

> And years ago, years ago, when I still only had one child, he told me he knew that I wanted out of the relationship and he said, "If I can't have you, I'm gonna make it so nobody can have you." And I didn't understand what he was talking about. And it was many, many years later that I realized he meant psychologically. He was going to destroy me psychologically so I wouldn't be fit to enter into another relationship. And it's basically true; I have not had another relationship. I'm afraid to go into a relationship. I don't trust men in general. So basically I live a solitary life, not by choice, but because I am afraid I'm going to end up in a relationship like that again. (84)

It is not unusual for police, courts, psychologists, and the general public to ignore psychological abuse. In many jurisdictions, the criminal justice system followed (and still follows today) what was informally called the "stitch rule": that the amount of harm done to you could be determined by how many stitches it took to sew you back up. Of course, if you did not have stitches, it was difficult to get any concern for your well-being. We have often described this to groups of men by asking them to recall the almost universal experience of a fight or bullying session in middle school, where they lost the fight and were humiliated. Many men can recall that humiliation twenty, thirty, or fifty years later, but they cannot recall just what their injuries were from that fight. Similarly, many battered women surprise the rest of us by claiming that a broken bone or a stitched-up cut really is not that big a deal: broken bones heal; psychological scars can last a lifetime.

This can also apply to the destruction of prized possessions. Once again, although this is something that has been long known, it has also been long ignored. For example, in the famed play *Trifles*,[7] first performed in 1916, Susan Glaspell provides the most important clue to the murder as the killing of Minnie's highly prized canary, no doubt by her husband. Glaspell recognized a century ago what eludes many of us today: that it can be worse to have your possessions ruined than to be beaten. Another example of both general destruction and specific harm to a pet was cited by Sev'er (1997):

> Laurette and Sue talked about the shattering of their treasured heirlooms in front of their eyes. Laurette's husband burned her books when she decided to take a few university courses. Daisy's husband slashed her favorite dress into ribbons so that she would not look pretty and "run away" with men. Ann's partner's violence extended to the cat she loved (and still keeps). He would raise the cat closer and closer to the revolving blades of the ceiling fan, and demand things that Ann did not want to do (such as swallowing large doses of sleeping pills). The partner kept her drowsy and docile and always told her that "she needed him." (580–81)

The entire relationship between physical violence and the emotional violence caused by the destruction of prized possessions was explained by a student of DeKeseredy's some years ago. This student was a photographer with aspirations to work for a high-profile magazine:

> Well, when my boyfriend broke my arm, I could go to the doctor and get a cast. When he punched me in the mouth and broke some of my teeth, I could go to the dentist and get them fixed. But, when he tore up my pictures, where

could I go for help? And, they were among the most important things in my life and I can't repair them.[8]

Another, admittedly extreme example has been given by historian Peterson del Mar (1996), quoting from a divorce petition from an impoverished California woman many years ago. She had "gotten a few things together" for the children on Christmas Eve, including gifts and a small tree. In this case, her husband never touched his wife or his kids, and certainly was not a traditional batterer. He came home late, drunk and angry:

> Upon entering the house and seeing the little tree, all fixed up, he became so angry that he took the tree and tore it to pieces, took all the little gifts and presents off of the tree and mutilated and destroyed them. . . . Not being satisfied with this, and while cursing and defaming the plaintiff, he took all of the table linen and mattress and sheets and quilts off the bed, took them to the kitchen and dumped them on the floor, gathered up all the food there was in the house and spilled these on the floor, put the cooking utensils on the floor and then took the stove pipe and dumped soot over the bed linen and food and everything he had put on the floor and then turned water all over this mess, then broke and tore up all the furniture. (124)

In this way, many women find that they have, over time, become controlled by a form of psychological abuse that creates "invisible chains" (Fontes 2015). Referred to as *coercive control,* this involves nonphysical behaviors that are often subtle, are hard to detect and prove, and seem more forgivable to people unfamiliar with the dynamics of violence against women. The primary objective of coercive control is to restrict a woman's liberties (Tanha et al. 2010). Common examples are stalking, threatening looks, criticism, and "microregulating a partner's behavior" (Kernsmith 2008; Stark 2007, 229).

Lisa Fontes has a Ph.D. in counseling psychology and has worked in the fields of child abuse, violence against women, and other family issues for over twenty-five years. She is also a survivor of coercive control as well as stalking, both during a relationship and after it ended. In her 2015 book written for the general public, she argues that exiting a relationship with a patriarchal, controlling man does not necessarily end the process of coercive control (Crossman, Hardesty, and Raffaelli 2016). In Box 1, Fontes describes what it feels like to be coercively controlled.

BOX 1. THE CONSEQUENCES OF COERCIVE CONTROL

From Fontes 2015, 5

Victims of coercive control often feel like hostages. Over time, being grilled, criticized, and shamed may come to seem routine. Victims often blame themselves as they feel despairing and disoriented. It can be hard for them to figure out exactly what's wrong. Isolated and humiliated, some women lose confidence and accept their partner's view of reality. They may have trouble deciding whether their partners are doing and saying hurtful things out of love and concern—as claimed—or out of cruelty. They may feel confused as they are told again and again that they themselves have triggered their partner's behaviors by doing something wrong. At the same time, to keep the peace in their relationship, victims may detach from family and friends, contacting them less and less often until they lose touch with many of the people they care about most. Unfortunately, the victims typically do not see the connection between their partner's control and their own isolation until time has passed. Losing self-confidence and close relationships at the same time can be paralyzing.

Women who get caught in the web of a controlling man are no different from other women. They just had the bad luck to become involved romantically with a controlling person at a time when they were especially vulnerable. Once a controlling man has caught a woman in his web, he will do everything he can to prolong the relationship.

Kirkwood (1993) describes this as "the web of emotional abuse," where, like a spider's web, a number of factors (fear, degradation, objectification, deprivation, overburden of responsibility, and distortion of subjective reality) are all intertwined so that the whole is more powerful than the sum of the parts. She reports that "the insidious nature of emotional abuse [is] that it is experienced as a subtle, nearly invisible process through which the fundamental components of its impact are ingrained in women, and as a result their escapes are complex and powerful" (60–61).

However, not all forms of coercive control are the same; some are more extreme than others. This is why Fontes (2015) states that coercive control exists on a continuum, and she defines the most extreme cases as examples of *coercive entrapment*. These means of denying women liberty are, according to her, "strategies . . . intensified by structural inequalities that further deprive victims of resources. The victim feels trapped, isolated, fearful, and threatened almost constantly. She may lose a sense of herself as an independent human being" (9).

Nickie was interviewed by DeKeseredy and Schwartz (2009), and her experiences exemplify what it is like to be hurt by coercive entrapment:

> I was his property that he wanted to own me. And I was his. That's how he looked at it. I was his property, and that's all that I felt I was to him, was just a lay, you know. But that's all he wanted me for was to satisfy himself. . . . He would deprive me. It was more of a mental torture, emotionally, mental torture than physical except in the sex it was physical. "You're mine and I'm gonna have you whether you want it or not. I want you." He was in control. And that's what it's all about with men like that. They have to be in control. (72)

All told, coercive control is an integral component of separation/divorce assault. As Stark (2007) puts it, its "cumulative effect . . . can be a hostage-like state of physical paralysis, subjugation, and chronic fear that has no counterpart in any other crime in private or public life" (244). This, then, is another one of the major reasons for using a broad conceptualization of separation/divorce violence against women, one that includes the physical, sexual, and emotional attacks on women while they work to try to remove themselves from the relationship, in addition to attacks after physical separation. For the purposes of this book, it is defined as the misuse of power by a partner or ex-partner against a woman, commonly resulting in a loss of dignity, control, and safety as well as a feeling of powerlessness and entrapment, and experienced by the woman as the direct target of physical, psychological, economic, sexual, verbal, and/or spiritual abuse. Separation/divorce violence also includes persistent threats or forcing women to witness violence against their children, other relatives, friends, pets, and/or cherished possessions (DeKeseredy and MacLeod 1997).

There are sound, empirically driven reasons for including harms done to children, other relatives, friends, pets, and/or cherished possessions in our definition. For instance, during the course of women's dangerous exits, "children can become unfortunate pawns in the violent games" played by male ex-partners (Polk 1994, 143), often being used to control the mothers (Beeble, Bybee, and Sullivan 2007). The son of one rural woman interviewed by DeKeseredy and Schwartz (2009) is just one example of a child who had a legitimate fear of being killed due to the abuse he and his mother endured during the process of leaving her husband. Agnes said, "My son automatically locks the doors when he gets into the house. He only sleeps with the dog. He has to have the dog in his room at night because that's his warning signal" (90).

Agnes's son is alive. Luke Schillings, however, is among a group of children who have died as a result of male ex-partners' attempts to regain control over the women who leave them. In over three-quarters of murder-suicides in Canada involving a child victim like him, the offender experienced intimate partner relationship problems (Jaffe et al. 2014). Luke lived in Ontario, Canada, and despite pleas from his mother, the Ontario family court process allowed his father, Paul, to have unsupervised access visits. The first visit was also the last. Paul strangled and burned 3-year-old Luke to death and then committed suicide at the crime scene (Kingston Frontenac Anti-Violence Coordinating Committee 2015).

What Paul Schillings did is referred to by social scientists as *retaliating filicide* or, in layperson's terms, the "deliberate murder of a child to cause harm and suffering to the other parent" (Jaffe et al. 2014, 12). Not enough attention is paid to the intersections of violence and abuse after separation with a family court system that is increasingly likely to force abused mothers into ongoing contact with their abuser (Dragiewicz and DeKeseredy 2008; Fields 2008). The limited research on outcomes for children following separation/divorce that considers the quality of the relationship prior to and following divorce indicates that continued exposure to "high conflict" is harmful for children (Jaffe, Lemon, and Poisson 2003; Jaffe et al. 2014). The courts have all but ignored these findings on harm to children from continued exposure to violence against women and the sizeable body of research on how exposure to woman abuse harms children. For example, children exposed to their mothers' being beaten by their fathers are significantly more likely to engage later in delinquent acts. One way to sharply reduce the number of children in juvenile court would be to end the violence against their mothers (Schwartz 1989). Interestingly, much of the academic literature has focused on how battering changes the mother's behavior, such that the child's problems are the fault of the mother's child-rearing deficiencies. Greeson and colleagues (2014) recently turned their attention to this issue, and they discovered that it was the battering behavior of the father that affected the children negatively, not the mother's changed parenting.

Similarly, courts are influenced by the extensive family studies research cited in support of "friendly parent" and other family preservation initiatives that simply ignore the existence of violence and abuse—and its effects—in the home. In an ideal world, it always sounds nice to proclaim goals in favor of family preservation, and courts and legislatures commonly proclaim these goals, but the end result of ignoring the research on abused women and the outcomes for children, or ignoring men's violence to focus on deficiencies in parenting skills by the mother, is to make it easier for more innocent children like Luke Schillings to be killed.

INTIMATE PARTNER VIOLENCE?

One thing that sets this book apart from many other contemporary materials in the field is that we do not use the term *intimate partner violence*. We understand why the term is popular and that it is used by many people who are concerned about doing the right thing. For example, numerous academics, practitioners, and activists are concerned that terms such as "woman abuse" or "violence against women" are not inclusive, since they do not include abuse against men.[9] We understand this, but we still feel that gender-neutral terms are problematic for two reasons. First, regardless of why people use this or other gender-neutral terms (e.g., "domestic violence"), such language suggests that violence results from ordinary, everyday social interactions in the family or other intimate relationships that have gone wrong and that women are just as responsible for the problem as men (DeKeseredy and Schwartz 2013; Meloy and Miller 2011). This is not a minor linguistic technicality. Modern society is rife with various efforts to blame women for men's violence. For example, during the fall of 2014, it was not uncommon to hear people (including many sports broadcasters) across North America publicly state that National Football League player Ray Rice was not entirely to blame for delivering an extremely brutal punch to his fiancée's face in an elevator that was caught on video. To many, this claim was buttressed by her public defense of his violent behavior. The Baltimore Ravens used their Twitter account on May 23, 2014, to send out a message they claimed was from her, saying that "she deeply regrets the role that she played that night in the incident." Evidently the story was that she had talked back to him, which of course fully justified (to many people) an exceptionally strong professional athlete hitting her hard enough to knock her unconcious, so that she had to be dragged out of the elevator. The message that women are responsible for men's behavior is of course internalized by many women and men in society, and it is used to justify (to many) a great deal of brutal violence.

It is also common for many of the people who use gender-neutral definitions to assert that women are as violent as men. For decades, some antifeminist researchers have made this claim and continue to do so today (e.g., Dutton 2012; Straus 2014). There is ample scientific evidence that disproves this assertion, but it is beyond the scope of this book to review the large body of relevant research that demonstrates, without a doubt, that women are the primary targets of intimate violence in adult and adolescent heterosexual relationships.[10] This is not to argue that men are not the primary targets of non-intimate violence, or that women never harm men. It is to argue that the primary offenders are men and the primary targets are women, except perhaps when the very political and highly flawed Conflict Tactics Scale is used to show that women are violent.

For these reasons, we feel that it is essential to clearly name what it is that we are talking about. Although it may be perfectly legitimate in certain contexts to be talking about both male-on-female and female-on-male violence, this is not one of those contexts. The violence we are talking about is primarily perpetrated by men, and the persons who are the objects of that violence are primarily women. Thus, we use the terms "violence against women" or "woman abuse" throughout this book. Of course, there are times we will use other terms, such as in direct quotes or when describing a situation. Certainly one can say that someone was killed by an intimate partner, or that the violence took place in a domestic setting. The problem comes when naming an entire class of behavior "intimate partner violence" or "domestic violence," when the topic under discussion is in fact male violence against women.

THE ANTIFEMINIST BACKLASH

We would be remiss not to point out that an enormous audience exists today for those whom Schwartz and DeKeseredy (1994) refer to as "people without data," whose declarations that women are as violent as men are disseminated by the mainstream mass media and via the Internet. As the term implies, this refers to the large group of columnists, politicians, bloggers, and media trolls who find it simple to dismiss mountains of careful and expensive research in favor of ideological belief, personal opinion, or a few examples plucked out of the universe. One of the latest groups of people to fall under this category is a cohort that masculinities theorist Kimmel (2013) identifies as a "new breed of angry white men" who are experiencing *aggrieved entitlement:* "It is that sense that those benefits to which you believed yourself entitled have been snatched away from you by unseen forces larger and more powerful. You feel yourself to be the heir to a great promise, the American Dream, which has turned into an impossible fantasy for the very people who were *supposed* to inherit it" (18, emphasis in original). The "American Dream" Kimmel refers to is one in which white men are superior to and receive more privileges than women and ethnic minorities. Their rage is expressed in many contexts and ways. In one of the most extreme, in 2015 one of these men, Dylann Roof, killed nine people of color inside the Emanuel African Methodist Episcopal Church in Charleston, South Carolina. In addition to a history of racism, he also had a sense of aggrieved entitlement. Just before shooting, "He just said, 'I have to do it.' He said, 'You rape our women, and you're taking over our country. And you have to go'" (cited in RT 2015, 1).

Roof's actions are at the extreme end of the Angry White Men behavioral continuum, but even the most cursory look at the Internet will turn up many examples. Kimmel (2013) reminds us: "The Internet provides . . . a man cave, a politically incorrect locker room, . . . where no one knows that you're the jerk you secretly think you might be. That's a recipe for rage (115). Many Internet sites, such as National Public Radio, are beginning to close down reader comment sections to stop the enormous flow of vitriol. Such comments show up in virtually every possible site. Sometimes they are organized. For example, when Raphael published *Rape Is Rape* (2013) it was to rave reviews, including five-star reviews from every Amazon reviewer who was verified as a purchaser of the book. However, another forty one-star reviews were posted by people who had not purchased the book, mostly repeating the same accusation that a minor fact on one page was an error, which invalidated the entire point of the book (that there are rape deniers who are actively involved in a backlash against women). Generally, there is no sexual assault story too horrific not to attract to any newspaper or media source large numbers of people who attack the victim and claim that the offender was innocent. This can easily be checked by any reader, but perhaps one significant example would be the story about an 11-year-old girl in Cleveland, Texas, who was gang-raped by at least twenty-one men as old as 27. *The New York Times* published a story that blamed the girl for such things as occasionally wearing makeup, and it cited community concerns for the fate of the rapists or for the town's reputation (McKinley 2011). As the story made news around the world, discussion boards turned up people everywhere who were concerned about what clothes the child wore, why her mother did not protect her, whether she acted older than 11, and more. Of course, there were more people defending her, but, if hordes of people will defend men in their twenties who raped a fifth-grade child by claiming that she wanted it or deserved it, imagine the numbers defending men in more typical rapes. In one of the criminal cases resulting from the child rape, the defense lawyer based his entire argument on a claim that the child was a seductress spider who enticed and entranced a man in his twenties into her web, which was an abandoned trailer ten miles from her home, crowded with other men who were taking part and filming the acts (Marcotte 2012).

The point of this discussion is that, though there may be more people than ever before who are sensitized to issues of sexual assault, there is an incredibly strong backlash against victims. If large numbers of people can insist that an 11-year-old girl deserved her fate (twenty-one men have thus far been sentenced for this crime), then how hard is it to imagine a lack of support for adult women beaten by their husbands or cohabitors?

The antifeminist recipe now has a new ingredient—Women Against Feminism (WAF). There have always been females opposed to feminism, but many of the recent WAF Internet postings mirror or echo the words of angry white men, supporting rape myths and the claim that women are as violent as men in intimate relationships (DeKeseredy, Fabricius, and Hall-Sanchez 2015). WAF's birth was generated by feminist responses to yet another angry white man's killing spree. On May 23, 2014, in Isla Vista, California, Elliot Rodger, after uploading a YouTube video entitled "Elliot Rodger's Retribution,"[11] murdered six people and injured fourteen before killing himself. His misogynistic diatribe explained that he was still a virgin at age 22 despite being "the perfect gentleman," and he announced his campaign to punish females for not having sex with him, and men for being sexually active.

Some of Rodger's words resemble those used by many men who commit intimate femicide during or after the process of separation and divorce: "If I can't have you, no one will." The concept of entitlement is widespread among men, showing up in a variety of venues related to their dealings with women. Rodger's words, actions, and video were the catalyst for the creation of #YesAllWomen on May 24, 2014 (Dvorak 2014). This is a feminist viral social media campaign on Twitter and Facebook that brings attention to gendered violence, sexual harassment, and sexism. It was created partly in reaction to the Twitter hashtag NotAllMen, which challenges feminist arguments and garnered much attention shortly after Rodger's rampage. Like some other feminist antiviolence social media campaigns, #YesAllWomen targets the cultural practices that perpetuate and legitimate violence against women, helping young women to share their experiences through what Rentschler (2014) terms "feminist response-ability," which "signifies the capacity to collectively respond to sexual violence and its cultures of racial, gendered and sexuality harassment" (68).

However, there are many women who sharply oppose the efforts of feminists and claim that they greatly exaggerate male patriarchal practices and discourses, censor "reasonable behavior," and demand "'special rights' beyond those of men" (Marwick 2013). Those affiliated with WAF are highly visible examples of antifeminist women. They created a Tumblr page, a

Twitter hashtag, and campaigns on Facebook, YouTube, and other social media in response to #YesAllWomen and to the Who Needs Feminism campaign. It primarily involves white, college-aged women posting pictures of themselves holding up handmade placards stating why they oppose feminism. Most posts begin with "I don't need feminism because" followed by reasons centering on personal responsibility or a lack of oppression. In a spectacular show of a lack of empathy, many argue that they personally are not victims, so they do not need feminism.

DeKeseredy, Fabricius, and Hall-Sanchez (2015) contend that these and similar narratives provide three key services to angry white men. First, they give many women a false sense of safety. Second, they make thousands of women who are abused on a daily basis invisible. And third, they buttress attempts to deny the existence of a dominant rape culture and "the cultural normalcy" of male-to-female violence in private places (Meloy and Miller 2011).

Today, there is extensive support for groups like WAF that mock, taunt, and disregard female survivors of male violence. Such a response is ironic at a time when crime discussions generally in the United States are still dominated by a "crime control" model that calls for more support for crime victims, strong support for massive imprisonment, and extensive support in many quarters for more executions, felon disfranchisement, and even corporal punishment of minor offenders (Alexander 2012; Holloway 2014; Wakefield and Wildeman 2014). Thus, at the same time that the public generally is against criminals and in favor of harsh punishment, many of the same people have very different views when men take violent actions against women, which they view as being in their sphere of entitlement. According to Estrich (1987), this is done by claiming that only certain "facts" constitute "real rape" or sexual assault. It is possible to maintain a view that "real rape" (typified by an attack by a total stranger on a chaste or modest woman) is truly a crime and deserves harsh punishment. If there are any grounds to blame the woman, however (such as an 11-year-old girl who wears makeup and acts older), or acquaintance rape in general, it can easily be dismissed as "boys will be boys," or some sort of exaggeration by the woman, or something for which she was asking.

There is an interesting symmetry between WAF postings and the men's rights activists' claims. Burleigh (2014), in fact, seriously suggests that most of the posts on WAF are sock-puppets, or postings by antifeminist and misogynist men under assumed online identities. DeKeseredy and colleagues (2015) found the claim that men are raped and victimized as often as women to be a major theme in WAF postings. Most of the posts they examined highlight this subject, which can be compared to posts reported in antifeminist, backlash research (Dragiewicz 2008, 2011, 2012). Similar to claims commonly stated by angry white men's rights organizations are WAF posts like these:

> It ignores the plight of men. They get raped just as much as women, and usually never win in custody battles. It twists tragedies to suit its own agenda (i.e., Elliot Rodger killings—he killed more men than women). So the male victims don't matter, huh? But when feminists find this out, they use their equality definition so they don't look like complete idiots.

> Men have problems too.

> The feminist community has shown fabricated statistics on rape of women, and has neglected statistics of men raped, as well.

> Equality is not something that will be gained by erasing victims of crimes women commit.

> Men experience physical abuse, sexual abuse, rape, domestic violence, body image pressures, etc. Keep on ignoring that in your rage-fuelled hate spiels.

Though women are far more likely than men to be physically and sexually abused in intimate, heterosexual relationships, it is the voices of the WAF community—people without data or research—that get heard more by the general public. One reason for this is that conservative women who publicly attack feminist and other progressive women are often featured in mainstream newspapers and television shows, especially on Fox News, which is the most-watched news station in the United States (Gedeon 2013). To some degree, this is due to the nature of news: stories attacking experts are more newsworthy than the reports of experts themselves. Of course, news media traditionally also feature viewpoints with which they personally agree.

There has been a steady growth of backlash politics against research that shows the extent of physical and sexual assault against women. We were first introduced to this backlash in 1993, soon after the release of the Canadian

National Survey, a nationwide scientific survey of violence in dating relationships (DeKeseredy and Kelly 1993), when the project was subjected to strong antifeminist attacks in the Canadian media (Currie and MacLean 1993). Although these people were, at the time, on the margins of political discourse, these angry white men were becoming mobilized and gained strength to the point where they had considerable influence over the federal Canadian government under Prime Minister Stephen Harper (Dragiewicz and DeKeseredy 2012). In the United States, comparable groups of angry white men had many more sympathetic political ears and garnered much support during the presidency of George W. Bush.

Angry white men's attempts to reassert patriarchy and white superiority are getting stronger. One group concerned about this is the Southern Poverty Law Center (SPLC), which monitors racist hate organizations and now features men's rights groups in its annual survey of hate (Kimmel 2013). It reports:

> Misogynists in the men's and fathers' rights movements have developed a set of claims about women to support their depictions of them as violent liars and manipulators of men. Some suggest that women attack men, even sexually, just as much as men attack women. Others claim that vast numbers of reported rapes of women, as much as half or even more, are fabrications designed to destroy men they don't like or to gain the upper hand in contested custody cases. (Potok and Schlatter 2012, 1)

The overlap in arguments between the fathers' rights and men's groups, and the kinds of concerns as expressed by the SPLC, makes it essential to take the WAF online community seriously. Youth today spend more time on their computers than they do in face-to-face relationships (J. Klein 2012), and social media such as Facebook, Twitter, and Tumblr enable people to reach larger audiences. In this way, antifeminist men and women can become aware of a large "support group" and become motivated to join the "Angry White Men's choir." With social networking sites now key arenas of political struggle and resistance, addressing WAF and the rage of angry white men should be deemed by progressive scholars and activists to be a "national political issue, not a therapeutic one" (Kimmel 2013, 284).

The relevance of all this to our book is that many of the attacks have focused on separation proceedings, alimony and child support payments, child custody cases, and family law in general. As described in later chapters, angry white men are also negatively affecting the family court system and increasing the risk of homicide, rape, and child abuse. What, then, is to be done? Answers to this important question are provided in the final chapter, which is designed to provide some hope for the thousands of women struggling to find peace for themselves and their children.

SUMMARY

What is separation/divorce and what is violence against women? One objective of this chapter was to answer these two important questions. Our offerings, however, are subject to much debate and "these disagreements are not mere academic exercises" (Renzetti, Edleson, and Kennedy Bergen 2011, 1). Our intended outcomes are to get society in general to broaden its understanding of separation/divorce and to view nonphysical harms as equally—if not more—injurious as physical ones. As described in the previous section, the consequences sought by those who fundamentally oppose our understanding of gendered violence and gender equality is the reassertion of patriarchy and the maintenance of all its injurious symptoms.

We have another important goal. This chapter, along with those that follow it, accentuate Stark's (2007) focus on the need for the media, professionals, policy-makers, and the general public to understand the ever-present dangers that mothers and their children face during and after separation or divorce from an abuser. Most battered women eventually manage to leave (Campbell et al. 1994), but many of their partners attempt to "renew the relationship" with violence against them and/or their children (Block 2000). Often, too, these men are relentless, as described by a southern Ontario, Canada, woman interviewed by Dragiewicz and DeKeseredy (2008):

> That's what they do and they bully and they bully and they bully until you will break. He's controlling in every other sense, and he uses that in the meantime. . . . There was yelling and screaming and cursing. You know, you are this and you're that and you will never get anywhere without me. I'm going to bury you and you have no lawyer. It's ridiculous, and there are times that he's been at my home, that he's kicked in my door because he doesn't get his own way, and he kicks the side of my house. And I can't do anything about it because he didn't actually hurt me. And the police say they don't

want to get involved with family situations. So you're dealing with all of that and emotionally I see where women go in and I had enough. Let him do whatever he wants, because I can't take it anymore. . . . It's enough. (27)

A significant amount of suffering is described throughout this book, and much of it is punctuated with the stories and voices of perpetrators and survivors of abuse, as told to us over many years of work in the field. This includes not only academic research but also decades of work in the shelter movement, with activist organizations, and doing government research. Many lessons were learned doing this work, and one of them needs to be made explicit as we end this chapter. Despite experiencing harms that very few of us could possibly imagine, the women you will read about here are not simply passive victims or weak people who are unable to take steps on their own behalf. They may have been battered, but they are not beaten (MacLeod 1987), and most of the survivors of separation/divorce assault use a variety of techniques to resist patriarchal dominance and control (DeKeseredy and Schwartz 2009), some of which are invisible to those unfamiliar with the complex process of "getting out" (Goetting 1999). These women may have been caught in a trap, but the vast majority find means to "triumph against all odds" (Sev'er 2001).

CHAPTER TWO

The Extent and Distribution of Separation/Divorce Assault

> He wasn't violent during the marriage, but during the separation. When I
> started to change, that's when it started. During this time he was violent
> about once a month, including in front of the kids. He usually took the
> phone off the wall when it happened.
>
> Cited in Kurz 1995, 67

We know that violence against wives has existed for at least as long as we
have had written records. However, the academic research literature before
the 1970s is particularly meager. This is not to suggest that academics were
unaware of disputes, conflicts, or divorce, or that police, courts, social service workers, or legislators were unaware of such violence. In fact, for many
generations there have been countless forums where violence against wives
has been discussed in detail, including in courts and legislatures. Rather,
whereas academics commonly discussed marital conflict and divorce, they
did not find the violence by men against their wives to be worthy of research
and study. For example, the important research publication *Journal of Marriage and the Family*'s 1971 special issue on family violence was the first time
since the journal's inception in 1939 that the word "violence" appeared in
the title of an article. It was not uncommon for discussions of "conflict" to
appear, according to O'Brien (1971), but "apparently violence, as such, was
either assumed to be too touchy an issue for research or else thought to be so
idiosyncratic as to be unimportant as a feature in 'normal' families" (692).
One of the few studies of family violence in any academic field before 1971, in
an era when there was virtually no examination of the men who beat women,
was a piece in one of the top psychiatric journals entitled "The Wife Beater's

Wife" (Snell, Rosenwald, and Robey 1964), which was an attempt to divert blame to women for bringing on their own beatings.

Throughout the research literature before 1971, family violence was considered to be something engaged in either by the mentally ill or by poor minority and immigrant men who presumably had "different" values (Gordon 1988; Pleck 1987). Child abuse had long been periodically rediscovered by researchers (Olafson, Corwin, and Summit 1993). In the 1960s, there was a wave of concern and legislative action in the United States after Henry Kempe invented the term "child abuse syndrome" (Kempe et al. 1962), drawing on the work of radiologists who had begun to doubt the word of parents that an extraordinarily large number of child injuries were accidental (Pfohl 1977; Parton 1979). Still, there was no other suggestion in the literature that violence was a regular feature of American families. After that 1971 special issue of *Journal of Marriage and the Family*, research on violence against women mushroomed in the 1970s (Gelles 1980). Since then, it would be hard to keep track of all of the new journals in the field, let alone the thousands of articles published across a broad swath of the literature. Just as one isolated but powerful example of the proliferation of theoretical, empirical, and policy work, the peer-reviewed journal *Violence Against Women* is now published fourteen times annually, when the norm for journals is three or four issues, or occasionally six. And there is competition: articles on a broad range of harms experienced by women are now routinely published in a large and growing variety of journals dedicated to this problem, such as the *Journal of Interpersonal Violence*, *Aggression and Violent Behavior*, and *Trauma, Violence, and Abuse*. Certainly, we now know much more about separation/divorce assault than we did when the very first study of this form of woman abuse was done over forty years ago.

The early studies of separation/divorce violence by such authors as O'Brien (1971) and Schulman (1981) helped spark contemporary empirical and theoretical work. This was expanded by small-scale studies done by Ellis (1988) and by Ellis and Wight (1987) on "post-separation woman abuse." Still, the field did not begin to fully develop until the early 1990s, which saw the publication of a spate of scholarly books, journal articles, and book chapters (Brownridge 2009; DeKeseredy and Dragiewicz 2014), most of which were influenced by variations of feminist understandings of violence against women.

How many women are victimized by lethal and nonlethal physical and sexual separation/divorce assault? What are the key risk factors associated with these harms? This chapter seeks to answer these questions. Generally, our orientation to answering them is feminist and sociological. Of course, not all readers will agree that this is a reasonable way to proceed. It is not uncommon, particularly for conservative commentators (e.g., Dutton 2010) to argue that feminist sociological approaches to research are biased and that authors who pay attention to the gendered dynamics of abuse are politicizing the topic rather than offering a "rational, empirically informed analysis." However, some points warrant attention here.

One of the major debates in the field is over the nature of value-free inquiry. Many mainstream and conservative researchers believe that they can be value-free and that they have no point of view. It is not uncommon for people who support mainstream points of view to believe that they are completely unbiased and that those who dispute the prevailing view are biased. For example, when *The Washington Post* reported the results of an Association of American Universities study of 150,000 students from twenty-seven universities that showed 23 percent of all undergraduate women had been victimized by some form of sexual assault, the paper felt the need to find and highlight a dissenting voice for balance. They chose a history professor who claims specialties in Lyndon Johnson and American foreign policy to opine that the apples of a confidential victimization study came up with incidence results higher than the oranges of widely assumed underreports to police, "which I think is somewhat dubious" (Anderson, Svurluga, and Clement 2015).

Anyone who is exposed to media today is aware of a common claim that findings the reader does not like must be biased. In the field of violence against women, there is a constant conservative attack on feminist research. Typically, attacks that gain the most traction in the mainstream media consist of quotes from people who have never done research on violence and often have never done social science research at all. Over twenty years ago, we began writing about "people without data" attacking scientific sexual assault research because it "sounds dubious" (Schwartz and DeKeseredy 1994).

It is a central claim of critical criminology that there is no truly value-free research (Schwartz and Brownstein 2016). It has been widely known and reported throughout history, from the Talmud to the influential columnist H. L. Mencken in the 1920s, to social theorist Max Weber, to writer Anaïs Nin in the 1960s: *We don't see things as they are; we see them as we are.* Our preconceived notions have much to do with what and how we see, interpret, and categorize. Or, as Cao (2004) puts it, people "do not see the world 'as is,' but they learn to see it" (16). No one has a monopoly on truth, and there are different ways of knowing, which is at the core of all social scientific work.

Thus, those who refer to feminist sociologists or criminologists as "ideologues" and who portray themselves as "objective scientists" are actually advancing their own political agendas, such as reasserting patriarchal authority (Dragiewicz 2011). As Goldenberg (2006) observes, "The appeal to the authority of evidence that characterizes evidence-based practices does not increase objectivity but rather obscures the subjective elements that inescapably enter all forms of human inquiry" (2621). Feminist scholars, in contrast, put their politics in the spotlight for all to view. They are committed to eliminating structured social inequality and its highly injurious symptoms, such as woman abuse (DeKeseredy and Dragiewicz 2007). The blinders that many scientists wear allow some of them to denounce feminist researchers as members of a "special interest group" (Johnson and Dawson 2011). In the same way that many white people are unable to see white privilege, scholars who embrace the ideology of objectivity do not recognize that they are also advancing an agenda: one that promotes a distorted understanding of rape, femicide, and other forms of violence and abuse by ignoring their deeply gendered dynamics.

The sociological research presented in this chapter is no more or less scientific than other perspectives. For example, there is ample evidence of feminists gathering and analyzing rich quantitative and qualitative data on woman abuse. Frequently, too, feminists conduct representative sample surveys of woman abuse and test hypotheses derived from their own theoretical work (e.g., DeKeseredy and Schwartz 2013; Johnson 1996; Smith 1990) as well as those from mainstream perspectives like routine activities and collective efficacy theories (Schwartz et al. 2001; DeKeseredy et al. 2003). Indeed, there is much empirical diversity found in the feminist sociological/criminological literature on violence against women, which reflects the view that research methods are tools that can be used in a variety of ways to achieve a variety of goals. Think of something as simple as a shovel. It can help build a rape crisis center or a prison. We use multiple research methods to reveal how broad social forces combine with personal and interpersonal factors to engender woman abuse and other major social problems.

There is another equally important reason for our focus on sociological studies of separation/divorce assault, which presumes that there are forces in society that operate on all men and women and that move some men to become violent. Much research in psychology supposes that violence is caused by personal problems or individual issues. By focusing on the individual offender or survivor, such studies strip away the influence of society and can leave the impression that violence and abuse are rare problems that only affect men or women with personality disorders (Dutton, Osthoff, and Dichter 2009). However, woman abuse is not minor, rare, or private. Every day, separation/divorce assault affects women around the world in numbers that would "numb the mind of Einstein" (Stephen Lewis, cited in Vallee 2007). If only a small number of men hurt the women who leave them or are trying to leave them, it would be easier to accept individualistic interpretations. Unfortunately, as we shall see in this book, the types of violence reviewed here are deeply entrenched in our society. Therefore, though we incorporate empirical contributions made by other disciplines, we rely primarily on sociological research to answer the above questions.

FEMICIDE IN THE CONTEXT OF SEPARATION/ DIVORCE WOMAN ABUSE

Our first stop is to investigate the death of women in separation and divorce settings. It is not at all unusual for people to blame the victim or at least to express dismay that she did not leave the relationship to stop being beaten. Unfortunately, for many women the problem is much more complex than a "bumper sticker" solution. Many women are killed trying to escape an abusive relationship, and many more are prevented from leaving by the fear that they will be killed or their children could be killed. Too often, that fear is well founded.

However, it can be very difficult trying to analyze data on femicides that occur worldwide during and after separation/divorce, mainly because

BOX 2. WHY MEN KILL IS NOT A MYSTERY

Anyone who has access to the Internet or reads a newspaper is exposed to almost daily accounts of men who murder their former wives, girlfriends, casual dating partners, or even women they wanted to date but did not. Perhaps today's story is about a man who kills his own children to get back at his wife for winning custody over them (because he was violent and dangerous, no doubt). Perhaps bystanders such as the woman's relatives or her new boyfriend or husband are killed by the former partner.

Most of these tragedies happened simultaneously in August 2015 in Houston, Texas, when David Conley, who claimed to be angered that his ex-girlfriend had changed the locks on her house, was charged with breaking in through a back window to tie up and then execute one by one the ex-girlfriend, Valerie Jackson, her husband, Dwayne Jackson, and all six of her children. One of the children was his own son.

Conley had been charged before with felony assault charges for an attack he made inside the same house. When Conley lived with Jackson, eighteen months earlier, Child Protective Services had filed a lawsuit asking for the children to be removed from the home because they were in immediate danger, but the judge turned it down and returned the children to Conley (Silverstein 2015).

After a senior police official reported that police could not understand why someone would do such a crime, journalist Amanda Marcotte suggested that "the urge to write off this level of horror as incomprehensible— as a form of unfathomable evil—is understandable" but that such murder "is committed almost entirely by men who feel off-the-charts levels of male entitlement—men who feel so entitled to control a woman just because they've dated or married her that they resort to violence to reassert control" (2015).

Conley made this sentiment clear in a bizarre series of jailhouse interviews, when he reported that as "the man of the house" it was his responsibility to deal with the children who were being unruly because they were not being properly disciplined (Arnold 2015). Marcotte reports that, with the frequency of these events and the ease with which men report their motives, "Domestic violence, even when it ends in tragedy as horrifying as the Texas murders, is probably the least mysterious form of violence there is" (2015). In Box 8 we point out how this case is typical of mass shootings in America; it just does not get much media coverage.

government statistics worldwide do not separate out this category. As stated by the World Health Organization (2012), "police and medical data-collection systems that document cases of homicide often do not have the necessary information or do not report the victim-perpetrator relationship or the motives for homicide, let alone gender-related motivations for murder" (63). In the United States, for example, most data on intimate femicide are derived from the Federal Bureau of Investigation's *Supplementary Homicide Reports*. In 2010, of the 12,664 homicides included in the reports, 50 percent did not include the contexts of the murders or the type of relationship (Dobash and Dobash 2015; Federal Bureau of Investigation 2012).

European data sets are also problematic. In their critique of a survey of homicide data in thirty-six European countries,[1] Dobash and Dobash (2015) point out that:

Comparisons across countries are difficult, if not impossible, because some European countries have no specialized national institutions or procedures for collecting, collating, and recording homicides. Barely mentioned . . . is the problem of missing data. European homicide researchers have concluded that these and other problems make it difficult to make valid comparisons and the safest approach is to compare trends over time using regional rather than country-specific patterns. (5-6)

Regardless of the above methodological problems, most, if not all, of the world's leading experts on femicide would agree with the material presented in Box 2. Many attribute the killing of former intimate partners to some form of mental illness, or, as in the narrative of Jody Hunt presented in Chapter 1, that they "just snap" (whatever that means). An alternative narrative is that such violence is indeed common and easily understood.

Femicide is highly visible in contemporary news media. In the United States, there are daily reports of men killing their former wives and girlfriends, children, friends, other family members, new partners, and/or bystanders. In Australia, this is weekly news. Such killings are also a prominent feature of entertainment, serving as common plot devices in television shows, gaming, books, and movies (DeKeseredy and Corsianos 2016; Herbst 2005). Despite this visibility, as noted in Chapter 1, the real causes of femicide are not typically reported by the media, and they have not been as popular topics in some academic circles as debates about the incidence and prevalence of sublethal forms of violence.[2] Of course, there are also those who insist that domestic violence is not a gender issue (Dutton 2006, 2010; Felson 2002), but it is our position that knowledge about fatal violence is essential to understanding male-to-female violence in general and separation/divorce woman abuse in particular. This is important for several reasons. First, intimate femicide is the background context for woman abuse. Second, separation and divorce are risk factors for fatal violence. Third, fatal woman abuse is a significant portion of all lethal violence against women. Finally, homicide is an important measure of separatioin/divorce woman abuse. We will take up each of these points in turn.

Intimate Femicide Is the Background Context for Woman Abuse

As noted in several parts of this book, abusive men repeatedly verbally threaten to kill female intimates (and/or their children and other loved ones) if they leave. These threats, which constitute one of the nonlethal forms of violence, are used to establish and maintain control of female partners. As Wilson and Daly (1993) state, "A credible threat of violent death can very effectively control people, and the . . . evidence on risks to estranged wives suggests that such threats by husbands are often sincere" (12).

An unknown number of abusive men also kill pets and destroy prized possessions to convey credible threats of homicide (Ascione et al. 2007; DeGue and DiLillo 2008; Volant et al. 2008). Below is an example of one of these behaviors included in an interview that Ptacek (1999) had with a woman who sought legal assistance:

> He has repeatedly threatened to kill me, threatened to burn down my home, threatened to wreck my car, pushed and shoved me, thrown things at me like broken furniture and household items every time I have tried to discuss divorce/separation. He would not leave voluntarily. I would have

to get a restraining order and if I didn't I wouldn't live to get to probate court. (80)

Children see and hear threats and assaults against their mothers more frequently than most people realize (R. Klein 2012), and it is not unusual for children to recognize the underlying threat of femicide. One 11-year-old girl reported that, had she not disclosed the abuse of her mother, "Well [we'd] probably still be with Dad and Mum and probably somebody would've been seriously hurt by now, somebody would've, could have even died by now" (cited in Mudaly and Goddard 2006, 83). One particularly common arena for such threats is in the context of child custody disputes during the process of separation/divorce. Think about what this woman experienced:

> My former husband had laid down in bed beside me. . . . He just laid down very quietly. And . . . he said, "If I killed you, I would get the kids." That was all he said. And just the way he said it—he was very calm and cool how he said it. So, the next morning, I was so terrified, I went to my family doctor and I said, "I want you to have this on record because, if I'm killed, I don't want him to have the kids because he's not good for them." (Varcoe and Irwin 2004, 85)

These examples illustrate how threats to kill abused women, their loved ones, and pets are central, rather than peripheral, to woman abuse by male intimate partners. This does not mean that many women are not battered without these threats, but that such threats are common.

Separation/Divorce Are Key Risk Factors Associated with Intimate Femicide

Chapter 1 makes explicit that woman-initiated departures are dangerous exits. For instance, Wilson and Daly's (1993) analysis of thirty-seven Chicago wife-victim cases found that each homicide was preceded by a wife's decision to terminate the relationship. Also interesting to us is their finding that the decision to divorce preceded actual relationship separation, a finding supporting the claim made in Chapter 1 that residency status is not an adequate indicator of relationship status or estrangement.

Currently, the literature on risk factors associated with lethal violence identifies separation and divorce as multiplying the risk of femicide by as much as nine times.[3] Returning to data presented in Chapter 1, the risk may be highest during the first two months of separation. During this time, as well, stalking often occurs and is strongly associated with femicide. Stalking is "the willful, repeated, and malicious following, harassing, or threatening of another person" (Melton 2007a, 4). To be discussed in greater detail in Chapter 3, stalking involves a variety of fear-inducing behaviors such as unwanted phone calls and emails, showing up at a woman's home when such a "visit" is unwanted, and sneaking into a person's home or car to let her know that the offender had been there (Black et al. 2011). Fontes (2015) provides a case study of a man who used multiple means of stalking his ex-partner, which is generally the case:

> After he moved out, Nate stalked Elizabeth for more than two years. He sprinkled flower petals on her driveway, extended the process of picking up his possessions, sent numerous harassing emails, tracked her movements, involved her in a court case, spread rumors around town, and came onto her property when she'd asked him not to. He broke into her office and propped up a picture of himself on her desk. He began dating and quickly moved in with the only single woman in her office, using his connection with his new girlfriend to continue stalking her. (174)

We often hear of the stalking experiences of movie stars and other celebrities, but most stalking quietly occurs in our own neighborhoods and typically involves men targeting current or former female intimate partners (Black et al. 2011; Klein and Hart 2012). For example, McFarlane and his colleagues' (1999) analysis of 141 femicides and 65 attempted femicides revealed that 36 percent of the victims were killed by their ex-partner and 34 percent of attempted femicides were perpetrated by ex-partners. They also found that former intimate partners were more likely than current intimates to stalk both femicide and attempted femicide victims. Sixty-nine percent of the femicide victims were stalked while in current relationships, compared to 88 percent of such victims stalked after ending a relationship. Among attempted femicide victims, 63 percent of women in current relationships were stalked compared to 68 percent in terminated unions. In both groups, the differences probably are not as important as the very high rates of stalking for all femicide and attempted femicide victims.

Stalking is also strongly correlated with nonlethal physical assaults and psychological abuse, and it escalates when women leave their male partners

(DeKeseredy and Schwartz 2009; Mechanic et al. 2000). Actually, a prior relationship between the victim and the offender is one of the most powerful predicators of stalking, together with explicit threats and a history of substance abuse (Basile and Black 2011; Rosenfeld 2004).

McFarlane and colleagues' (1999) research cited above supports some claims made earlier in this chapter. Their data show that the perpetrator had threatened the children if his partner left him in 13 percent of femicides, hurt a pet on purpose in 11 percent of femicides, threatened to take the children if she left him in 15 percent of femicides, and left threatening notes on the victim's car in 10 percent of such murders. These behaviors were not all completed by male ex-partners. Still, the use of threats against female partners "if you leave" indicate that estrangement played a role in these cases, at least in the mind of the abuser.

Intimate Femicide Is a Significant Portion
of All Lethal Violence against Women
Fatal violence is relatively rare compared to most other crimes (Newburn 2013), but homicides perpetrated by current and former intimate partners constitute a significant portion of all killings of women and children. For example, the United Nations Office on Drugs and Crime's (2011) *Global Study on Homicide* found that, in selected countries in Europe, 35 percent of female murder victims were killed by spouses or ex-spouses, as compared to 5 percent of male victims. The U.N. report points out that studies from Australia, Canada, Israel, South Africa, and the United States show similar or higher rates. Another way of looking at the same data, it said, is that women were 77.4 percent of all persons killed by a spouse or ex-spouse.

Australia has shown similar numbers, with women as 75 percent of intimate partner deaths, and prior violence identified in 44 percent of cases (Cussen and Bryant 2015). Intimate partner homicide is the most common category of homicides of women and the least common category of homicides of men (Chan and Payne 2013). An Australian study of same-sex intimate partner homicides from 1989 to 2010 found similarly gendered patterns, where presumably men were predominately the offenders: of thirty-two victims, 88 percent were men and 13 percent were women (Gannoni and Cussen 2014).

In the United States, the offender is not identified in roughly one-third of homicide cases. Of those cases from 1980 to 2008 where the perpetrator was identified, 16.3 percent of all homicide victims were killed by an intimate partner. However, this number is misleading because it obscures marked sex differences. Actually, in 2008, 45 percent of female murder victims and 4.9 percent of male murder victims were killed by an intimate partner (Cooper and Smith 2011). Official U.S. data sources like the *Supplementary Homicide Reports* combine current and former boyfriends and girlfriends in the same category, making it impossible to determine how many of these were cases of separation/divorce homicide. Given these limitations, domestic violence fatality review teams (DVFRTs) are able to identify a greater share of femicides related to woman abuse, allowing for a more comprehensive and accurate analysis.

Domestic Violence Fatality Review Teams
Because of the under-identification of intimate femicides in official records like the *Supplementary Homicide Reports*, DVFRTs are often the most comprehensive source of information on these crimes. Forty-one American states have these interdisciplinary teams, which often combine representatives from criminal justice and health care agencies, the two groups most in contact with victims and perpetrators (Wilson and Websdale 2006).

DVFRTs identify homicides and suicides caused by intimate partner violence, examine interventions and events that occurred prior to death, and make recommendations to prevent similar deaths in the future. Though initially created to spot risk factors and systems failures contributing to domestic violence deaths, the teams are increasingly addressing collateral killings, near-deaths, and suicides, and they interview surviving family members to identify best practices for lowering death rates (Websdale 2003). Rather than focusing on who was at fault for deaths, DVFRTs concentrate on identifying risk factors and improving systems' responses to prevent future deaths.

One of the first DVFRT reports, the Charan case in California, involved a woman who was separated from her abuser in 1991. That review uncovered the need for improved communication and coordination of agencies, data collection, and access to services and training, and it specifically criticized the family court for its lack of interest in protecting battered women and their children. Santa Clara's county-based review prompted by that case found that more than half of the deaths of intimate partners were separation/divorce killings (Websdale, Town, and Johnson 1999). Florida's 1994 review also highlighted "[a]ttempts to break away from the perpetrator, including divorce, separation, and estrangement (approximately 70 percent of cases). In a number of cases of breaking away, researchers identified accompanying relationship difficulties regarding such matters as child custody/visitation" (Websdale, Town, and Johnson 1999, 69).

The state of Washington's fatality reviews are among the most comprehensive. A review of thirteen years of intimate partner deaths from 1997 to 2010 reveals that "in at least 46% of homicides by abusers, the domestic violence victim had left, divorced, or separated from the abuser or was attempting to leave or break up with the abuser. For cases not reviewed in depth, information on the status of the relationship is often incomplete, so the number of victims who were in the process of leaving abusers is likely higher" (Fawcett 2010, 17).

Australian fatality reviews also find that separation is strongly related to intimate femicide. In New South Wales, "two-thirds of all intimate partner homicides where a female was killed, the victim and perpetrator had either recently separated or were in the process of separating" (NSW DVDRT 2015, 22). Similarly, in another part of Australia, the Queensland Domestic and Family Violence Death Review Unit identified actual or intended separation as a risk factor for femicides in 43 percent of cases where men killed female intimate partners (Office of the State Coroner 2015). Comparable findings are available in Canada, such as the Ontario Domestic Violence Death Review Committee's (2009) finding that pending or actual separation was the most common risk factor for deaths, with separation and history of violence against the victim identified in 75 percent of cases.

Homicide Is an Important Measure of Separation/Divorce Woman Abuse
Since we do not know how many cases of woman abuse exist, we do not know the percentage of them that result in homicide. Certainly, the number is relatively smaller, but it remains true that homicide is a key measure, partially because it is almost always reported to or discovered by the police.

Accordingly, the statistics are less open to dispute than nonlethal woman abuse estimates, which continue to be hotly contested. As Wilson and Daly (1993) put it:

> Such problems of subjectivity and possible reporting biases can be largely circumvented when the focus is on homicide. Homicide is of course a relatively rare outcome of assaults and threats of violence, but it provides a relatively objective window on the sources of variable risk of violence, without the numerous reporting biases that bedevil analyses of lesser manifestations of interpersonal conflict. (5)

Nonetheless, homicides related to a history of woman abuse are still underidentified. The context of prior violence may simply not be known, or other factors, such as drug use, the deaths of children, or multiple deaths, may overshadow the history of abuse and its relevance to the killing.

Many homicide studies categorize deaths by relationship between the victim and perpetrator, and some disaggregate current and former spouses, but few disaggregate current and former girlfriends/boyfriends. Campbell and colleagues (2007, 247) note that, in the United States, the *Supplementary Homicide Reports* database for homicides misses or misclassifies many intimate partner homicides, primarily because there is no category for exboyfriend/ex-girlfriend perpetrator, which may be as much as 20 percent of femicide cases. Biroscak, Smith, and Post (2006, 393) found that by combining data from multiple sources, including death certificates, newspaper articles, law enforcement reports, and medical examiners' records, researchers could identify 34 percent more intimate partner homicides than the *Supplementary Homicide Reports*. Merging information from all of these sources also identified 22 percent more cases than were reported in newspapers alone.

Another problem is that these relationship status categories do not reflect emotional separation or the communication of an intent to separate. As stated in Chapter 1, this relationship stage is extremely important. It is not easy to discover how many homicides, even in troubled and broken relationships, resulted from a woman's attempt to separate from or divorce an abusive partner. We will examine issues related to separation and children's risk in greater detail in Chapter 5.

Femicide Summary

Separation/divorce femicides challenge the claim that terminating a relationship automatically reduces women's risk of violence.[4] The words of Moracco, Runyan, and Butts (1998) echo some of those featured in Chapter 1: "The large proportion of victims of partner femicides who had separated or were separating from their mates demonstrates both that battered women *do* leave their abusers and that leaving or threatening to leave can be deadly" (441, emphasis in original). As will be revealed in Chapter 5, the continued and escalated risk of fatal violence during and after exiting relationships is especially pertinent for abused mothers as well as family court personnel, custody evaluators, politicians, and family lawyers, who overwhelmingly labor under the misconception that the danger ends at separation/divorce. This incorrect belief is reproduced in divorce research that does not take violence into consideration. This literature, which emphasizes cooperative parenting and joint custody, has been enshrined in family law practice in many jurisdictions and dangerously applied to cases with a history of violence. This results in forced exposure to violence and abuse, including femicide, murders of children, and killing of collateral victims.

Not all women have an equal opportunity of becoming a victim of intimate femicide. In the United States, an important risk factor is being African American, with these women two to three times more likely to be killed by men than are white women. Native American and Hispanic women also have higher rates than white women, but lower than African Americans (Basile and Black 2011; Campbell 2008). Unsurprisingly, the number-one risk factor for intimate femicide is a history of male violence against a female partner (Auchter 2010; Campbell 2007; Johnson and Dawson 2011). A risk factor suggests that it is not automatic or guaranteed that a batterer will become a murderer, but, looking at the perpetrators, one thing they are most likely to have in common is that they had previously battered intimate partners. There are other important correlates, some of which are discussed in greater detail in Chapters 1 and 4. The ones most commonly identified in the literature are past use of a weapon to scare or harm the victim, simple possession of a weapon, past threats of suicide or homicide, stalking behavior, jealousy, and alcohol and/or drug abuse by the perpetrator (Adams 2007; Cambell et al. 2003; Dobash and Dobash 2015; Ellis, Stuckless, and Smith 2015).

Note that most of the data presented in this section refer to femicides in general. Are there risk factor variations in separation/divorce femicide? For example, are African American men at higher risk of killing their ex-partners than white males, or the reverse? Are younger men more likely to kill during and after their partners' exit than are older men? To the best of our knowledge, sound empirical answers to important questions like these have not been reported in the literature thus far. A somewhat telling statement on this dearth of information is that the words "age," "race," "ethnicity," "socioeconomic status," and "region" are not found in the subject index included in Ellis, Stuckless, and Smith's book *Marital Separation and Lethal Domestic Violence* (2015). This is not an indictment of their work but, rather, support for our observation. We do have sound scientific data on the motives for separation/divorce femicide (much of which is covered in Chapter 4), but the next logical empirical step is to examine sociodemographic similarities and differences for lethal separation/divorce assault.

WHAT WE KNOW ABOUT MALE PERPETRATORS OF SEPARATION/DIVORCE ASSAULT

Two variables briefly mentioned in Chapter 1—patriarchal dominance and control and male peer support—have been found to be powerful determinants of violence during and after the process of exiting.[5] However, both are also relevant in other contexts, such as dating and marriage. For example, data scattered throughout DeKeseredy and Schwartz's (2013) book on male peer support reinforces what Bowker (1983) said more than thirty years ago about all-male subcultures of violence:

> This is not a group that is confined to a single class, religion, occupational grouping, or race. It is spread throughout all parts of society. Men are socialized by other subculture members to accept common definitions of the situation, norms, values, and beliefs about male dominance and the necessity of keeping their wives in line. These violence supporting social relations may occur at any time and in any place. (135–36)

In their work interviewing survivors of separation/divorce sexual assault, DeKeseredy and Schwartz (2009) found that three types of male peer support in particular stood out: frequently drinking with male friends; informational support; and attachment to abusive peers. Informational support refers to the guidance and advice that influences men to abuse their female partners, and attachment to abusive peers is defined as having male friends who also abuse women (DeKeseredy 1988). These factors are identical to those found to be highly significant in predicting which men on college campuses will admit to being sexual predators (DeKeseredy and Schwartz 2013).

In addition to hunting with rural sexist male peers (see Hall-Sanchez 2014), frequent drinking with friends is often associated with the development of a particular kind of masculinity that objectifies women and endorses male behavior that can be physically and sexually violent (Campbell 2000; DeKeseredy and Schwartz 2005). Thirty-three (77 percent) of the women in DeKeseredy and Schwartz's (2009) study of rural women abused after separation said that their former partners often drank alcohol, and twenty-seven (63 percent) said their partners spent large amounts of time with their male friends and that most of the time together involved drinking alcohol. Furthermore, as is the case with college men who sexually abuse women, "nights out drinking with the boys" were seen by many respondents as contexts that often supported patriarchal conversations about women and how to control them.[6] As one interviewee stated: "Um, they're basically like him. They sit around, talk about women, and gossip. They're the biggest gossips there ever was. But they sit around and brag how many times they get it and how they keep their women in line and, you know, just like crap, you know" (cited in DeKeseredy and Schwartz 2009, 67).

The social settings this woman and other respondents described are also examples of the factor of informational support, although these were not restricted to group drinking events. For instance, one interviewee's abusive partner spent much time with his cousin who "hated women" and who often called them "fuckin' bitches" and "whore sluts" (DeKeseredy and Schwartz 2009, 67). Her partner also had a married brother who "hit his wife every so often" (68). Another woman said that her ex-partner's friends "love to put women in the ground. Women are nothing but dirt" (68). In addition, most of the women's partners' peers were patriarchal. For instance, Lynn said that "they just think women are their property and they can lay 'em anytime they want to. That's just their whole attitude about it" (68). Twenty women interviewed (47 percent) said that they knew their partners' friends also physically or sexually abused women, which indicates that attachment to abusive peers also contributes to separation/divorce assault. One interviewee said that *all* of her ex-partner's friends hit women or sexually assaulted them, and several women said that they directly observed their partners' friends abusing female intimates. Jackie is one such participant: "I watched a friend of his who shoved a friend of mine up against a wall . . . and try to, you know, have his way with her" (68).

A few perpetrators also enlisted the aid of their friends to sexually abuse some of these women. Such male peer support could involve forcing women to have sex with the man's friends, which is what happened to this person:

> Well, him and his friend got me so wasted. They took turns with me and I remembered most of it, but, um, there was also drugs involved. Not as much on my behalf as theirs. I was just drunk. And I did remember most of it, and the next morning I woke up feeling so dirty and degraded and then it ended up getting around that I was the slut. . . . And in my eyes that was rape, due to the fact that I was so drunk. And I definitely don't deserve that. And I was hurting. I was hurting the next day. (Cited in DeKeseredy and Schwartz 2009, 68)

Some women who were forced to have group sex were also beaten after going through brutal degradation experiences. Lorraine recalled an incident that occurred during the end of her relationship: "He wanted me to have sex with a few people. Okay, like I was telling you earlier, and I didn't want to. . . . And, uh, I finally did. And then I got beat for it because I did. I tried not to, but then when we did, I got beat" (cited in DeKeseredy and Schwartz 2009, 70).

In South Africa, a version of this kind of gang rape is referred to as "streamlining." It is, according to Jewkes and colleagues (2006, 2951), "essentially a rape by two or more perpetrators. It is an unambiguously defiling and humiliating act, and it is often a punishment, yet at the same time it is an act that is often regarded by its perpetrators as rooted in a sense of entitlement (Wood 2005). Streamlining is sometimes an act of male bonding, a 'favor' to the boyfriends' friends (Niehaus 2005; Wood 2005)."

One of the more difficult questions involved in this analysis, and one that needs more study, is: How do we move beyond Bowker's (1983) findings that male peer support groups exist throughout society? Many findings in other settings show a strong statistical relationship between the existence of a male peer support group and the commission of violent acts against women (e.g., Schwartz and DeKeseredy 1997; Schwartz and Nogrady 1996; Franklin, Bouffard, and Pratt 2012). Extensive theoretical analyses have attempted to account for this correlation (e.g., DeKeseredy and Schwartz 2013). However, the question that remains unanswered is the direction of the causal arrow. Did male peers teach the partners of the women in these studies to commit separation/divorce sexual assault, or did abusive men simply seek the friendship and support of violent peers who would agree with and support their actions?

Returning now to patriarchal control, its relationship to the harms covered in this book are described in greater detail in Chapter 4, but it is worth mentioning that studies have consistently found patriarchal control to be a major determinant (Brownridge 2009; DeKeseredy 2011; Dobash and Dobash 2015).[7] For instance, 79 percent of the rural Ohio women discussed above said that their partners strongly believed that men should be in charge and in control of domestic household settings. Joan is one such participant, and she said, "He didn't allow me to socialize at all. My place was at home with the children, and that's where I was most of the time. The only thing I went out for was if they had a parent-teacher conference at school. I went for that. But no, I had no outside contact" (cited in DeKeseredy and Schwartz 2009, 71).

The women, who all reported sexual assault, for the most part reported that they were raped during or after separation and divorce because their partners wanted to show them "who was in charge." Hall-Sanchez's (2014) qualitative study done in roughly the same geographic area uncovered similar results. Debbie, for instance, told her:

> I remember one time . . . I did try to get away from him and it was rough and it was "you're gonna do this because you're my wife!" and "you said that we were back together again!" Because I didn't want to get hurt. Because I knew if I started a fight with him then, it would've gotten ugly. I felt terrible. . . . I just wish this was over, you know. . . . I just don't want this. And it went on and on and finally he just, it was over. And I remember going outside on the deck and cryin' and cryin'. . . . I felt filthy and it was my husband. . . . And I threw up and I got sick and screamed and . . . I felt horrible. Just dirty. (505)

Offenders' alcohol and drug consumption are often deemed to be two other key risk factors associated with lethal and nonlethal types of separation/divorce assault (DeKeseredy and Schwartz 2009; Ellis and DeKeseredy 1989; Sharps et al. 2003). As mentioned, DeKeseredy and Schwartz found that offenders spend extensive amounts of time taking drugs and drinking "booze" with male peers. This same finding was replicated by other researchers. Close to 90 percent of the women who participated in Hall-Sanchez's (2014) rural Ohio study of male peer support, hunting, and separation/divorce sexual assault study stated that this was the case. One of them, Gina, said: "He had his group of friends, you know. Everything involved a case of beer. . . . But that was just normal. All of them would drink while they went hunting. All of them would drink while they went fishing . . . be out in the garage workin' on stuff, drink. It was normal for that whole group to do that" (503).

Still, findings that related alcohol and drug use to separation/divorce assault were not found by all researchers (see Fleury, Sullivan, and Bybee 2000; McMurray et al. 2000), making the overall research findings "inconsistent" (Brownridge 2009). Of course, there could be a number of reasons for this. One reason may be that the use of alcohol and drugs is so widespread in some communities that it does not stand out among the men who are involved in violence against their partners and ex-partners. Dobash and Dobash (2015) identify some other methodological issues, such as the fact that different researchers may be using different definitions of how much use is necessary to count as abuse.

Gun ownership is another strong correlate of intimate femicide during and after separation and divorce (Campbell et al. 2003; Dobash and Dobash 2015; Liem and Oberwittler 2013). This is a particular problem for rural women, because the rate of gun ownership in the United States is higher in rural than in suburban and urban places (Donnermeyer and DeKeseredy 2014). Websdale (1998) observes:

> Rural culture, with its acceptance of firearms for hunting and self-protection, may include a code among certain men that accepts the casual use of firearms to intimidate wives and intimate partners. In urban areas it is more difficult for abusers to discharge their weapons and go undetected. People in the country are more familiar with the sound of gunshots and often attribute the sound to legitimate uses such as hunting. (10)

Whether it is for this reason or for others, there is a relationship between rurality and femicide. Gallup-Black (2005) found not only that the U.S. rates of intimate partner homicide were higher in rural than in urban areas but also that, over the twenty-year study period, the rate went steadily down in urban and suburban areas but dramatically rose in rural areas. By the end of the study period, the rural rate was six times the rate of the metropolitan areas. Similarly, in Canada, close to 50 percent of domestic homicides involving firearms occurred in rural communities, though rural homes account for less than 20 percent of Canada's population (Donnermeyer and DeKeseredy 2014; Royal Canadian Mounted Police 2013; World Bank 2013). Back in the United States, in DeKeseredy and Schwartz's (2009) study, 58 percent of the forty-three battered women they interviewed said their male partner had guns, and some were threatened with them. Guns are still related to intimate femicide when intimate partners live apart (Campbell et al. 2003). Hall-Sanchez (2014), who completed an extensive review of the literature on gun ownership in this context, concluded that "[o]wning a gun is highly correlated with using it to threaten an intimate partner" (497). This is what happened to one of DeKeseredy and Schwartz's interviewees when her partner found out that she wanted to leave him:

> And I mean the one night he'd come home and pull a double barrel and cock both barrels and said he was going to kill me. And it was like, wait a minute here, you know, it was two o'clock in the morning. I was sound asleep and I got up at four to go to work. But he'd always keep pressuring me, "If you leave me, I'll find you. I'll kill you. If you leave me, I'll find you, I'll kill you." (2009, 48)

Hall-Sanchez's (2014) recent qualitative work provides support for the claim that rural hunting culture is closely associated with separation/ divorce assault and keeps women caught in a trap. She found that hunting was an integral part of the rural male peer support subculture that promoted and justified separation/divorce assault and other forms of male-to-female violence in her participants' communities. She states:

> Regardless of why these men participated in the hunting subculture, the excruciatingly imperative reality is that it allowed them access to a legal and justifiable weapon that could be (and oftentimes was) used to intimidate,

threaten, control, and hurt their female partners. This fact alone has a profound impact on the lives of rural women experiencing violence in their intimate relationships, especially when they are expressing a desire to or actually separating from their abusive male partners. (502)

The effect of the mass media on men involved in this violence is an area that has also begun to be analyzed in the academic literature. Recent years have featured an unprecedented level of the pornographic degradation, abuse, and humiliation of women. We are not referring to erotica, which is "sexually suggestive or arousing material that is free of sexism, racism, and homophobia and is respectful of all human beings and animals portrayed" (Russell 1993, 3). Rather, our concern is with what the pornography industry coins as "gonzo." Such images and writings are the most profitable in the industry and have two primary things in common. First, females are characterized as subordinate to men, and the main role of actresses is the provision of sex to men. Second, in the words of Dines (2010), gonzo "depicts hard core, body punishing sex in which women are demeaned and debased" (xi). These images are not rare. Actually, a routine feature of contemporary pornographic videos is painful anal penetration, as well as brutal gang rape and men slapping or choking women or pulling their hair while they penetrate them orally, vaginally, and anally (DeKeseredy and Corsianos 2016).

Pornography transcends videos, pictures, and adult novels. In addition to living in a "post-*Playboy* world" (Jensen 2007), we exist in a "striptease culture" (McNair 2002). The sexual objectification and degradation of women exists in a wide range of contexts, including strip bars, live sex shows, and even advertising (DeKeseredy and Hall-Sanchez 2016). McNair (2002) correctly points out on the back cover of his book that "sex and sexual imagery now permeate every aspect of culture." Unfortunately, much, if not most, of what he is referring to is harmful, and we are starting to see a strong association between pornography and separation/divorce sexual assault, at least in rural communities. For example, 65 percent of the estranged partners of the women who participated in the study conducted by DeKeseredy and Schwartz (2009) viewed porn, and 30 percent of the interviewees reported that this type of media was involved in the sexually abusive events they experienced.

DeKeseredy and Hall-Sanchez (2016) conducted a study that involved two stages: (1) secondary analysis of the rural Ohio interviews, and (2) "back talk" interviews with twelve women harmed by separation/divorce sexual assault who were from rural Ohio towns similar to those where DeKeseredy and colleagues' participants lived. The back-talk approach is a recent development in qualitative social sciences (Hall-Sanchez 2013). Yet "back talk" as a display of resistance or form of opposition in narrative has deep roots in African American history (Collins 2000). It meant "speaking as equal to an authority figure . . . daring to disagree and sometimes it just meant having an opinion" (Hooks 1989, 5). As a form of testimony, it meant to "bear witness, to bring forth, to claim and proclaim oneself as an intrinsic part of the world" (Collins 2000, 2). Therefore, the roots of "talking back" date back prior to the era of slavery, yet the use (and validation) of this participatory action component in qualitative research is relatively new.

Back talk as an independent methodology is beginning to take shape as a recognized methodological tool to obtain new and original data. Back-talk interviews are frequently used in community-based studies where researchers "go back" to communities, presenting their results to glean reactions and additional questions/concerns/suggestions for future research (Hall-Sanchez 2014). These discussions generate rich qualitative interactive data to supplement a previous or ongoing study or as new data to be further analyzed on their own (Wilkinson 1998). Back-talk interviews empower participants, providing opportunities to exercise a greater role in the research processes. Scholars can also responsibly disseminate sensitive issues to potentially diverse and highly politicized audiences, contributing to a more reflexive and socially responsible research culture (Frisina 2006; Hall-Sanchez 2013).

In addition to collecting supplementary data to update the findings reported in DeKeseredy and Schwartz (2009), stage two provided a safe space for women to "talk back" critically to their findings. The results (including key themes) were presented to the participants, and they were asked to comment based on their own experiences. The sample was recruited using techniques employed by DeKeseredy and his colleagues. Still, DeKeseredy and Hall-Sanchez's reanalysis of the original data set yielded an increase (from twenty-eight to thirty-two) in the number of women with partners who viewed porn. Furthermore, there was an increase in the number of women who stated that pornography was involved in their sexual assaults, with more than half of the total sample (N = 24) reporting this harm.

Broadening the definition of porn to include other sexually explicit and degrading elements of U.S. culture was one of the most significant factors that helped produce these findings. However, scattered throughout some of the forty-three original transcripts was also relevant information on Internet, video, and magazine pornography that was likely not detected earlier, especially when the women did not label the images as pornography. The secondary analysis of the original study reveals five significant themes: learning about sex through pornography; imitation and comparison; introducing other sexual partners; filming sexual acts without consent; and the broader culture of pornography (e.g., sex work and fetishes). The back-talk stage of this study strongly suggests that the connection between pornography and violence against women is still as strong, if not stronger, than when the original data were collected. Of the twelve women interviewed, nine reported that their abusive experiences were related to their ex-partners' use of pornography. Moreover, most of the women's hurtful experiences mirror the above themes. Six interviewees discussed learning about sex through pornography, seven mentioned imitation/comparison, three described the introduction of other sexual partners, three talked about sexual acts filmed without their consent, and three women discussed the influence of the broader pornographic culture.

For example, Evelyn's ex-husband often imitated violent rape scenes filled with degrading and foul language:

Um, forceful, nasty, demeaning. I wouldn't say particularly violent, except that he would pin me down and wouldn't let me get up and he, he was, he had taken martial arts classes and could anticipate every move I made before I moved. . . . It was just horrible . . . like sex would go on and on and on and he couldn't get off until I was uncomfortable and after reading everything I got the idea that he can't get off unless I'm uncomfortable and it progressed through the marriage to where it wasn't just being uncomfortable, it has to be worse than that. He had to, he, he didn't hit me that often. He did hit me though during the marriage but not like during sex he didn't smack me around and stuff, um, but he would call me just really foul names and try to make me feel as horrible about myself as I could in the bedroom. It was always a sex thing. You had to feel bad about yourself during sex and you know, until I was screaming at him, "get off of me!" Cussing at him, you know, fighting with him and then he would get off. So, one day I decided, you know, I'm going to test this. I'm going to start right at the beginning and see if it works and it did. He got off before he even got his pants down because I started the fighting even before he got me in the bed and it worked and I knew, I knew that he was sick and this was never going to end. (Cited in DeKeseredy and Hall-Sanchez 2016, 13)

Gail's experience highlights themes of imitation and the addition of "other people" found in the wider study:

Just degrading like you know, stupid. I got called stupid a lot you know and even if it was like joking around, you know, it became serious. "Oh you're stupid" and then it just became name calling. . . . "Oh you're a fuckin' retard," you know it just got worse and like . . . then it was like other things that he encouraged me to do. Um, him and his friend watched a lot of porn and encouraged me and his friend's wife to make out so it was like things that he wanted that he was trying to get me to do for his own pleasure you know. It was like, even if I felt uncomfortable, you know, just drink a little bit more and it will be ok, you know. (Cited in DeKeseredy and Hall-Sanchez 2016, 13-14)

In addition to confirming that pornography consumption is associated with separation/divorce sexual assault, DeKeseredy and Hall-Sanchez demonstrate that it is necessary to avoid using the word "pornography" in questions and instead to ask behaviorally specific questions because they generate more valid and reliable woman abuse data (Jacquier, Johnson, and Fisher 2011).

One problem with this work is that it has all been done in rural America. Obviously, we need data gathered from people living in urban and suburban communities to determine how widespread the relationship may be between pornography consumption and separation/divorce assault or, for that matter, assaults within intact relationships. Since many of these women were assaulted prior to separation, we know that this happens in such relationships also. What we do not know is whether the problem is worse for separated and divorced women, or whether these hard-to-believe high numbers would be found throughout society.

Similarly, we need data from other countries on this subject to see if this is mainly a U.S. phenomenon or if it affects men (and therefore women) in other countries. Certainly, however, any beginning hypothesis would be that the use and influence is widespread. Given how lucrative the pornography business is, it is rather unlikely that only a small number of people use it (Lehman 2006).[8]

What about other characteristics that are commonly examined in social scientific research on other topics, such as age, race/ethnicity, and employment status? Unfortunately, there are no adequate empirical answers to this question. The bulk of the research on correlates of separation/divorce assault (especially the research on nonlethal variants) focuses on women,[9] an issue to be addressed in greater detail at the end of Chapter 4.

REGIONAL VARIATION IN PHYSICAL AND SEXUAL ASSAULT

One of the recurrent themes of this book will be the problems of obtaining useful and correct statistics.[10] The previous section discussed many of the problems of obtaining or compiling data about femicide, and there are many similar problems in obtaining statistics about nonlethal physical and sexual assaults during and after separation/divorce. For example, the bulk of the research on separation/divorce violence has used a methodology that asks respondents both about assaults and about their marital status. Thus, though we know that separated women report intimate assault much more often than currently married women, few studies tell us much about the timing of the victimization. Did the woman separate or divorce her partner because they were victimized? If so, this would account for her currently being separated or divorced? Or were women already separated or divorced being victimized after leaving? This would look the same—women who reported assault were divorced or separated—but would involve very different dynamics. For close to forty years, we have seen study after study repeating the same methodological shortcoming. Another related problem is that few studies present data that allow a comparison of rates of separation/divorce violence to rates of violence in marriages that remain intact (Brownridge 2009).

Another way of stating this is that the bulk of the many studies done are asking questions at one point in time in the life of their respondents.

Campbell et al. (1998) discuss the "fluidity of relationships." Is a couple separated or together? The answer might differ monthly. People will stop living together but maintain a friendly and often sexual relationship. Life can get complicated. Overall, people change, life changes, and circumstances change. We have known for many years that large numbers of women return to live with their batterers after leaving, often for excellent reasons (promises of reform, economic hardship, family pressure, fear of retaliation, and more). Shelter houses often claim that their clients typically have to leave several times before making a break. Of course, we all often forget that these women married or formed intimate relationships with these men because they had love or other strong attachment feelings, and we rarely discuss how difficult it can be to simply walk away from such feelings.

One statistical way of dealing with at least some of these issues is to engage in longitudinal studies that follow a group of people over a period of time. Victimization can then be measured over the entire period, and some conclusions can be drawn as to the cessation of violence as time passes after a breakup or the continuation of such violence. An excellent example of the use of such a methodology was a study conducted by Fleury, Sullivan, and Bybee (2000). This was actually part of a much larger inquiry about services to battered women, but, as part of that research, women were interviewed every six months for two years about their victimization. The women in the final subsample had all spent at least one night in a shelter house, and they were then followed up for two years. Within this group, 36 percent were assaulted by a male ex-partner during the two-year follow-up, some multiple times. These were all women who were involved with the male at the time that they entered the shelter house but who left them afterward. Unsurprisingly, the time of greatest danger for the women was in the first ten weeks after sheltering. Presumably many of them left the relationship at that point. Of the women who were assaulted again, 51 percent were assaulted during those first few weeks. However, the passage of time was no guarantee of safety, as 8 percent of the first assaults after shelter came eighteen to twenty-four months after shelter. It might be notable that most of the assaults were on the severe end of the researchers' scale, and almost half resulted in injury. Fleury and colleagues note, however, that their methodology still undercounts separation/divorce physical assaults. All of these women were threatened and assaulted before entering shelter, as it is a common tactic used to attempt to gain control over women and to prevent them from leaving. Any women who were successfully terrorized by their batterer into maintaining their relationship were, by definition, excluded from the sample used. Anecdotally, we know that many women believe that their male partner will kill them if they leave, and they make a rational and intelligent choice to stay alive by not leaving.

Campbell and colleagues (1998), in another well-designed longitudinal survey, present a small-scale contextual analysis that sacrifices generalizability for in-depth understanding. Although they found that violence continued after breakup, they did not use categories that make it possible to directly compare their findings to other studies. Rather, they centered on the decision-making of women in abusive relationships and found them intelligent, rational, and forward-looking in their plans to end or reduce violence in their lives. Actually, there has been a large group of longitudinal studies that followed battered women over a period of time but almost always to answer a fairly narrow (albeit legitimate) question that is different from ours. Campbell and Soekin (1999), for example, focused on questions of health and mental health; Anderson and colleagues (2003) measured the level of depression over time; and Hardesty (2002) was interested not in the extent of violence after separation but in the effect of such violence on post-divorce parenting. Aldarondo (1996) looked at continuation or desistence patterns in intact families only, while Grisso and colleagues (1996) conducted a longitudinal study of inner city women in poverty to ascertain their levels of injury. Jacobson and colleagues (1996) conducted a longitudinal study to attempt to predict which marriages broke up and which had the partners staying together. As we can see, all of these studies have been valuable, but none told us the extent to which women are the victims of physical and sexual violence when they plan to leave, are leaving, or after they have left an intimate relationship.

Although many questions remain to be answered, we certainly have the research in hand to state clearly that there are great dangers and risks for women contemplating or completing leaving abusive relationships, and it might even increase the risk for her simply to enter shelter (Dugan, Nagin, and Rosenfeld 2003). It is beyond the scope of this chapter to review every relevant study showing the dangers involved in leaving, since this has been done elsewhere (see Brownridge 2009; DeKeseredy and Schwartz 2009). However, Brownridge's (2006) summary of the current state of knowledge in this field is still fully accurate today:

> In short, studies that allow a comparison of violence among separated, divorced, and married women show a consistent pattern of separated and divorced women being at elevated risk for violence compared to married women, with separated women having by far the greatest risk for post-separation violence. It appears that separated women have as much as thirty times the likelihood, and divorced women have as much as nine times the likelihood, of reporting non-lethal violence compared to married women. (517)

This is not the end of the inquiry. It was extremely important to discover that separated and divorced women are at higher risk of receiving violence, but are all separated women at the same risk? Or, for that matter, all married women? Clearly not. Some separated women evidently have a lower risk than others. Fleury and colleagues (2000) made a first effort to identify the characteristics of women who were at higher or lower risk. Unsurprisingly, one important factor related to decreased risk was living in a different town than the ex-partner. That is certainly no guarantee of safety, as at least anecdotally many in the field have heard of cases where a man traveled hundreds or even thousands of miles in order to attack a woman who had broken up with him. But, for obvious reasons, living in a different city seems to reduce the risk. Women who were breaking up from longer term relationships were at greater risk than women leaving shorter relationships. Fleury and colleagues (2000) suggest that this may be due to a psychological investment, in that men might batter in a short-term relationship but also accept a breakup more easily. This might be somewhat supported by another finding from this study that the likelihood of physical attack by an ex-partner increased with the number of threats that the woman reported receiving during the relationship.

Women Living in Rural America

In looking at all of the factors that raise or lower the risk of separation/ divorce violence, at times there is more information about the problems faced by rural women than for women living in other areas. For instance,

DeKeseredy and Schwartz's (2009) exploratory qualitative study strongly suggests that rural separation/divorce sexual assault is a major problem; their data challenge the notion that rural areas are nonviolent idyllic retreats. Furthermore, as Websdale (1998) and others (e.g., Donnermeyer and DeKeseredy 2014) point out, there are social practices that oppress both rural and urban females, but they operate differently in rural areas. For example, extensive attention has recently been paid to the relations between poor men of color and the police in urban and suburban areas (Brunson and Gua 2015). In rural areas, police officers are often friends with some of the men who batter their current or former intimate partners. They hunt and fish, play sports, and drink with them, and are thus less inclined to arrest batterers because of what is referred to in Australia as "mateship norms" (Owen 2012; Scott and Jobes 2007). For example, Rockell (2013) describes one rural woman abused by her husband who was a retired member of the state police force and who had convinced her not to file a report because his former "troopers" would not believe her. However, he turned around and filed a complaint and had her arrested when she burned his golf hats and shirts in a trash bin as a way of fighting back.

In rural sections of the United States and Canada, widespread violence against women exists alongside community norms that prohibit women from publicly talking about their experiences and seeking social support (Brownridge 2009; DeKeseredy and Schwartz 2008; Krishnan, Hilbert, and Pase 2001; Lewis 2003). Although urban abused women encounter many barriers to service (R. Klein 2012), rural women by comparison simply have fewer social support resources to draw on (Lohmann and Lohmann 2005; Merwin, Snyder, and Katz 2006). Those that do exist are likely to cover very large geographic areas (DeKeseredy and Schwartz 2009; Logan et al. 2005). This imposes major physical barriers to drawing on these services, in addition to the geographic and social isolation that some of these women already have. So, for example, a major city might have a variety of shelter houses, some catering to women of a particular language or ethnic group, but a single house might serve three or four rural counties, where there is probably inadequate (if any) public transportation (Lewis 2003; Logan et al. 2006). Another factor exacerbating rural women's plight is that rural women are less likely to be insured than are urban and suburban residents (Mueller and MacKinney

2006; Patterson 2006), which restricts their access to some of the physical and mental health-care services that do exist (Basile and Black 2011).

This insurance question reminds us of our major question: We know that separated women are more likely to be physically attacked by former partners, but are all separated women at equal risk, or are there other factors such as place of residence that affect these chances? One of the ways to study this is through the National Crime Victimization Survey (NCVS), a U.S. government sophisticated survey that asks people about recent nonfatal victimizations. Using aggregated 2002–2009 data, Rennison, DeKeseredy, and Dragiewicz (2013) found that rural divorced and separated females are more victimized than their urban and suburban counterparts. Unfortunately, the NCVS does not have a question about cohabiting, although we know from other studies that cohabitors have a very high risk of being assaulted by intimate partners. There is little information available about this group in rural communities, but 67 percent of the cohabiting women interviewed by DeKeseredy and Schwartz (2009) in rural Ohio reported that they were sexually assaulted when they stated that they wanted to leave their abusive relationships.

DeKeseredy and Schwartz (2009) studied a particular type of separation/divorce attack, which was sexual assault. They claimed that this harm may be more prevalent in rural areas than in urban and suburban places, but they could not generalize their qualitative findings. Rennison, DeKeseredy, and Dragiewicz (2012) examined 2002–2009 aggregated NCVS data and found that 54 percent of rural women who were divorced or separated—as compared to 36 percent of urban women—were victims of an intimate rape/ sexual assault. When converted to rates, they found that 3.1 separated /divorced rural women (per 1,000) were victims of intimate partner rape/ sexual assault, which is significant higher than the proportion of 1.7 suburban women and 1.4 urban women that experienced the same violence while divorced or separated. Most of the power in this relationship came from separated women, where the statistically significant difference was between a rate of 8.7 (per 1,000) for rural separated women, 0.9 for suburban separated women, and 2.5 for urban women.

This research adds to the growing number of studies of rural woman abuse, such as those conducted by Bachman and Saltzman (1995), Brownridge (2009),

DeKeseredy and Hall-Sanchez (2016), DeKeseredy and Schwartz (2009), Hall-Sanchez (2014), Peek-Asa and colleagues (2011), and Wendt (2009). Yet there is still much we do not know about separation/divorce rape and sexual assault in nonmetropolitan areas. Although we have discovered that rural communities are different in victimization than suburban or urban communities, there are still many different rural communities that may vary greatly on these issues (Weisheit, Falcone, and Wells 2006). For example, a number of Native American and Indigenous rural populations in North America (Wells and Falcone 2008) are marked by extensive violence against women. Only about 3 percent of the 35 million Canadian residents identify themselves as Aboriginal, but it is estimated that they are 12.5 times more likely to be victims of robbery or of physical or sexual assault than non-Aboriginal people (Donnermeyer and DeKeseredy 2014; Perrault 2011; Siegel and McCormick 2012). In the United States, nearly 50 percent of the women who identified as Native American or Alaskan natives reported having experienced rape, physical violence, and/or stalking by an intimate partner at some point in their lifetime.

In another attempt to look at this question, DeKeseredy and Rennison (2013a) framed the question as: "Do the characteristics of female victims of intimate separation/divorce non-lethal assault differ across urban, suburban, and rural communities?" They used aggregate 1993–2010 NCVS data to look at all NCVS nonlethal violence responses, but this time they looked at geographic region (urban, suburban, or rural) of the victim's residence as their dependent variable. Although the use of geographic area as a dependent variable may appear unusual, their approach has been employed in fields such as taxonomy and biology and, increasingly, in criminological research. This strategy does not treat geographic region as a dependent variable in the classic sense (see Harrell 2001 for more information), but it allows the use of multinomial logistic regression on non-ordered nominal categories. For some variables it was *less* likely that the victim would live in a rural area, including being black or Hispanic, being college educated, being employed, or having children in the household. Victims with less than a high school education were *more* likely to live in a rural area.

Such results should not be highly surprising. Substantially larger proportions of two high-risk groups of women—African Americans and Hispanics—live in metropolitan areas. Low educational attainment is a key risk factor for violence against women generally (Macmillan and Kruttschnitt 2005), and individuals in rural places are less likely to earn a college degree because of the lower socioeconomic status that characterizes rural areas (Byun, Meece, and Irvin 2011). Those in rural areas who achieve a higher level of education are more likely to move away due to the eroding economic base that characterizes many rural places today (Brown and Schafft 2011; Weisheit, Falcone, and Wells 2006). Even so, prior to DeKeseredy and Rennison's research, it was unclear whether rural, urban, and suburban women's educational levels put them at greater or lesser risk for separation /divorce assault. They found that the victims of such harm with less than a high school diploma are more likely to live in an urban or a rural environment—but not a suburban area. Furthermore, woman abuse victims with a four-year degree or higher are more likely to live in an urban and suburban place—but not in a rural setting. It is unclear what accounts for these differences, but several studies show that many men find women's educational and labor market gains threatening, and the "narrowing of the male-female status gap" results in violence as a form of backlash (LaFree and Hunnicutt 2006; Russell 1975; Xie, Heimer, and Lauritsen 2012), which is an issue covered in greater detail in Chapter 4. Why this effect is found in some areas and not others, and reasons for the differential effect of education across areas, require greater attention. This may be due to the fact that educational attainment levels are lower in rural communities than in suburban ones (Council of Economic Advisors 2012).

Employment was found to differentiate separation/divorce assault victims. For example, an employed victim was more likely to live in a suburban versus a rural area. Or, stated differently, unemployed victims are more likely to live in rural settings. This finding may reflect the lack of employment opportunities in rural areas and the loss of employment in a family business or on a family farm following the dissolution of a marriage.

In sum, DeKeseredy and Rennison found more similarities than differences among separation/divorce assault victims living in urban, suburban, and rural areas. Their data suggest that the demographic profile of these victims of woman abuse is similar across geographic regions. Whereas eleven out their thirty-six statistic comparisons indicated significant differences in victims across the three areas, twenty-five of the comparisons did not.

DeKeseredy and Rennison's research, then, highlights the complex relationship between several variables and geographic area.

One salient problem that cuts across all of the rural separation/divorce assault studies done by Rennison and her colleagues (including the work reviewed previously in this section) is the use of three crude categories to operationalize geographic areas: urban, suburban, and rural. This categorization is based on the NCVS categories. Although this technique allows for comparisons with previous research on regional variations, it masks significant difference within these geographic areas. This pitfall, of course, is endemic to most large-scale U.S. victimization surveys. Not all rural places are the same, nor are suburban and urban communities (Donnermeyer and DeKeseredy 2014).

Unfortunately, two important potential correlates of separation/divorce assault are missing from this analysis: stalking and pregnancy. In both situations, the NCVS added questions at some point, but there were too few cases to be used in regression models. This is unfortunate because the research community still does not know for sure whether pregnant women are at higher or lower risk of being physically abused (Campbell et al. 2011). Certainly, women who were beaten during pregnancy were also assaulted before they were pregnant (Basile and Black 2011; Jasinski 2004). Nevertheless, DeKeseredy and Schwartz's (2009) qualitative study suggests that exiting and/or attempting to exit a patriarchal abusive relationship may be especially dangerous for pregnant women.

Tanya, for instance, is one woman they interviewed who was pregnant and raped during the process of leaving her male partner:

> He did it because I was his and he felt he could. And it was his way of letting me know that, ah, first of all, of letting me know that I was his. And secondly, letting me know that um, that I wasn't safe anywhere. And I, when were together, when he had forced me to go back together with him, ah, he, ah . . . raped me as another form of possession. And I think also as a reminder of what could happen. And ultimately, at one point, I believed that he raped me as part of his means of killing my unborn child. (Cited in DeKeseredy and Schwartz 2009, 72)

Research on demographic, geographic, and other variations in nonlethal physical and sexual types of separation/divorce assault is, surprisingly, still in a state of infancy, and many more empirical questions need to be answered and probably will be in the coming years. It is also time to devote more theoretical attention to the problems covered in this chapter and to gather rich qualitative and quantitative data from men. These two concerns are addressed in greater detail in Chapter 4. Yet, some rich information derived from a small number of studies of women's experiences tell us much about the characteristics of men who partake in lethal and nonlethal forms of separation/divorce assault, and these data have been presented here.

SUMMARY

Despite all of the data recently gathered on separation/divorce assault, there are still quite a few major gaps in the field. For example, though we presented extensive information in this chapter on the relationship between male peer support and separation/divorce assault in rural America, there has been no such study of this relationship in urban and suburban communities. Obviously, this is a major gap, and one that needs to be filled.

Overall, this chapter and the next one show that separation/divorce assault is multidimensional in nature. The various assaults that women endure often overlap in nature, which is not surprising since this is also the case for those people abused in a wide range of marital, cohabiting, dating, and other intimate relationships. These types of attacks might include sexual victimization, physical violence, psychological and at times terroristic abuse, economic abuse, the abuse of loved pets, stalking, and the destruction of prized possessions. For example, of the women reported in DeKeseredy and Schwartz's (2009) study, 80 percent reported experiencing two or more of these forms of separation/divorce assault. Still, there is a great deal left to learn about the extent and distribution of some of these acts. For example, it is unclear from reading psychological abuse data gathered by the Centers for Disease Control's National Intimate Partner and Sexual Violence Survey which groups of women in the United States are the most vulnerable and which groups of men are most likely to be perpetrators.[11]

The research presented here undoubtedly underestimates the extent of separation/divorce assault. Even with all of the methodological refinements over the past thirty years, Smith's conclusion in 1987 is still true: obtaining accurate estimates of the extent of any type of violence against women in intimate relationships "remains the biggest methodological challenge in survey research" (185). Certainly some victims of most types of crime do not fully report their victimization, but the problem is particularly acute in this field for a variety of reasons. This is a crime where the victims are often too embarrassed to report and very often suffer from a fear of reprisal if they do report. People who are regularly victimized may run the events together in their minds, making it difficult to figure out just how often they were assaulted. Some feel that intimate victimization is a private matter, not to be disclosed, whereas others may think that their victimization is not important enough to mention. The numbers that we do gather are, to some unmeasurable degree, underestimating the true level of the problem (Schwartz 2000). Further, as mentioned in Chapter 1, definitional issues may serve to undercount the problem by defining some assault situations out of the problem. If women must be physically separated for an assault to count as separated/divorced violence, then the violence against women trying to leave or preparing to leave will not be counted.

We could learn much more about these issues by devoting more attention to the characteristics of the perpetrators. Depending almost completely on homicide statistics, surveys of women, and interviews with women is problematic because these data sources do not reveal the reality of abusive men. Scully (1990) was talking about rape when she suggested that "such insight is acquired through invading and critically examining the social constructions of men," (4), but of course this is true of all instances of male-to-female violence.

New Technologies and Separation/Divorce Violence against Women

Online harassment against women made the news when Reddit CEO Ellen Pao resigned over what she called "the largest trolling attack in history." That came after Reddit began taking down revenge porn and banning harassment earlier this year. When Reddit removed sections of the online discussion site where heavy harassment occurred, Pao and other employees received death threats and had their private information posted online.

Snider 2015[1]

New technologies are part-and-parcel of many of our daily lives, especially if we use the Internet, something that is no longer a luxury but treated as a basic necessity by most people and most communities. Some antipoverty advocates come close to claiming that free use of the Internet should be a human right. The argument is that any inability to access this technology due to financial constraints blocks low-income people from equal opportunities to education, employment, government services, and contemporary civic participation (Monsebraaten 2016). As scholars, educators, and activists, we certainly would be much less efficient at doing our work without access to the Internet and the variety of sites, resources, information, and opinion that are made possible by new technologies. Within a very short time, only a decade for many people, we have gone from a society where information was housed mainly in print, and often held only in libraries and repositories, to one where people now argue that "it is difficult to imagine a life without the ability to look up information online within seconds"

(Clevenger and Marcum 2016, 3). As a number of people have noted (most famously comedian Louis C.K.), many people today who needed serious research skills and time to look up information only a very short time ago, now get angry and truly upset when they are on a device that takes an "extraordinarily slow" few seconds to locate and present the requested data.

Contemporary technologies ranging from smart phones to drones are extensively used throughout the world today to achieve numerous positive objectives, such as remaining in constant contact with friends and relatives or writing books like ours, or just to provide exceptionally fast communications through email, messaging, video messaging, or many other means. There are now many examples of humanitarian deeds made possible in recent years only by using newer technologies, such as crowdsourcing funding for good ideas, paying the medical bills of heroes, or bringing together people to support good works. A section in Chapter 6 briefly describes how new technologies can be used to help curb woman abuse.

Unfortunately, there is also a dark side to the recent use of new technology. Many people devote exceptional energy to attempting to maintain these newer information areas as safe places for all of us, but, as leading experts on information technology (IT) point out, "Despite all these efforts, technology is persistently used either as a facilitator or as the arena for crime perpetration, from facilitating illegal prescription drugs to collection of donations under false pretences" (Vargas Martin, Garcia-Ruiz, and Edwards 2011, xxii). Their assertion is supported by an ever-growing body of scientific evidence and more attention being paid to the use of new technology in such areas as hacking computers, spreading viruses, recruiting children for sexual acts, and identity theft. What has been missing is that, until recently, the bulk of the research on the negative features of new technologies either ignored or overlooked the fact that technology is now a tool used by men to exert control and power over their current and former partners (Navarro, Clevenger, and Marcum 2016).

All of the authors here are familiar with women who find themselves under increasing control by the men in their lives. For example, some years ago Walter DeKeseredy overheard a woman at an exercise center tell another women that her husband had given her a cellular phone for Christmas. The recipient of this information responded, "Oh that was nice of him." The first woman, however, replied, "Not really. Now he can monitor me more and easier than he ever did before." Because of what was, at that time, brand new technology, this woman's partner achieved an additional method of control and victimization. Being so monitored can range from something annoying to something life-threatening. Navarro (2016), for example, describes a woman who tried to escape an abusive husband only to have him show up at her place of hiding to attack her again and steal her car. It turns out that his cell phone company allowed him to track her phone, which she could not stop or turn off. Navarro asks the reader to empathize: "Imagine how you would escape a dangerous relationship. How would you escape knowing that your bank/credit cards, cell phone, and movements were possibly being tracked by the perpetrator? What would you do?" (129).

Certainly, some new technologies are powerful instruments of separation/divorce violence against women, and the main objective of this chapter is to focus on this issue.

CYBERSTALKING

As stated in Chapter 2, stalking is "the willful, repeated, and malicious following, harassing, or threatening of another person" (Melton 2007a, 4). Chapter 2 also confirmed that stalking is strongly correlated with physical, sexual, and psychological abuse, and it escalates when women leave their male partners (DeKeseredy and Schwartz 2013; Melton 2007b). Stalking involves a variety of fear-inducing behaviors, some of which are what Navarro (2016) refers to as "low-tech" and others are what she terms "high-tech," although the widespread availability of these items, and the ability for people without technical knowledge to use them, may make such distinctions less useful. Low-tech methods do not require that the stalker obtain particularly sophisticated technological knowledge, and for that reason the use of such methods is widespread and common. The literature is filled with examples of such low-tech stalking, such as monitoring phone calls (Belknap, Chu, and DePrince 2011; Hand, Chung, and Peters 2009),[2] using information included in fax headers to locate women who have fled abusive male partners, using phone calls and electronic mail (email) to threaten, harass, or insult survivors, or disrupting email communication by flooding a victim's email box with unwanted mail. It might include sending a virus program or impersonating the victim online to harm their economic or personal reputation, making repeated phone calls to them, or perhaps making numerous phone calls to their place of employment in an attempt to get them fired (Burke et al. 2011; Cavezza and McEwan 2014; Melander 2010). Yet another low-tech technique is "electronic dumpster diving," which is the use of public information sites to get information about women to use for harassment purposes (Navarro 2016).

Higher-technology techniques may be used instead of low-tech strategies, or may be used in combination with them to cyberstalk. The examples offered below make it clear that "feeling safe" is no longer a simple function of putting some physical distance between the woman and her stalker. The newer high-tech technologies have "destroyed the concept of safety" (Navarro 2016, 128). One example is the installation of spyware on the computers and phones owned or used by the victim who is the object of the stalking (Southworth et al. 2007). One form of spyware that can be installed is a keylogger, which records every keystroke made on a keyboard without the user's knowledge or consent. This information is then sent to the person who installed the program or physical device. Keylogging is not new; in fact, in the early 1980s, the Soviet government installed keyloggers on IBM Selectric typewriters in the U.S. Embassy in Moscow and the U.S. Consulate in St. Petersburg (Malecki 2012). Today there are dozens of keylogging programs available for easy purchase.

Of course, as technologies change, the ability of high-tech criminals to capture information, and the ability of stalkers to exploit that information, similarly increases. Such devices become more easily and commercially available, and the price drops down to put such devices into the reach of a great many people. This is also true of another form of spyware, screenlogging, which consists of using the screen capture feature on most computers to regularly send images of what is on the screen to the stalker. Other new programs can capture mouse clicks, so that even very high-tech programs that require a password to be entered by choosing figures or numbers on a screen can be broken by capturing where on the screen the mouse was clicked, so that a password can be calculated. Once a password can be captured, or calculated through monitoring of on-screen pixels, a stalker (or other criminal) can gain access to bank, insurance, and work records, whether for profit or just to cause trouble.

Other "high-tech" devices that Navarro (2016) says can be used by stalkers to harass their victims are also easily commercially available. As just one example, typing in "hidden spy camera" on Amazon's[3] website brings up thousands of devices, including a variety of cameras hidden in clock radios, smoke detectors, clothes hooks, picture frames, pens, a thermometer, and even a bottle of water. For a better picture, one can turn on the video camera in a tablet, laptop, or phone. Many of these are activated with a motion detection device, some have DVR recorders, and some are less expensive than lunch in a chain full-service restaurant.

We know that these types of stalking occur during and after separation/divorce, but as of yet we do not know the true extent and distribution of these problems. Furthermore, of the small number of studies that have been done on cyberstalking, an even smaller number document gendered patterns of female victimization and male offending that are similar to the stalking that is found in other contexts (Crisafi, Mullins, and Jasinski 2016). Research specifically designed to measure the incidence and prevalence of separation/divorce cyberstalking is definitely needed. Still, what we do know, which is a good start, is that male former partners constitute the largest group of known cyberstalkers (Crisafi, Mullins, and Jasinski 2016; Working to Halt Online Abuse 2013). It is certainly worth accepting as a reasonable assumption that the motivations for former partners to engage in online stalking are the same as the motivations we know about for offline or non-cyberstalking. Such motivations include obsession, jealousy, revenge, a desire to control the victim, and a wish to reestablish a relationship (DeKeseredy and Schwartz 2013; Melton 2007b). Regardless of what causes men to stalk, their illegal behavior generates much fear and concern. As one woman told interviewers: "I'm afraid that he will feel like a man with nothing to lose and he will kill me. That's what I am afraid of. I think he would rather see me dead than to see me happy or to see me with someone else" (cited in Logan et al. 2006, 22).

In light of the femicide data presented in Chapter 2 and information included in this chapter, women who exit relationships and are stalked are not overreacting and suffering from irrational fears. Rather, being fearful is a legitimate reaction to something that is, at minimum, very anxiety-inducing and, at maximum, very dangerous and occasionally fatal. An unknown

number of abusive men who eventually kill their ex-partners not only stalk
them through conventional physical means but also use social network sites
to harass, intimidate, and humiliate them (see Box 3).

SOCIAL NETWORK SITE INTRUSION

Although a number of early experiments and prototype networks have to be
considered when writing a history of the Internet, the network merger that
created the Internet we know today, and its impact on culture, communications, and entertainment, only dates back to the mid-1990s. From something that only scientists and academics were using, and even then in
limited numbers, the Internet has exploded into massive use throughout
society. A Pew Research Center survey conducted in September 2014 found
that Facebook, the most popular social networking site, includes as mem-

TABLE 1

Who Uses Social Networking Sites?

Internet users	Percent of Internet users within each group who use social networking sites
All	74
Men	72
Women	76
18–29 years of age	89
20–49	82
50–64	65
65+	49
High school grad or less	72
Some college	78
College+	73
Less than $30,000 per year	79
$30,000–$49,000	73
$50,000–$74,999	70
$750, 000+	78

SOURCE: Duggan et al. 2015.

bers 71 percent of all Internet users (Duggan et al. 2015). Of course, many other platforms are popular, particularly with younger users who might be regularly sending out tweets on Twitter, participating in Black Twitter, posting pictures on Instagram, Flickr, or Snapchat, posting to Tumblr or Google+ texting through Kik or WhatsApp, or perhaps checking out the gossip on Yik Yak. The use of various social media is widespread throughout the world. Table 1 shows how social media has been integrated into U.S. society, from data collected by the Pew Research Center in January 2014. It would certainly be reasonable to assume that these numbers would be higher if collected today.

There is a large literature on the positive attractions of electronic social networking. There are also extensive warnings about how teenagers could get into trouble with unmonitored use of these sites, with special attention being placed on the dangers of child molesters or exploiters lurking on sites or harvesting sexual photos that unsophisticated teens thought would be private. An example that will be widely used of this danger came when two Virginia Tech freshmen were charged with meeting 13-year-old Nicole Lovell online and convincing her to run off in the middle of the night in a bizarre murder plot aimed at providing excitement for them (Silverstein 2016). Although there has been extensive public discussion of the danger of social networking sites to young people, Crisafi and colleagues' (2016) review of the empirical literature on social network site intrusion reveals a disturbing trend that does not garner near as much academic attention.

The work by Crisafi and colleagues shows that most of the data about social networking intrusion as a form of separation/divorce violence against women come from studies of social networking on Facebook. For example, Lyndon, Bonds-Raacke, and Cratty (2011) found that over two-thirds of the 411 people in their sample of college students who used Facebook and had recently broken up from a serious relationship made contact with that ex-partner through Facebook, doing things like writing poetry or music lyrics on their target's Facebook wall. However, 18 percent used Facebook to publicly harass their ex-partners, including such abuse as creating a fake Facebook profile of an ex-partner to humiliate or embarrass them, or writing negative things about their ex-partners on friends' Facebook walls, often venting at depth about their ex-partner's behavior.

Some of these abusive acts only start during or after the dissolution of a relationship, but an unknown quantity of men who victimized women in ongoing relationships continue to do so through Facebook after their female partners leave them (Darvell, Walsh, and White 2011; Dimond, Fiesler, and Bruckman 2011). Moreover, postings by Internet-linked men's and fathers' rights groups might encourage abusive men to hurt their ex-partners on social networking sites by portraying violence as an acceptable solution to their problems (Crisafi et al. 2016). Keep in mind what Paul Elam, founder of A Voice for Men, stated in one of his blogs:

> There are women, and plenty of them, for which a solid ass kicking would be the least they deserve. The real question here is not whether these women deserve the business end of a right hook, they obviously do, and some of them deserve one hard enough to leave them in an unconscious, innocuous pile on the ground if it serves to protect the innocent from imminent harm.

The real question is whether men deserve to be able to physically defend themselves from assault . . . from a woman. (Cited in Kimmel 2013, 118)

Elam is not, by any means, a lone wolf. There are many men who take his words to heart, or who would be happy to make similar arguments if they had an audience. Similarly, the antiwoman organization Return of Kings, led by Daryushi Valizadeh, also known as Roosh, has a growing following and holds public meetings that claim certain misogynistic acts are acceptable. Return of Kings has received considerable attention from the mainstream media, particularly in Australia, and on social networking sites. Much of the mainstream publicity came when Roosh announced that there would be an International Meeting Day at multiple sites in forty-three countries on February 6, 2016, and then canceled all of the meetings at the last minute. Online articles written by him and other members of Return of Kings assert that misogynists are better for women than feminists, that women should not be able to vote, that rape on private property should be legalized, that transgender women who have sexual relations with heterosexual men are rapists, and that women are biologically determined to follow the orders of men. LaCapria (2016), writing on the website Scopes (a site that attempts to separate fact from rumor or hoax), suggests that the entire Return of Kings website hosted by Valizadeh was from the beginning a "troll" site more concerned with upsetting people than truly believing its own articles, such as the assertion that feminists can be turned into sex slaves. Still, Valizadeh's Return of Kings website, which was developed in 2012, has about 14,000 Facebook "likes" and publishes roughly fifteen articles a month (Moloney 2016). Obviously, even if this is a troll site to promote misogyny or the message that legalizing rape is good for women because it will give them the incentive to learn how to protect themselves, it is a site with numerous regular readers. Consider this statement included on a Return of Kings webpage:

> Even while women have redefined themselves as butch, buzz cut wearing, cursing, tattooed, pierced, masculine, empowered career drones who can slut around as much as they want until they decide to settle down with a nice guy, they have somehow been able to retain this idea that they are the gentler sex. This is despite evidence that they are the more violent physical aggressors in domestic disputes, and certainly the more emotionally manipulative. According to them, they must be wined and dined and pleased and catered

to at all times, they are better parents, they would make better leaders, and they should be courted and spoiled the way our grandfathers would treat a lady.

Although remember, they are not responsible for their actions and if they drink alcohol that they legally buy at a bar, a place that exists as a location where single men and women can go to meet each other and grease the wheels for sexual interaction. This can now be equated to violently raping her if she is unhappy.[4]

These diatribes are similar to the antifeminist sentiments reported in Chapter 1, and, for reasons presented there, it is necessary to take antifeminist online communities seriously. Still, an important question remains: Is there a strong correlation between visiting social network sites like Return of Kings and the types of social network intrusion discussed here? In other words, does the encouragement of online male peer support groups have the same effect on men's behavior that we have shown takes place in face-to-face peer support (DeKeseredy and Schwartz 2013)? An answer to such questions that we often use is, "This is an empirical question that can only be answered empirically." The literature seems to be silent on this question; there have been, as far as we know, no major empirical studies to determine if there is a correlation or a relationship between online support and behavioral cyberstalking action.

Similarly, there needs to be additional empirical work on the extent and the breadth of psychological damage done by social network stalking and intrusion. Of course, anecdotally we know that such damage might be long-term, and theoretically even lifelong, since anything posted on the Internet never truly disappears and can reappear at awkward or difficult times in the future. As one would expect in a field like the Internet that is, even theoretically, only twenty years old, we have a lot more to learn about the physical health effects of such torment and abuse (Bauman, Toomey, and Walker 2013). However, we do know that there are teenagers committing suicide directly and indirectly because of bullying (Klomeck, Sourander, and Gould 2011; Kowalski, Limber, and Agatston 2012). We know that the effects of cyberbullying can be severe for adolescents. In a study of 1,963 American middle schoolers, Hinduja and Patchin (2010) found that the victims of cyberbullying were more likely to have suicidal thoughts and to have made

New Technologies and Violence

suicide attempts. There is no way of knowing how many students succeed in these attempts directly due to cyberbullying, but the researchers contend that these reactions suggest the need for vigilance on the part of school officials, who are too often either unprepared to deal with these newer issues or unaware of the seriousness of the problem (J. Klein 2012).

Certainly researchers studying teenagers have found that cyberbullying has ill effects, including suicide (Kowalski, Giumetti, and Schroeder 2014). A meta-analysis of thirty-seven studies on bullying and suicide suggested that the relationship between the two is strong (Kim and Leventhal 2008). Indirectly, cyberbullying can cause depression and decreased self-worth, which can cause suicidal thoughts (Hinduja and Patchin 2010). We know that suicide is one of the leading causes of death among American youth, but it remains difficult—if not impossible—to estimate how many of these deaths were the result of cyberbullying.

If the effect of cyberbullying against the widely studied youth population is still in its adolescence, then our knowledge base about the effect of such bullying among adults is absolutely in its infancy. Researchers commonly believe that adolescence and schooling are difficult terrains for youths to master and that massive social pressures combined with fewer emotional resources and reserves make the teenage years particularly difficult. Yet it is also widely known that such effects can be lifelong, with triggers to a memory of bullying even forty or fifty years later producing a reaction in older adults (Kowalski, Limder, and Agatston 2012). Many people presume that the passage of years gives people the reserves to cope with bullying. Unfortunately, there does not seem to have been much research on this question; at this point, it remains a presumption. We presume, however, that targeted bullying from former partners can result in reactions as strong in adults. Knowing that the physical and psychological reactions resulting from social network intrusion and the abusive use of other new technologies are severe for youths, we see no reason not to assume that these reactions can be similar for many adults.

PORNOGRAPHY

We briefly discussed the relationship between pornography and separation/ divorce sexual assault in Chapter 2. We are also seeing strong correlations between porn and woman abuse in other intimate contexts, such as marriage/cohabitation, dating, and "hooking up." Although we might not yet fully understand the specific dynamics of how it operates, there is ample evidence that violent pornography is a component of woman abuse and that many abusive men are graduates of what Bancroft (2002) refers to as "the Pornography School of Sexuality" (231).[5] Maybe, then, it would be best to follow Jensen's (2007) advice: "Rather than discussing simple causation, we should consider how various factors, in feminist philosopher Marilyn Frye's terms, 'make something inviting.' In those terms, pornography does not cause rape, rather it helps make rape inviting" (103).

The Internet was nowhere near an integral part of people's lives as it is now when early studies of the relationship between porn and woman abuse were conducted between the early 1980s and late 1990s. The pornography of that era did not have the high rates of aggression and violence that exist today (Bridges and Anton 2013). Of course, there is conversely no way of knowing whether the men who watch today's porn are at greater risk of abusing current or former female partners than men who consumed violent sexual materials prior to the advent of the Internet. What we do know today is that we "certainly have enough evidence to warrant identifying pornography as a risk factor . . . associated with sexual violence among some populations" (Shope 2004, 68). We also have enough evidence linking other forms of woman abuse to men's use of porn (DeKeseredy and Corsianos 2016). One of the key reasons for the connection is the contemporary porn industry. This is not to say that other reasons are less important, but they are given in-depth coverage in other sources (e.g., DeKeseredy and Corsianos 2016), and examining them is beyond the scope of this book.

For years, feminists have argued that North America and other parts of the world are *rape-supportive cultures*, where values and beliefs that support and encourage the sexual victimization of women are widely available to all men (Cross 1993; Schwartz and DeKeseredy 1997). This does not mean that all men adopt such attitudes and values, but that they are so prevalent in popular culture that they are readily and commonly available to all men, available and seemingly culturally approved for men who choose to adopt them. A rape-supportive culture also refers to "the set of cultural expectations, practices and standards that seek to erase the realities of sexual violence through a certain kind of story—one that says if a woman is assaulted, it's because of what she was wearing, drinking, doing or saying—not because of the person who assaulted her" (Healey 2016, 1). Probably the relationship is fairly complex, as these attitudes existed before the porn industry, but pornography reflects, amplifies, and provides support for such attitudes, making it an integral part of today's modern and expanded rape-supportive culture.

In a 2009 book, DeKeseredy and Schwartz examined sexual assault against divorced and separated women, specifically centering on rural areas. This is, of course, a smaller subset of the problem that is being examined in this book. However, an important conclusion of the 2009 book, as mentioned in the section of this book dealing with rural issues, is that in many cases pornography is an important feature of violence against women. Men who viewed pornography, either alone or in groups, tended to demand that the women in their lives duplicate or replicate the scenes, often violent, that they had watched in porn. Pornography served a role, though its extent is unknown, in teaching these men that the proper role for women to play was to serve and service their sexual needs, that women were a commodity and as such were property owned by the men. They learned that these possessions were theirs as long as they wanted them, not as long as the women wanted to be in a relationship. The most extreme statement of this were the men who felt that "if I can't have you, no one can."

It is, of course, difficult to lay all of this at the feet of pornography, because, as we said, these attitudes were around long before pornography as we know it today existed. However, pornography plays an major role in underscoring, expanding, legitimizing, and spreading these beliefs. The role of technology is not only to invent and promulgate new ideas but also to take older ideas and spread them wide and fast. Certainly, in Western history, there have been songs or jingles that spread around the country in a period of months and began to have an effect on people's beliefs. Today, because of the Internet and various forms of the media and social media, the effect can be days or even hours, and it can spread from a local phenomenon to every corner of the globe. In some cases, the harm is much greater than before. For centuries, people who were jerks tried to get even with people who broke up with them by spreading rumors and stories and by trying to ruin their reputation. This could be exceptionally painful, and it could require the victim to move a few villages away, but today there are methods of harassment that can reach like-minded people 10,000 miles away fairly instantly, and they can remain in circulation permanently.

IMAGE-BASED SEXUAL ABUSE

An electronic variant of abuse that is currently garnering increased scholarly, media, and legislative attention is *image-based sexual abuse,* which is also referred to as *revenge pornography, nonconsensual pornography,* or *involuntary pornography* (Franks 2015).[6] In Box 4, a rationale for using the term image-based sexual abuse instead of the more popular revenge porn is made, based on the arguments of McGlynn and Rackley (2016). Their reasoning is becoming widely accepted among academic experts in the field, if not yet by the general public. Regardless of which terminology one prefers, many of the images and videos discussed here are typically made by men with the consent of the women they were intimately involved with but then distributed online without their consent, typically following women's termination of the relationship (Salter and Crofts 2015). Image-based sexual abuse websites and blogs first appeared on the Internet in 2000 and started to gain U.S. national attention in 2010 following the creation of IsAnyoneUp.com. In their history of revenge porn, Lamphere and Pikciunas (2016) note:

> The creator, Hunter Moore, a 25-year-old man from Sacramento, California, began the website which featured sexually explicit photos, a link to the person in the photo's Facebook, Twitter, and/or Tumblr, as well as personal information about the person. The site allowed anonymous submissions of photos of any person to its database, and at one point it had reached a rate of over 30 million views per month. (148)

Leading experts in the field, such as La Trobe University's Nicola Henry, state that there is a "massive potential audience for revenge porn" (cited in Marriner 2015, 1). Most revenge porn sites, though, are underground, and people "trade" nonconsensual images for *bitcoins.* Also referred to as a type of money known as *cryptocurrency,* bitcoin is, briefly, a variant of digital currency and is decentralized. In other words, no single bank or institution controls the bitcoin currency. Moreover, users can hold multiple bitcoin addresses, which are not linked to names, addresses, or other personally identifying information (CoinDesk 2015).

Few studies to date have actually measured the extent of image-based sexual abuse (Crisafi, Mullins, and Jasinski 2016), but it is estimated that there are now more than 3,000 such sites, and the bulk of the perpetrators are male ex-husbands, ex-boyfriends, and ex-lovers (Lamphere and Pikciunas 2016; *Economist* 2014). Furthermore, McAfee Security's *Love, Relationships, and Technology Survey* (2013) uncovered that one in ten ex-partners threatened to post sexually explicit pictures of their former partners online, and 60 percent of these threats were carried out. Note, too, that an internal evaluation of 1,244 people done by the Cyber Civil Rights Initiative (2016) found that over 50 percent of victims stated that their naked pictures appeared next to their full name and social network profile. Over 20 percent of victims reported that their email addresses and telephone numbers appeared next to their photos, and over 80 percent of victims experienced severe emotional distress and anxiety (Citron and Franks 2014).

Another relevant study is worth mentioning here because it is national in scope. Powell and Henry (2015) surveyed 3,000 Australians aged 18 to 54 and found that one in ten stated that someone had posted online or sent to others nude or seminude pictures of them without their permission; 9.6 percent reported that someone threatened to post such images or to send them to others. Certainly, the data are alarming, but the researchers state that their survey was not specifically designed to focus on image-based sexual abuse and thus there is no way of knowing the motives behind the threats and actual sharing. Nor were the researchers able to determine whether the images were shared by a current or former intimate partner, relative, friend, acquaintance, or stranger. It is also unknown whether the images were accompanied by personal or identifying information for the purpose of humiliating or harassing victims. This missing information is vital because, as Powell and Henry put it:

> While sharing any nude or semi-nude image without permission of the person depicted can be considered harmful behavior, the context around the image itself and the circumstances in which it is shared can increase the severity of the harm and the impact on the victim. This is an important consideration for future research into seeking to understand the prevalence and nature of image-based sexual exploitation. (2)

The harm done by image-based sexual abuse is irreparable, as demonstrated by Holly Jacobs's experiences. She is the founder of the advocacy

BOX 4. WHAT'S IN A NAME? IMAGE-BASED SEXUAL ASSAULT

Various students of language of many backgrounds have long argued that the very words we use to label behavior or actions tend to influence our attitudes and beliefs about that behavior. For example, "getting played" sounds much less offensive and less in need of intervention than "criminal sexual assault." Using an accurate descriptive term can be important when the goal is to label that behavior as wrong. This applies to the topic here, which is commonly known as *revenge pornography*.

What might legitimately be termed "revenge porn" is only one part of the complex problem of *image-based sexual abuse*. The limited term applies when a sexual partner or ex-partner, who is legitimately in possession of private sexual videos or pictures, decides to exact revenge by sharing them, such as to websites. One problem is that, even in this limited example, partners share private images for many reasons in addition to private revenge. For example, they might be trying to make money, they might think it is funny to do so, or they might see it as enhancing their own reputation. Some people who post images to revenge-porn sites have stolen the images and may not even know the people involved. Calling these images revenge porn places all of the attention on the motivation of the offender, sometimes incorrectly, and none of the attention on the harm that such behavior does to the victims. It also involves a presumption that revenge porn consists of images created with the consent of the victim but then shared, which is not always the case. There are entire genres of such imagery, such as hidden camera or upskirt videos, where the notion of "revenge" is not applicable.

Thus, the field is in need of a term that emphasizes the problem involved. This is not an issue of condemning pornography but rather one that underscores the abusive nature of having sexual images publicly shared without the victim's consent. As McGlynn and Rackley (2016) point out, "[I]t is a form of harassment and often part of a pattern of coercive, domestic abuse. It is also a breach of the fundamental rights to privacy, dignity and sexual autonomy, with women (and victims are mostly women) being forced off-line and blamed or targeted" (1).

> Possibly most important, McGlynn and Rackley point out that using the words "image-based sexual assault" links the behavior not to pornography but to sexual violence generally, allowing the user to locate the nonconsensual use of private sexual images on a continuum with other abusive attacks on women. Attempts to gain support and protection for victims might be easier to conceptualize if the target is not pornography but nonconsensual and tremendously harmful attacks on autonomy and integrity.

group End Revenge Porn, and her ex-boyfriend hacked into her Facebook profile and posted sexually explicit images for relatives and friends to see prior to disseminating more material through revenge-porn websites and emailing material to her employers (Miller 2013). Revenge porn sites were then used by groups of men to harass and abuse Jacobs (Salter and Crofts 2015). She stated on her website:[7]

> Due to this act, I have had to legally change my name, stop publishing in my field (I am a Ph.D. student), stop networking (giving presentations, going to conferences), change my email address four times and my phone number three times, change jobs, and explain to human resources at my school that I am not a sexual predator on campus. (Cited in Salter and Crofts 2015, 236)

Sexting is now a common practice, and it is also a means of engaging in image-based sexual abuse. Sexting involves sharing compromising photos, videos, or written information with other people via texts or other electronic media (J. Klein 2012, 115). Generally, however, it is done with a smartphone or tablet (Lamphere and Pikciunas 2016; Weins 2014). In most cases, the original aim of the person sending out the photos, particularly for adolescents, is to share flirty or sex-themed pictures with intimate friends, under the presumption that they will not be shared. And, of course, this is usually exactly what happens. However, sometimes the recipient is not as trustworthy as the sender hoped, and the photo gets shared with others. Our major concern here is the vicious and purposeful attempt to ruin the life of the sender, in revenge for breaking up the relationship, by posting such photos widely or on sites that not only make them widely available (worldwide, to boot) but also identify the image by name, e-address, or other information that allows predators and trolls on the Internet to directly contact and harass the woman depicted. This new technology is causing lifelong damage to numerous people. It is worthwhile for all adolescents, and in fact for adults, too, to remember this warning by the National Campaign to Prevent Teen Pregnancy and Unplanned Pregnancy and CosmoGirl.com:

> There is no changing your mind in cyberspace—anything you send or post will never truly go away. Something that seems fun and flirty and is done on a whim will never really die. Potential employers, college recruiters, teachers, coaches, parents, friends, enemies, strangers, and others may all be able to find your past posts, even after you delete them. And it is nearly impossible to control what other people are posting about you. Think about it. Even if you have second thoughts and delete a racy photo, there is no telling who has already copied that photo and posted it elsewhere. (National Campaign 2012, 2)

The two organizations that issued this warning also conducted a national U.S. survey to uncover information on what Wastler (2010) defines as "downward distribution":

+ 38 percent of teen girls and 39 percent of teen boys say they have had sexually suggestive text messages or emails—originally meant for someone else—shared with them.
+ 25 percent of teen girls and 33 percent of teen boys say they have had nude or seminude images—originally meant for someone else—shared with them.
+ 37 percent of young adult women and 47 percent of young adult men have had sexually suggestive text messages or emails—intended for someone else—shared with them.
+ 24 percent of young adult women and 40 percent of young adult men say they have had nude or seminude images—originally meant for someone else—shared with them. (National Campaign 2012, 3)

Sexting is a relatively new phenomenon. Although Brown, Keller, and Stern (2009) assert that sexting can be dated back to an earlier era when images were taken and printed out with the relatively instant Polaroid camera, others argue for dating the phenomenon to the earliest published report on sexting: a 2004 report in the Canadian national newspaper *The Globe and Mail*. That article concerned a story about a sexually explicit text message shared between famous professional soccer player David Beckham and his assistant (Lamphere and Pikciunas 2016). With a phenomenon this recent, there certainly are no reliable estimates yet of the number of women who are harmed by sexting during and after separation/divorce. Since the primary mechanism to take and send these photos are the suddenly ubiquitous cell phones with cameras, the widespread use of sexting had to wait until cell phones came into wide use. However, another reason why we do not know much about adult sexting is that research thus far on the subject has focused on the prevalence of youth and young adult sexting. This social scientific literature is fast growing (Jaishankar 2009; Lamphere and Pikciunas 2016; Reed, Tolman, and Ward 2016). Still, there is so little known today that extensive research will be necessary before we have a solid basis for discussion.

In the United States, at least thirty-four states and the District of Columbia have instituted some sort of law against image-based sexual abuse, although the laws range from misdemeanors to felonies, depending on the state, and occasionally depending on the age of the offender (Cyber Civil Rights Initiative 2016). In England and Wales, a new law on the subject went into effect in April 2015, and, at the end of one year, the government reported that 206 men had been prosecuted. However, to illustrate the difficulty of depending on such laws, the BBC's research found that, in the first months of the law, by December 2015, a survey of 75 percent of the nation's police forces uncovered 1,160 reports to the police of revenge porn violations. Prosecutors reported that they were unable to gather sufficient evidence in most cases (BBC 2016).

It is reasonable to presume or speculate that the problem of revenge porn will only get worse. There is no particular reason to believe that men are reducing their use of sexist, racist, or homophobic comments or verbal attacks. Certainly this is nothing new. As far back as we know, men have been making these remarks in public, whether in bars or pubs, the workplace, or any other meeting ground. The difference is that, today, the same mean-spirited comments can gain a wider audience than a few men who happen to be present. Hundreds or thousands of people can read comments and, as noted above, some comments and images can stay on the Internet for the foreseeable future. With the constant stream of new technologies, it is easy for gender-related offenses to take place. One home of such comments is Yik Yak, which has been specifically designed to host anonymous gossip of up to 200 characters within a limited geographic area, sort of like an electronic bulletin board. A great many Yik Yak posts are neutral or positive, and the application has become popular with college students who want to build community or keep up with a wide circle of friends and acquaintances. The problem is that the same technology can be used to carry hateful, racist, sexist, or other hurtful comments. One such example took place in the fall of 2014 at Eastern Michigan University. There, students in the classes of three female professors posted more than a hundred demeaning Yik Yak posts about the women, including sexual remarks, insults about their appearance, and derogatory terms for women and their anatomy, earning them a write-up in *The New York Times* (see Mahler 2015). The women were unaware of the comments for quite some time, until one of their other students brought them evidence of the posts.

The Eastern Michigan University example is neither isolated nor unusual. Since its birth in November 2013, Yik Yak has "been causing havoc on campus as a result of students posting threats of harm, racial slurs, and slanderous gossip" (Schmidt 2015, 1). Another example of this came from the University of Maryland, where a female guest speaker was threatened with rape on Yik Yak. Danielle Citron, a Maryland law professor, was reported as saying that "[w]hat followed were other threads suggesting she should be raped, with kind of graphic descriptions of how. I imagine if it's reported as abuse, they take it down, but sometimes the harm is already done. If you think about it, a rape threat is frightening to someone. And so, yes you take it down, but you take it down two days later and the person is pretty scared" (cited in Bennett 2014).

Perhaps, then, it is most appropriate to end this section with Funnell's (2011) concluding statement in her piece titled "Sexting and Peer-to-Peer Porn":

> So while digital technology and social media have no doubt enhanced many aspects of our lives, they have also extended the ways in which women and girls can be violated, humiliated, and abused. To deal with this will require more than mere education for young people about the risks associated with technology. It will require an entire cultural shift, which, as its starting point, acknowledges and seeks to redress the ingrained misogyny, sexism and degradation of girls and women that underscores so much of our current culture. (40)

SUMMARY

Six years ago, Goodmark (2011) observed, "When the first domestic violence and stalking laws were passed, no one could have foreseen how technology would facilitate abuse, stalking, and harassment" (195). Undoubtedly, by the time you finish reading this chapter, there will be new electronic sites for inflicting pain on current or former intimate female partners as well as on other groups of people. Yet social scientific theoretical and empirical developments have not kept pace with the rapid spread of cybercrimes such as those identified in this chapter.

Perhaps researchers will never be able to keep up with the ever growing and ever changing electronic technologies. However, whatever conceptual, empirical, and theoretical work that is done in the future must take gender seriously and draw heavily from feminist schools of thought and the masculinities literature. This is not simply a political statement. Rather, the fact remains that there is a strong relationship between gender and the risk of being targeted by the harms covered in this chapter that cannot be adequately accounted for through the use of mainstream theories. The same people who made this observation—Reyns, Henson, and Holt (2016)—make another good point: "[T]here is a need to better measure the extent to which victims of interpersonal online victimization are targeted by former or current intimate others online" (91). We hope that some social scientists will respond to this call and advance our understanding of intimate relationship status variations in electronic means of woman abuse.

We would be remiss if we did not at least briefly mention that it is not only women's ex- or current partners who engage in electronic forms of woman abuse. An unknown number of women who come forward to report offline victimization (e.g., rape) are intimidated, bullied, and stigmatized in social media, especially if they seek criminal charges against high-profile athletes, actors, and other celebrities. This, in turn, influences other abuse survivors to suffer in silence. Of course, these are not the only reasons why most female victims of harassment, physical violence, and sexual assault do not come forward. Even so, the use of social media to cause the above effects is yet another reminder that every new technology can be misused in our rape-supportive, patriarchal culture (DeKeseredy and Dragiewicz 2013).

CHAPTER FOUR

Explaining Separation/Divorce Violence against Women

> Positivist data never really get underneath simplistic surface correlations, and lack sophistication and validity at the basic *conceptual* level, the foundation stone of social science. The quantitative data that positivists produce about changes in crime rates are a classic example: they rely on narrow legally-defined conceptualizations of crime without asking whether they truly represent the harms that impact negatively on people's lives.
>
> Hall and Winlow 2015, 10 (emphasis in original)

The above statement made by two eminent British critical criminologists brings us back to the issue of underreporting raised in Chapter 1. There we argued that a narrow conceptualization of separation/divorce results in many behaviors not being counted when investigating violence against women. Hall and Winlow (2015) also remind us that much criminological research, including a sizeable portion of that done on violence against women, is dominated by *positivism*, which assumes that human behavior is determined and can be measured (Curran and Renzetti 2001). The problem is that some measurement is theoretically based and scientifically grounded, but "in much of the social sciences reality has been lost in a sea of statistical symbols and dubious analysis" (Young 2013, viii). Our agreement with Young does not mean that we are among those criminologists arguing against any study with measurement and statistics. In fact, we have extensive backgrounds in self-report and victimization survey work.

However, there are good and bad analyses and numbers. As feminists, following Young (2013), we advocate the type of statistics that offer "the counter-voice to neo-liberalism and conservatism" (217). Additionally, good numbers are, to again quote him, not purposely "chosen . . . to fit the favored model and the model is finessed and meticulously adjusted to fit the data" (16). They are statistics generated by progressive surveys that define and categorize crime publicly, "not as officially processed through official categories" (MacLean 1991, 230).

Young's *The Criminological Imagination* (2013), informed by Mills's *The Sociological Imagination* (1959), is a powerful critique of orthodox criminology by advocating linking theory with research. Of course, the reason for these critiques is that many researchers do not have a strong theoretical backing for their empirical investigations. In North America, where the bulk of separation/divorce violence against women research is done, this has been a particular problem. However, as made explicit in Chapter 1, there are not fierce empirical, theoretical, or ideological debates within the group studying the issues covered in this book. Still, some are more theoretically inclined than others. The main objective of this chapter is to review our own offerings and those made by our colleagues, based on our belief that theoretical developments are important precursors to empirical analysis.

THE MALE PROPRIETARINESS THESIS

Many recent theories of both lethal and nonlethal separation/divorce violence build on Wilson and Daly's (1992, 1998) *male proprietariness thesis*, which is a variant of evolutionary psychological theory (Ellis, Stuckless, and Smith 2015).[1] Evolutionary psychological perspectives on crime, as Lilly, Cullen, and Ball (2015) succinctly describe them, are

> efforts to explain psychological traits, including tendencies toward criminality, in terms of adaptations that contributed to survival and were then transmitted to later generations until they became part of the biological heritage of certain people. The differences between males and females in tendencies toward law violation, for example, are traced to contrasting natural selection processes among primates that tend to lead to survival and reproduction of more aggressive males and more social females. (381)

According to Wilson and Daly (1992), marital separation escalates the risks of spousal homicide because it challenges "male sexual proprietariness"; this is "the tendency [of men] to think of women as sexual and reproductive 'property' they can own and exchange" (85). For example, a wife rape survivor interviewed by Bergen (1996) was frequently told by her abusive partner, "That's my body—my ass, my tits, my body. You gave that to me when you married me and that belongs to me" (20). Correspondingly, one of DeKeseredy and Schwartz's (2009) interviewees told them that she was repeatedly sexually assaulted because "it was his way of letting me know that, ah, first of all, of letting me know that I was his" (38). These views were common enough to have made their way into many laws, which for generations in Anglo-American law codified the notion that sexual assault could not be a criminal act, since by agreeing to marriage a woman has agreed to sex with her husband at all times in the future (Schwartz 1982). Of course, though such attitudes permeate popular culture in many areas, at least as legal principles they have been repudiated in virtually every juris-diction worldwide (Caringella 2009).

Proprietariness refers to "not just the emotional force of [the male's] own feelings of entitlement but to a more pervasive attitude [of ownership and control] toward social relationships [with intimate partners]" (Wilson and Daly 1992, 95). Certainly, many threats to kill women are tactics men use to terrorize their wives or cohabitors and to "keep them in line."

Again, as stated in Chapter 1, this book focuses on women-initiated exits because any "unilateral decision" to leave puts them at especially high risk (Brownridge 2009; Wilson and Daly 1993). When women emotionally or physically leave a relationship, sexually proprietary men "feel deprived of the power of ownership and thus feel justified in trying to take back their possession(s) by whatever means they can, including physical force" (McMur-ray 1997, 551). Until fairly recently, men had the law, tradition, and culture in most places to help husbands prevent their wives from leaving them.

How often was this power used to commit violent acts against wives? Of course, it is difficult enough to discover the exact amount of violence against women perpetrated around the world today. Trying to count acts from long ago is significantly more difficult, particularly as the more it was approved by law and culture, the less likely it was to be commented on in documents. However, it is generally accepted that most societies in most of the world were patriarchal, and that part of male power was the definition that men are in charge of the family. It was not unusual (and still is not) for male political and religious leaders to claim that part of men's duties was the chastisement of women and children when needed, and that this "chastisement" could involve physical violence. Christianity has been filled with documents, from Friar Cherubino to Martin Luther, reinforcing male authority in the family (Lentz 1998). The notion that violence was "correction" or "chastisement" always confused judges, since the person in charge seemed to need the ability to correct improper behavior. Numerous histories cite documents from assorted eras showing that woman abuse was at minimum tolerated and at times condoned as a legitimate use of authority. Of course, there are numerous similar documents, speeches, and authority denouncing the use of violence by husbands (Lentz 1998). Still, on balance, it seems to be difficult to find any society in any part of the globe that did not have a significant part of the female population subjected to husband violence, and that remains true today (United Nations General Assembly 2006).

In Colonial and early American history, there were a few courts that upheld the right of men to "chastise" their misbehaving wives, but courts were unanimous that this could not extend to aggravated assault. By the 1870s, it was the view of all British, Scottish, and Irish courts, plus all American states, that such violence by men was not allowed (Calvert 1975). In fact, in England, Lord Chancellor Halsbury ruled in 1891 that most of the claims of common law, such as the right of chastisement or the rule of thumb that allowed wives to be beaten with sticks, had never been part of British law. "In the same way such quaint and absurd dicta as are to be found in the books as to the right of the husband over his wife in respect of personal chastisement, are not, I think, capable of being cited as authorities in a court of justice in this or any civilized country" (Stedman 1917, 242–43). Yet all of these authorities discussed how such "common law" traditions are believed and acted on by "the lower classes" with great frequency. Such history and tradition is even today cited regularly as justification for wife-beating around the world, by men who feel a sense of proprietariness over their wives (DeKeseredy and MacLeod 1997; Dobash and Dobash 1979).

We are left, then, to try to understand just why it is that men developed laws, or at least strong beliefs, that justified, at the minimum, painful physical force to "chastise" their wives. Four beliefs contributed to these laws and practices:

1. Women were considered the property of men, first of their fathers, then of their husbands.
2. Women were considered "naturally" subordinate and childlike and were therefore expected to obey their husbands and to be dependent on them both economically and in terms of rational guidance.
3. Men were believed to have authority over their wives within the home.
4. The appropriate place for women was believed to be in the home. (DeKeseredy and MacLeod 1997, 9–10)

In modern time, these beliefs have been augmented by a belief in romantic love—a type of love characterized by emotional extremes, psychological suffering, isolation, and possessiveness (Fontes 2015). In some ways, this may have made things worse for the wives of possessive men. Peterson del Mar (1996) argues that, in the past, great emphasis was placed on women doing what they were told. Now, with the rise of an emphasis on marital intimacy and love, women became responsible for emotions: it was her fault if he did not feel good about his life. Battering became less instrumental, where it was designed to get women to do something specific. Now, he argues, it became more expressive, an attempt to maintain a patriarchal society and to protest women's moves toward independence.

Throughout the twentieth century, American states and national legislatures progressively expanded the grounds for divorce and passed new laws forbidding physical and sexual violence within marriage. This inability to marshal outside support for their behavior has meant that proprietary husbands must rely on their own spouse-controlling resources to a greater degree. Their violence is a form of informal social control (Black 1983). The use of violence as a means of such control escalates when female partners separate, because separation is an extreme public challenge to male partners who believe they own their wives/cohabiting partners and therefore have the right to control them (Ellis and DeKeseredy 1997).

There is some empirical support for the relationship between male sexual proprietariness and separation/divorce assault.[2] Yet, logically, a constant such as proprietariness cannot explain a variable (changes in the frequency and severity of violence). In other words, if proprietariness is part of the makeup of a great number of male partners, why do only some men beat, rape, and kill their intimate partners? There are empirical data showing variations in men generated by a variety of patriarchal or macho ideology scales (e.g., DeKeseredy and Schwartz 1998; Smith 1990). Even the pioneers of this thesis—Wilson and Daly—recognized variation in male proprietoriness-related violence over time and across cultures (Wilson and Daly 1998). Nevertheless, they assert that male proprietariness is a function of the biologically evolved psychology of all men.

Certainly such a view is not without its critics. Dobash and Dobash (2015) argue that, though cultural and individual factors are important, working out evidence of biological roots to a way of thinking in a far distant part of prehistory is extremely difficult if not impossible. They suggest that debates over the "ultimate" source of such thinking are not needed. It is enough to point out that the thinking exists. "Possessiveness and jealousy are relevant and important issues when men murder an intimate partner whether the root source is social cultural, psychological, and/or biological" (2015, 27). Overall, Ellis, Stuckless, and Smith (2015) wrap up the general feeling in the field that "Daly and Wilson's evolutionary psychological explanation of the empirical generalization linking separation with femicide is a significant intellectual achievement" (91). Still, both Ellis, Stuckless, and Smith (2015) and Dobash and Dobash (2015) conclude after extensive analyses that jealousy/possessiveness is but one of several determinants of separation/divorce femicide and nonlethal violence that occurs during and after the process of exiting a relationship.

THE CHALLENGE THESIS

One alternative theory to Daly and Wilson was developed by Ellis and DeKeseredy (1997) with the *challenge thesis*.[3] This was one of the early theoretical developments in the field of separation and divorce violence against women studies, and it is included here in chronological order to show where we and the field have been. This perspective includes the concept of male proprietariness but as a building block to describe events that the earlier theory could not adequately explain. The findings indicate that a few men kill their estranged wives/cohabiting partners, but most do not. Ellis and DeKeseredy's inclusion of interventions invoked by mechanisms of *loyalty/love*, *voice*, and *exit* in a more elaborate challenge thesis was used to account for variations between estrangement and intimate femicide. These mechanisms were derived from the work of economist Hirschman (1970), in which he defines voice as "an expression of protest or dissatisfaction," exit as "leaving or buying a competitor's products or services," and loyalty as "attachment or relatively inelastic demand for services/products" (2). Ellis and DeKeseredy note that, in applying these three mechanisms to intimate relationships, three modifications are necessary. First, Hirschman applies these mechanisms to "the concept of random and more or less easily repairable lapse" (592). In Ellis and DeKeseredy's theory, they are applied to systematic recurring harms inflicted by males on their intimate female partners. Second, Hirschman conceives of exit, voice, and loyalty as "recuperative mechanisms" (592). Ellis and DeKeseredy view them as mechanisms for disintegrating or severing as well as reintegrating intimate relationships. Third, for Hirschman, voice ends with exit (43). In Ellis and DeKeseredy's application of these mechanisms to intimate relationships, however, escalated violence following exit is frequently encountered.

This theory is too complex to fully describe here (see Figure 2), but we will outline five main elements of it. First, Ellis and DeKeseredy's model locates male intimate partners on a *continuum* of proprietariness, because, as stated above, a constant cannot explain a variable.

Second, female intimate partners are located on a continuum of resistance. Evidence of this is provided by researchers such as Bowker (1983), DeKeseredy and MacLeod (1997), DeKeseredy and Schwartz (2009), Goetting (1999), Haselschwerdt et al. (2016), and Sev'er (2002). In the present case, loyalty/love, voice, and exit constitute different points on a continuum of resistance/change.

Third, mechanisms of resistance/change are linked with the choice of different kinds of interventions (Haselschwerdt et al. 2016). Thus, loyalty/love tends to be associated with the choice of marital counseling or voluntary participation in programs such as Alcoholics Anonymous. Voice tends to be associated with involving the police, neighbors, or friends. Exit makes the choice of shelters, women's support groups, lawyers, or mediators more likely.

Fourth, harms experienced by estranged wives/cohabiting partners can be located on a continuum of harms, ranging at one extreme from mass killings (such as the one involving Jody Hunt discussed in Chapter 1) to single

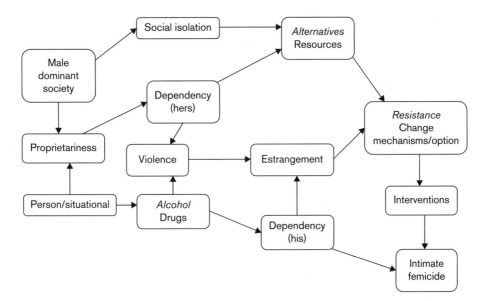

Figure 2. Elaborated model of male proprietariness effects. (From Ellis and DeKeseredy 1997.)

killings, aggravated assaults, sexual assaults, threats, stalking, and coercive control at the other end (Fontes 2015; Kelly 2012; O'Hagan 2014).

Fifth, person/situational factors are included in Figure 2 because Ellis and DeKeseredy claim that they help account for variations in male violence via their impact on proprietariness and deviance.[4] In this connection, Gondolf and Fisher (1988) include in their typology of batterers dangerous sociopathic and antisocial batterers who are generally violent,[5] substance abusers,[6] and those who have a history of "socially undesirable and criminal behavior" (66). It should be noted in passing, however, that though researchers are able to distinguish different types of abusive men, the value of these typologies to predict treatment success has been questioned (Tolman and Edleson 2011, 356).[7]

The Gondolf and Fisher (1988) typology suggests that sociopathic and antisocial batterers may be overrepresented among those who kill only their estranged partners. For them, femicide is the terminal point in a recurring and increasingly serious pattern of violence toward their partners. The fact that their wives/cohabiting partners are often killed within two or three months of separating may reflect a continuation of their pattern of violence rather than a reaction to separation as such.

Ellis and DeKeseredy (1997) point to another pattern in which males who have rarely or never abused or beaten their partners kill them and others as a reaction to separation. This type is not included in Gondolf and Fisher's (1988) typology of batterers because he tends not to be abusive. Rather, he is "highly dependent" on his partner and is "needy or clingy" (Adams 2007). He uses his emotional dependency rather than violence to control his intimate partner (Ellis and Kerry 1994), and he is willing to pay any price for her continued presence. For such a man, who tends to have a lower-status job and lower income than his wife/cohabiting partner, separation is likely viewed as abandonment. For that reason, separation tends to increase the likelihood of multiple killing—that is, femicide and suicide, or femicide, homicide, and suicide (Ellis, Stuckless, and Smith 2015; Polk 1994). Two men interviewed by Adams (2007) are examples of highly emotionally dependent perpetrators of separation/divorce femicide: "One killer said, 'I didn't realize how bad off I was emotionally. I thought in my heart that I could get her back.' When asked if there was anything his estranged partner could have said to have avoided being killed, another man said, 'If she told me she wouldn't leave me. I was so vulnerable I would have believed her'" (48).

Now we turn attention to how Ellis and DeKeseredy (1997) describe the ways in which interventions invoked by loyalty/love, voice, and exit affect intimate femicide. Some of them tend to decrease the risk of this crime by stopping the battering of women who stay. Others are aimed at preventing the killing of women who stay.

Co-residing Intimates: Interventions Invoked by Loyalty/Love
Being abused does not necessarily drive out love or loyalty (Fontes 2015). Nevertheless, there appears to be limits to the coexistence of loyalty/love and being battered. As the violence escalates in frequency and severity, and as it spreads to include the children, battering is likely to drive out feelings of love and loyalty (Browne 1987). Moreover, even first incidents of verbal or physical abuse have the potential for initiating the emotional separation process when the incident produces serious injuries, when the wife/cohabiting partner is abused again even after she changed the behavior that he

claimed caused his reaction, or when friends and/or relatives point out that she is neither morally blameworthy nor responsible for his violence (Ellis and DeKeseredy 1997).

Bowker (1983) identified a number of interventions that battered wives reported in a survey that seem to be invoked by loyalty/love. These include disclosure; seeking advice from friends, relatives, and neighbors; contacting professional counselors; and communicating a commitment to the relationship and an interest in reestablishing it. One indicator of the effectiveness of these strategies is that 37 percent of 144 surveyed battered wives included loyalty/love-invoked intervention in the general advice they gave to other battered women. Almost the same proportion (35 percent) included these interventions in a list of strategies that enabled or forced husbands to stop beating them. Unfortunately, loyalty/love-invoked interventions were not cross-classified with the stage in the progression of violence, so it is unclear whether their effectiveness varied with their timing.

Gondolf and Fisher (1988) believe that, regardless of the timing, loyalty/love-invoked interventions, such as voluntary participation in marital counseling, are unlikely to end battering by sociopathic and antisocial batterers, and they recommend excluding such men from counseling because "they are beyond the scope of conventional treatment" and "in order to avoid presenting another false hope to women" (66). Counseling, it seems, is a highly effective route by which dangerous husbands/cohabiting partners get their intimate female partners to return to them (Hamby 2014). The ethical problem comes when the treatment is known not to work, except to convince women to return.

In sum, Ellis and DeKeseredy (1997) contend that loyalty/love-invoked interventions are most effective in reducing the likelihood of intimate femicide when they are applied to "sporadic batterers"—that is, batterers who are in the first or initial stages of violence progression and who are neither generally violent nor serious alcohol or drug abusers with a lengthy record of criminal or deviant conduct. Failure to end violence by sporadic batterers via loyalty/love mechanisms increases the likelihood of both escalating resistance by wives/cohabiting partners and violence by the men from whom they are being estranged. Escalated violence/resistance increases the likelihood of intimate femicide (Dobash and Dobash 2015). Variations in intimate femicide, then, are for Ellis and DeKeseredy a function of variations in the effectiveness of loyalty/love-invoked interventions. In turn, the effectiveness of these interventions in ending battering depends on the timing of their invocation. The earlier they are invoked, the more effective they are deemed to be.

Co-residing Intimates: Interventions Invoked by Voice

Many abusive men are beyond the influence of loyalty/love as a mechanism of change and also of interventions invoked by loyalty/love. Although these informal help-seeking interventions are aimed at keeping batters from getting into trouble, voice and escalated voice may be more effective for these men precisely because the interventions they invoke can get batterers into trouble with the law, both criminal and civil.

To support their assertion, Ellis and DeKeseredy (1997) drew from Bowker's (1983) work, which is now obviously dated. Bowker found that, among the list of factors enabling or forcing husbands to end their battering, "fear of criminal or legal action" and "fear of divorce" were present in 51 percent of the cases. That these fears were instigated by threats (part of voice) is suggested in table 6-6 of Bowker's book. As shown in this table, threats decreased battering in 54 percent of the cases and increased it in only 13 percent of them. In an attempt to end their husbands' violence, many women carry out their threats by calling the police. That is, they move from voice to escalated voice. In other cases, their own raised voice (e.g., loud arguments) alerts neighbors or friends who call the police. Keep in mind, though, that contemporary research tells us that the presence of a "third party" or bystanders "minimally increases reporting to the police" (R. Klein 2012).

When the police are called, Ellis and DeKeseredy say, their arrival is, in and of itself, an intervention, and one that is likely to be more effective the faster the police arrive. A quick police response tells the victim that the police are treating the matter seriously. It may also provide an opportunity for intervention before the violence escalates further. They assert that a rapid police response can be the difference between an assault, an aggravated assault, an attempted femicide, and a femicide.

Even so, the positive effects of a rapid police response can be undermined by what the police do when they arrive at the scene, such as a lack of any action. Even worse are the many cases of dual arrests in which women

Explaining Violence

are criminalized for using self-defense or fighting back (Miller, Iovanni, and Kelley 2011). Laws that require the police to charge the primary aggressor are supposed to solve this problem, but, as Miller and Bonistall (2012) conclude:

> Responding police officers may still treat the woman as the primary aggressor as women tend to remember each violent incident (Dasgupta, 1999; Kimmel, 2002) and more readily admit to their use of violence (Dobash, Dobash, Cavanaugh, and Lewis, 1998). Additionally, women who are still experiencing emotional trauma from the battering situation may appear less credible than men who may be better able to describe the preceding events to their benefit (Miller, 2005). Criminalizing women for taking actions in self-defense may have many negative consequences, including denial of safe housing in a shelter, loss of custody of children, economic hardship, and unwillingness to call police in the future. (321)

Ellis and DeKeseredy, writing at a time when most scholars believed in aggressive policing, claimed that voice-invoked interventions that increase the confidence of the battered wife/cohabiting partner and that symbolize society's opposition to woman abuse will increase the probability and severity of the costs associated with battering and are fairly effective in ending abuse when they are invoked against two subtypes of "typical batterers: chronic and sporadic batterers." They go on to conclude that such interventions tend not to be effective against sociopathic and antisocial batterers for the reasons offered by Gondolf and Fisher (1988).

Ellis and DeKeseredy conclude this section of their theoretical model by stating that variations in the use of effectively implemented, voice-invoked interventions against chronic and sporadic batterers indirectly account for variations in intimate femicide via the contribution they make to ending battering. There is, today, no sound empirical support for this. As Hamby (2014) puts it, though large numbers of women continue to call the police:

> [I]t is widely known that the police response may have limited effectiveness in preventing future violence, may increase the retaliatory violence or other punishment by their partners, may put a victim at risk of being arrested herself, and in some communities, may expose victimized women or their partners to violence perpetrated by the police (Hirschel and Buzawa, 2002; Martin, 1997; Richie, 1996). Further, law enforcement involvement can also

be risky for women who may be worried about involvement from child protective services or immigration enforcement. (144)

In general, research on police activity has not found much effect of arrest or other interventions, or even the use of special domestic violence units that are claimed to be more sensitive than regular police patrols (Schwartz 2012). The most recent popular strategy, after an early simple evaluation in New York claimed some success, has been the "second responder approach," which sends a trained police officer or social worker back the next day to the scenes of battering calls. Unfortunately, every subsequent and more sophisticated evaluation has shown not only a complete lack of success but indeed a tendency for increases in further abuse (Davis, Weisburd, and Hamilton 2010).

Separated Intimates: Interventions Invoked by Exit
As a mechanism in this model, exit refers to the rather narrow definition of no longer sharing the same residence as the batterer. Many battered women who exit seek refuge from their violent male partners in shelters, which provide them with temporary, immediate refuge from violence and access to trained people who will listen to their concerns and offer advice. Does the earlier discussion about the dangers immediately after separation mean that women who enter shelters are at greater risk of being killed? For too many of them, the answer is yes (Dugan, Nagin, and Rosenfeld 2003). A central theme of this book is the point made by Dobash and Dobash (2015): "This is a dangerous time for women and those who might assist them. When separation occurs, issues of possessiveness and jealousy are elevated as are conflicts about the separation itself" (42).

Most shelters offer services for five days, one month, three months, or other short periods of time, and an abusive man may become even angrier because his partner left him. Moreover, shelters neither solve the problem of economic insecurity nor pay legal costs associated with separation/divorce (Hamby 2014). Hence, Ellis and DeKeseredy (1997) recommend that exit via shelter be associated with other interventions that enable battered wives and their children to live safe, autonomous lives. The provision of jobs, job training, child care, and housing would go a long way toward realizing this objective (DeKeseredy 2011; DeKeseredy and Schwartz 2009; Renzetti 2011).

Exit, via shelter or any other route (Haselschwerdt et al. 2016), is frequently associated with legal separation proceedings, at least for married women. These two decisions—to leave and to start separation proceedings—elevate the risks of intimate femicide because they represent a public, permanent, and costly challenge to male proprietariness. If children are present and/or the male partner expects to or has to transfer a significant proportion of his income or his possessions over to his wife/cohabiting partner, the costs and the risks are greater (Dragiewicz and DeKeseredy 2008).

Emotional separation, as stated in Chapter 1, especially if it is associated with a proprietary culture, also increases the likelihood of violence. Although lacking reliable data, Ellis and DeKeseredy speculated that emotional separation represents a significantly greater or more radical challenge to proprietariness. They also argued that women who continue to reside with husbands/cohabiting partners after they have told them of their intention to start legal separation proceedings are probably at greater risk of being killed than women who have physically separated but have not started such proceedings. What is more, they stated that, were the requisite data available, they would probably reveal the following risk rankings (from the highest to lowest risk): leave and start legal proceedings; stay, but communicate intention to start legal proceedings; go, but start no legal proceedings; and estranged but no communication about leaving or starting legal separation proceedings.

As discussed, women in the highest risk category—wives who are legally separated—have a six-fold increase in the risk of femicide (Ellis, Stuckless, and Smith 2015). Where physical separation and the initiation of legal separation proceedings occur at the same time, as stated in Chapter 1, the period of highest risk is the following two months. As time increases, risk decreases. Therefore, the intimate femicide rate is markedly lower among divorced women because divorces are usually granted one or more years following separation.

Following the decision to exit and to start legal separation proceedings, the next decision has to do with how the legal separation should be processed. In many, if not most jurisdictions, the choice is between *lawyer negotiations* and *mediation*. The research of Ellis (1994) and Ellis and Stuckless (1996) suggests that lawyer negotiations do not reduce the likelihood of violence as much as divorce mediation or conflict resolution (Ellis, Stuckless, and Smith 2015). To Ellis (2000), divorce mediation consists of a trained mediator leading negotiations between the separating couple, whereas conflict resolution is an attempt to reconcile the underlying issues that might lead to violence. Lawyer negotiations can be a similar system to working out everyone's desired outcomes, but it too often involves attempts to manipulate and "win." The use of affidavits that attempt to discredit the other partner, Ellis and DeKeseredy argue, is the mechanism that makes this process the least useful in reducing violence.

Other exit-invoked interventions that may also mediate the impact of extreme estrangement on intimate femicide include orders for exclusive possession of the matrimonial home, restraining orders with very strict access provisions and enforcement, supervised access to children, and significant jail time for men. Yet none of these interventions should be considered completely effective. For instance, there is some evidence that restraining orders, which are occasionally referred to as *orders of protection*, decrease physical violence over time.[8] Yet, as Hamby (2014) reminds us, "[T]hey are only pieces of paper. They are not magic force fields and they will not stop or even slow down a perpetrator who has no regard for the law" (147).

To sum up, Ellis and DeKeseredy (1997) contend that exit and exit-invoked mechanisms are effective in ending battering for most abused women. Even so, they may actually instigate lethal violence among extremely dependent husbands/cohabiting partners who may even have never abused their partners. Variations in intimate femicide, then, are partly a function of variations in the deployment of effective exit-invoked interventions, according to Ellis and DeKeseredy.

Summary of the Challenge Thesis

One of the key strengths of Ellis and DeKeseredy's (1997) offering is that it addresses the complexities of separation/divorce femicide. It builds on Wilson and Daly's (1993, 1998) work by integrating it with a theory of interventions. The problem is that the challenge thesis has never been empirically tested. In fact, given its complexity, it may very well have more value in summarizing the complex literature (a heuristic or teaching model) than as a predictive model to isolate and predict which specific men are most likely to commit violence or to be precluded from doing so. Such heuristic models are useful, and two authors of this book, Walter DeKeseredy and Martin Schwartz, have developed several that emphasize the concept of *male peer support*. Defined in Chapter 1, it is, again, the attachments to male peers and the resources that these men provide that encourage and legitimate woman abuse. This concept and male proprietariness are integral components of the next theory to be reviewed.

A FEMINIST/MALE PEER SUPPORT MODEL OF SEPARATION AND DIVORCE SEXUAL ASSAULT

In the middle of the past decade (see DeKeseredy and Joseph 2006; DeKeseredy and Schwartz 2009; DeKeseredy et al. 2006), Walter DeKeseredy and his colleagues wanted to achieve two goals.[9] One was to conduct the first North American qualitative study of separation/divorce sexual assault in rural communities, and the other was to advance a better theoretical understanding of this problem. At that time, rural crime research had not yet developed a theoretical framework that could synthesize the extant scholarly literature on what Hogg and Carrington (2006) refer to as "gendered violence and the architecture of rural life" (171). Further, the limited theoretical work that did exist on this topic ignored separation/divorce sexual assault. Of course, the neglect on the part of scholars to examine this problem applies to woman abuse research in general.

Even the marital rape literature can be defined as essentially atheoretical because it is restricted to presenting women's opinions about why their partners assaulted them or to constructing typologies based on the information provided by female respondents (DeKeseredy, Rogness, and Schwartz 2004; Mahoney and Williams 1998). For instance, Finkelhor and Yllo (1985) identified three types of rape: battering rape; force-only rape; and obsessive rape. These and other typologies of marital rape (e.g., Bergen 1996; Russell 1990) are reviewed elsewhere (see Mahoney and Williams 1998).

To fill the gap in rural crime literature, DeKeseredy, Rogness, and Schwartz (2004) crafted a research-driven theory that allows for a simultaneous consideration of broader macro-level forces and micro-level gender relations of central concern to feminist scholars. As presented in Figure 3, their offering moves well beyond answering the problematic question "Why doesn't she leave?" to "What happens when she leaves or tries to leave?" and

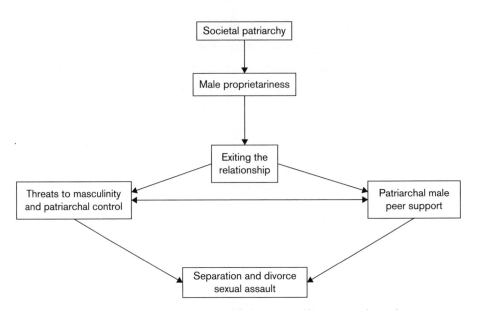

Figure 3. A feminist/male peer support model of separation/divorce sexual assault. (From DeKeseredy, Rogness, and Schwartz 2004, 684.)

"Why do men do that?" (Hardesty 2002; Stark 2007). As pointed out by many scholars and activists, the "Why doesn't she leave" question blames females for the abuse they endure in intimate relationships, rather than the person committing the criminal acts. And, as Stark (2007) notes, "It is men who stay, not their partners"; undeniably, "there is no greater challenge in the abuse field than getting men to exit abusive relationships" (130).

The fact that we critique the marital rape literature should not be construed as an all-out indictment of this body of knowledge. Marital rape researchers have identified several important risk factors (e.g., power, control, and an adherence to the ideology of familial patriarchy).[10] This identification was essential to later work in constructing and testing theories of separation/divorce sexual assault as well as other variants of woman abuse (Jasinski 2001). Some of the determinants mentioned by participants in marital rape studies done by Bergen (1996), Russell (1990), and others (e.g., Finkelhor and Yllo 1985) are included in the theoretical model depicted in Figure 3. Since this perspective is reviewed elsewhere (see DeKeseredy, Rogness, and Schwartz 2004; DeKeseredy and Schwartz 2009, 2013), it is only briefly described here.

When they first started thinking about theorizing separation/divorce sexual assault in rural places, DeKeseredy, Rogness, and Schwartz (2004) recognized that the best place to start was the theoretical literature on non-sexual forms of violence (such as beatings and femicide) that occur when women want to exit or have left a relationship.[11] The role of patriarchal dominance and control is central in this literature as well as in the marital sexual assault literature (Mahoney and Williams 1998; Maier 2014; McOrmond-Plummer, Easteal AM, and Levy-Peck 2014). Heavily informed by theoretical work on woman abuse done by DeKeseredy and Schwartz (1993, 2002), Ellis and DeKeseredy (1997), Rogness (2002), and Wilson and Daly (1992), DeKeseredy, Rogness, and Schwartz's model situates rural separation/divorce sexual assault within the larger context of *societal patriarchy*. This refers to the broader overall forces within North American society that maintain or hold in place male domination patters (recognizing, of course, that this system changes and flows, sometimes rather rapidly) (Schwartz and DeKeseredy 1997). Still, to this day, North America's *gender structure* is set up in such a way that "men and women are not valued equally, and men and women do not have equal access to society's resources and rewards" (Renzetti 2013, 8). Numerous examples could easily be presented here.

DeKeseredy, Rogness, and Schwartz (2004) view societal patriarchy as a constant that cannot explain a variable such as changes in the frequency and severity of male sexual assaults on women who want to or who have left them. Similar to a question posed by Ellis and DeKeseredy (1997), DeKeseredy and his colleagues ask: If we live in a patriarchal society that promotes male proprietariness, why, then, do some men sexually assault during or after separation/divorce, whereas most others do not? The answer is that there are variations in male proprietariness, and DeKeseredy, Rogness, and Schwartz use the definition of this concept that was offered in a previous section of this chapter.

Many women resist or eventually will resist their spouse/cohabiting partners' proprietariness in a variety of ways, such as arguing, protesting, and fighting back if they have been abused (DeKeseredy and Schwartz 2013; Haselschwerdt et al. 2016; Sev'er 2002; Websdale 1998). There are also many women, though the precise number is unknown, who challenge men's control by exiting or trying to exit a relationship, and this may involve emotional separation (see Chapter 1), obtaining a separate residence, and/or starting or completing a legal separation/divorce.

Exiting, or attempting to exit, in any capacity challenges male proprietariness, but exiting alone, like other single factors, cannot account for sexual assault. As DeKeseredy and Schwartz (2009) and Hall-Sanchez (2014) uncovered in rural southeast Ohio, many abusive men's peers are also patriarchal and reinforce the belief that women's exiting is a threat to male masculinity. In addition, numerous members of patriarchal peer groups view wife beating, rape, and other forms of woman abuse as legitimate and effective means of repairing "damaged patriarchal masculinity" (Messerschmidt 1993; Raphael 2001). On top of encouraging the use of violent behavior to maintain control, these men serve as role models because they, too, are abusive. Nearly half (47 percent) of the women interviewed by DeKeseredy and Schwartz (N = 43) stated that their partners' male friends physically and sexually assaulted women.

Hall-Sanchez's (2014) study of rural separation/divorce sexual assault reveals that hunting trips are key contexts of male peer support. One woman told her:

> He would leave on Friday morning and return late Sunday. I would see him pack a few clothes but mostly beer, bullets, and porn. What a combination, right? I never understood how all that went together but he would tell me that they would drink, go scout the stuff and set up their spots in the woods, and come back to camp and drink, shoot targets, watch porn, guy talk, play cards, you know the usual guy stuff. They would tell dirty jokes and look at porn. So weird but I guess that is what made them "real" men. No women allowed and that is how they wanted it. That was a place where they could get away with demeaning women and get a pat on the back for "puttin' their women in their place." I'm sure all those guys did the same thing so it's no wonder. Sundays were always bad for me. (503)

Male peer support in the rural communities examined by DeKeseredy and Schwartz (2009) and Hall-Sanchez (2014) not only involves contributing to the perception of damaged masculinity and to motivating men to use violence to regain control but also entails public ridicule because a man "can't control his woman." Thus, he is more likely to sexually assault her to regain status among his peers.

There is some empirical support for Figure 3 derived from qualitative research done by DeKeseredy and Schwartz (2009) and Hall-Sanchez (2014). A quantitative test, however, is much needed. At this point in time, it serves as a building block for future theoretical considerations. Obviously, there are other factors that contribute to separation/divorce sexual assault in rural communities. One recently discovered factor in rural southeast Ohio is male consumption of pornography. DeKeseredy and Hall-Sanchez's (2016) in-depth interviews with fifty-five women who wanted to leave, were trying or in the process of leaving, or had left their marital/cohabiting partners reveal that pornography is a major component of the problem of rural woman abuse. DeKeseredy and Schwartz (2009) also discovered this but did not devote as much empirical attention to this issue as did DeKeseredy and Hall-Sanchez.

DeKeseredy, Rogness, and Schwartz's (2004) model is not a predictive model, and it does not attempt to isolate specific perpetrators. However, several hypotheses derived from it could easily be tested using measures of male peer support, Smith's (1990) familial patriarchal ideology items, and several other quantitative techniques. This and other separation/divorce assault theories will, we hope, be evaluated in the near future using both quantitative and qualitative techniques.

A RURAL MASCULINITY CRISIS/
MALE PEER SUPPORT MODEL
OF SEPARATION/DIVORCE SEXUAL ASSAULT

In order to bring a richer understanding of rural life to Figure 3 and the discussion above, DeKeseredy and colleagues (2007) developed the theory presented in Figure 4.[12] Rural social and economic transformations, challenges to masculine identity, and male peer support are major components of this model.

Following Sernau (2006), these theorists assert that, in rural U.S. communities, "male privilege is persistent but precarious" (69). For example, prior to the end of the twentieth century, many rural men obtained an income from owning family farms, working in extractive industries (e.g., coal mining), or working in factories (Brown and Schafft 2011). Buttressed by a patriarchal ideology, most of these men's marriages were characterized by a rigid gendered division of labor in which men were the primary bread

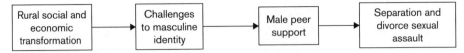

Figure 4. A rural masculinity crisis/male peer support model of separation/divorce sexual assault. (From DeKeseredy et al. 2007, 304.)

winners and women had "an intense and highly privatized relationship with domestic production," such as child-rearing and doing housework (Websdale 1998, 49). This is not to say that such gender relations are nonexistent today; they are still evident in a sizeable number of rural communities (DeKeseredy and Schwartz 2009; Lobao 2006). Consider the experiences of Angie, a southeast Ohio woman interviewed by Hall-Sanchez (2014). Her husband is "a traditional man's man." She also said that "His supper had to be waitin'. . . . Ready for him when he comes home and if it wasn't, I would pay for it" (504).

Today, after forty years of major challenges, rural men's power is more fragile (Donnermeyer and DeKeseredy 2014). In an environment where one source of men's power was their ability to operate in the outside economy, they have been hard hit by the declining number of jobs in both the extractive and the manufacturing sectors and by the fact that wages are lower in rural areas where jobs still exist. Meanwhile, "rural workers are less well prepared to obtain jobs in well-paying sectors; and rural economies are especially vulnerable to global competition" (Brown and Schafft 2011, 163).

In addition to these problems, there has been a major decline in the number of family-owned farms because many people cannot make a reasonable living from them (DeKeseredy and Schwartz 2013; Toews 2010). Today, many women seek employment or get jobs when their husbands become unemployed or when their farms become less profitable—another factor that has the potential for weakening the overall power of men (DeKeseredy and Schwartz 2009; Lobao and Meyer 2001). This transition in the arena of unemployment often generates marital instability, because many economically displaced men who cannot meet their perceived responsibilities as the man of the household feel deprived of intimate and social support resources that give them self-worth (DeKeseredy and Schwartz 2013; Harris and Bologh 1985). There are, of course, many ways that men can react to this set of problems, but what is most relevant here is how many unemployed rural men who strongly adhere to an ideology of familial patriarchy compensate for their lack of economic power. To reclaim their masculinity, they engage in behavior like the ex-husband of a woman interviewed by Hall-Sanchez (2014):

> I was working at the hospital and he was just laid off and couldn't find work. There really is no work here for men who work with their hands so he just became consumed with hunting. It was like it was a macho thing to do in this town. He could go out and shoot things and feel powerful and then go out drinking with his buddies and brag about that. It filled the void because he didn't have to admit that he wasn't bringin' home the bacon. No, he was still a real man 'cause now he could go out and shoot shit and come home and smack his woman around, take sex when he wanted. Yeah, I think that helped him get his balls back. He didn't have to feel bad about not working. (504)

Franklin and Menaker (2014, 826) show how a feminist variant of status inconsistency theory also helps explain the above man's behavior. In its original form, this theory asserts that people in roles that violate social norms, such as not being the male breadwinner, will experience negative social and psychological consequences stemming from role conflict (Stryker and Macke 1978). According to Franklin and Menaker, the original theory was based on access to resource accrual; feminist theory would suggest that, under traditional and patriarchal gender hierarchies, these status inconsistencies (losing the farm, unemployment) would could lead to negative self-worth and feelings of inferiority. They argue that these feelings, in turn, increase the likelihood that the man will resort to physical violence in the family to maintain control and regain power.

These recent changes in rural areas come on top of other social and economic transitions that have spawned what Hogg and Carrington (2006) have termed "the crisis in the rural gender order" (181). This crisis began more than a century ago with women's rights to own property and inherit wealth (often known as the Married Women's Property Acts), an increase through the past century in the number of rural women's associations, and the "delegitimation" of some forms of rural masculinity (such as stricter drinking and driving laws). Of course, such attacks on traditional masculinity are not inevitably tied to poor outcomes, because some unemployed rural men remake and redefine masculinity in positive ways. For instance, Sherman's (2005) study of families hurt by sawmill closures in a rural California community found some unemployed men who became active fathers and enjoyed spending time with their children while their wives worked. Of course, like the above hunter, some spend their time with their peers. As stated earlier in this chapter, many rural men have peers who view wife beating, rape, and other forms female victimization as legitimate and useful techniques for repairing damaged masculinity. Such men, as mentioned, serve as abusive role models.

When women terminate relationships because of their partners' substance abuse, violent behavior, obsession with hunting, or other problems generated in part by unemployment, rural men often perceive this as yet another threat to their masculinity. Many of them are influenced by their male peers to engage in separation/divorce sexual assault to regain control and to avoid losing status (DeKeseredy et al. 2007). Status is a factor that is also closely related to fear of ridicule, which is a mechanism of informal social control in many societies (Bierstedt 1957). For example, if abusive men's peers see them as failures with women due to separation/divorce, they may face group ridicule and lost status. This process is similar to the dynamics behind the presentation of self by males in rural pubs, as described by Campbell (2000). The male behavior he observed was not so much part of a need to demonstrate masculinity as it was dealing with a fear of being seen by peers as less than masculine. One solution that men in this position may see is to engage in control and abuse of the women to attempt to prevent a loss of status.

The bulk of rural criminology has been informed by mainstream place-based theories such as social disorganization and collective efficacy.[13] Figure 4, like Figure 3, does not reduce gender to an afterthought or to a control variable in a statistical equation. Rather, it is a rare attempt to examine the plight of women who have historically suffered in silence. Certainly, if battered lesbians, women of color, and female members of other ethnic/racial groups have been delegated generally to the margins of orthodox criminology (Carrington 2015; Potter 2015; Renzetti 2013), the same can be said about socially and economically excluded rural women who experience separation/divorce sexual assault and other types of male violence.

Male peer support theorists DeKeseredy and Schwartz (2013) note that, in addition to bringing marginalized abused women's experiences to the forefront of rural criminological analysis, Figure 4 responds to some of the problems in the state of male peer support theory and to research that needs to be done in the future. Topmost among these pitfalls, they assert, is the question of whether there are regional variations in male peer support for sexual assault and other types of woman abuse. There has been very little empirical and theoretical work on male peer support outside the mostly white, middle-class confines of large university campuses—for example, on working-class men of the same age in rural communities—to see if their experiences are the same. In addition, except for Figure 3, there has been no other previous attempt to apply male peer support theory to any variant of separation/divorce abuse. Thus, Figure 4 moves male peer support research and theorizing beyond the limited realm of academic settings and focuses on a very high-risk relationship status category. Moreover, it addresses the fact that rural women's individual experiences are part of a larger set of economic and social structural factors (Donnermeyer, Jobes, and Barclay 2006). The same can be said about the social and economic exclusion model of separation/divorce woman abuse in public housing presented in Figure 5.

THE SOCIAL AND ECONOMIC EXCLUSION MODEL OF SEPARATION/DIVORCE WOMAN ABUSE IN PUBLIC HOUSING

By the first years of the current millennium, only a few sociologists had collected data on violence against women in North American urban public housing complexes.[14] Among this small group of scholars were DeKeseredy, Alvi, Schwartz, and Tomaszewski (2003), Holzman, Hyatt, and Dempster (2001), Raphael (2001), and Renzetti and Maier (2002). The theoretical model presented in Figure 5 and crafted by DeKeseredy, Schwartz, and Alvi (2008) emerged out of some of the results uncovered by DeKeseredy et al.'s (2003) Quality of Neighborhood Life Survey (QNLS), which was administered in six public housing complexes situated in a large Canadian city. They found that separated women in their sample reported almost twice as much severe violence victimization than did married public housing women. Unfortunately, as will be explained below, the QNLS did not ask whether these women were

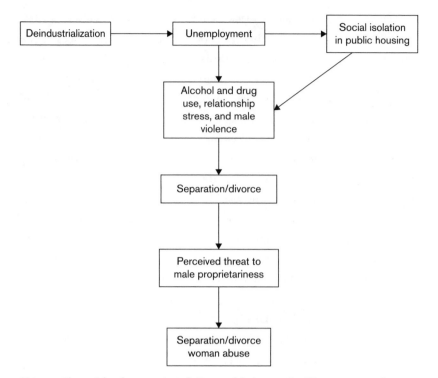

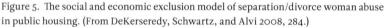

Figure 5. The social and economic exclusion model of separation/divorce woman abuse in public housing. (From DeKerseredy, Schwartz, and Alvi 2008, 284.)

victimized by the same person that they were separated from. Further, public housing in Canada may be different than in the United States, in that many more adult men may reside there, including married men. The model here uses this location to explain how some of the tendencies in modern society result in exacerbating the problem of woman abuse, at least among those living in public housing.

Figure 5 attempts to explain the finding of increased violence among separated women, and it builds on DeKeseredy and Schwartz's (2002) economic exclusion/male peer support model of public housing abuse, DeKeseredy et al.'s (2003) theory of post-separation woman abuse in public housing, and Sernau's (2001) web of exclusion model.

Briefly, DeKeseredy, Schwartz, and Alvi's (2008) model asserts that the rapid disappearance of manufacturing work that has occurred in North America since the 1970s has generated an alarmingly high rate of unemployed urban men and that this problem is not likely to subside in the near future with the ever increasing amount of corporate outsourcing to countries with lower pay scales. Often, particularly in Canada, these men end up living in socially isolated public housing communities. This isolation further contributes to unemployment because many employers believe that public housing residents are more likely than others to steal, be violent, miss work, and abuse substances (Wilson and Taub 2006). Another factor that fuels joblessness is the suburbanization of employment. Many low-paying jobs are now only found far away from inner-city housing estates. Thus, it is difficult to get or sustain a job if people cannot afford cars or expensive public transportation (Brown and Schafft 2011).

As can be expected, numerous jobless men use alcohol and drugs to cope with social and economic exclusion (Brownstein, Mulcahy, and Huessy 2014). Staying "clean and sober" is almost impossible in many poor places, especially if sizeable numbers of your peers and members of your family do not have the courage, motivation, or desire to abstain from using drugs and alcohol. When QNLS respondents in Canadian public housing projects were asked how many of their friends used drugs, such as marijuana, hashish, speed, or crack, more than a third of both men and women said that some, most, almost all, or all of their friends did so (DeKeseredy et al. 2003). For those respondents under the age of 30, 47 percent of the men and 50 percent of the women reported that their friends used drugs. Currie (1993) developed the *saturation model* to explain this problem, which also pertains to the issues uncovered in studying the methamphetamine community by Brownstein, Mulcahy, and Huessy (2014). Currie contends that, after decades and generations of limited economic opportunity, some urban areas become marked by pervasive hopelessness. Drug use becomes more widespread until it virtually saturates the entire community. People do not really make a conscious effort to become drug users but just seem to drift into what everyone else is doing.

Excessive drug and alcohol consumption generates a great deal of relationship stress and is strongly associated with separation/divorce violence as well as other types of intimate woman abuse (DeKeseredy 2011). Not surprisingly, many women do not wish to live with men who abuse substances and who are violent. Some women, particularly in public housing, will not leave their homes to avoid these men, especially if it is their name that is on the lease, but they "invert patriarchy" by evicting men deemed irresponsible, or who may be too difficult to house and feed (Bourgois 1995; DeKeseredy, Alvi, and Schwartz 2006). Regardless of how the relationship ends, many male public housing residents, like other "truly disadvantaged" men (Wilson 1987), are very patriarchal. Thus, they are prone to interpreting women ending relationships as a challenge to male proprietariness, which, if it is not already clear, can result in violent retaliation.

Some of the QNLS data partially support Figure 5 and Bourgois's (1995) argument that, by abusing women, many socially and economically excluded inner-city men are "desperately attempting to reassert their grandfather's lost autocratic control over the household" (500). Peterson del Mar (1996) similarly argued in a complex study of divorce petitions that the twentieth century was marked by violence that was less instrumental (specifically trying to get women to do something) and more expressive, protesting women's increased independence and attempting to reassert a perceived lost era of male dominance. Women who resist or challenge their partners' patriarchal expectations are at a substantially elevated risk of being assaulted. Certainly, we know this from the femicide literature reviewed previously in this book.

Yet the data used to support Figure 5 cannot tell us about some key issues. For example, the QNLS asked respondents only about their current marital status (i.e., married, divorced, separated, single). It was not designed to measure the number of separated/divorced female respondents who left their male partners because of male violence, drug/alcohol use, or unemployment, nor the number of women who were victimized by these men during or after the process of estrangement. It is at least theoretically possible that some women were separated or divorced from nonviolent men but later victimized by another man. There may also have been separated or divorced women in the QNLS sample who were victimized by men who did not live with these women. Many poor areas are marked by a number of men who do not want to be attached to one woman, preferring multiple partners (Franklin and James 2015; Wilson 1966), and such imbalances foster change in power relationships between men and women.

SUMMARY

The main objective of this chapter has been to review widely read and cited theories of separation/divorce violence against women. What most of the perspectives examined in this chapter have in common is an emphasis on two variables: male proprietariness, and male peer support. Additionally, it should be obvious that all the theories take gender seriously. This is because they were crafted by feminist scholars. To be sure, feminists are at the forefront of empirical and theoretical work on separation/divorce woman abuse.

What is sorely needed, however, are tests of existing theories using data derived from men (DeKeseredy and Rennison 2013b). This has been an ongoing issue in the area of separation/divorce assault research. The academic community studying violence against women is now at the point where it can confidently state that a substantial number of females experience abuse during and after separation/divorce, and hence it is time to use some different techniques to yield better answers to the very important question "Why does he do that?" (Bancroft 2002). This is not to say, though, that interviewing women or administering victimization surveys do not help achieve this goal. They certainly do, and the information women provide led to the development of the theories reviewed in this chapter.

Nevertheless, interviews with men are in short supply and so are self-report surveys administered to men. Arendell (1995) is one of a tiny cohort of scholars to glean interview data from men about separation/divorce assault, and what she stated in the 1990s still has some validity today:

> Men are relatively neglected in divorce research. A dearth of information on men's perceptions and actions persists even though divorce research increased dramatically over the past several decades, as the divorce rate remained strikingly high. This neglect of men, and particularly of divorced fathers, is not unique but is characteristic of fathers and fathering more generally. . . . Neither mothers' reports nor survey findings, however, give expression to fathers' view or experiences. (3)

Since this was written, there has been some movement to study men in divorce situations by scholars. However, though men and the role of men in parenting after divorce and other topics are being studied with greater frequency, there has been much less work on the topics covered in this book.

For example, we know that separation and divorce are major determinants of intimate femicide, yet Adams's (2007) interviews with thirty-one men who killed intimate partners is the first U.S. study that elicited information directly from male perpetrators. Also, there is a dearth of male self-report data on nonlethal separation/divorce assaults. This is somewhat surprising because there is a sizeable number of self-report surveys of men's experiences with other types of woman abuse in intimate relationships.

Self-report data from men may tell us much about what drives them to be abusive and may enable researchers to more effectively test some of the theories covered here. Several hypotheses derived from them could be tested using quantitative measures of male peer support and men's adherence to the ideology of familial patriarchy. Essentially, in recent years, Block and DeKeseredy (2007) and Brownridge (2009) are the only researchers to be guided by theoretical perspectives in the analysis of statistical data on separation/divorce assault. Block and DeKeseredy tested an element of Wilson and Daly's (1992, 1993) male proprietariness theory, whereas Brownridge's (2009) use of Canadian national victimization survey data was heavily informed by an ecological framework[15] and Ellis and DeKeseredy's (1989) DAD (dependency, availability, and deterrence) model, which is an attempt to explain marital status variations in woman abuse.

In sum, a variety of methods enhances a social scientific understanding of separation/divorce assault, and new techniques are always welcome. Perhaps, too, it is most fitting to end this chapter with a statement made thirty years ago by Hotaling and Sugarman (1986). As woman abuse researchers, we should always keep it in mind:

> While research on men's violence toward women raises a number of complicated issues, it is sometimes forgotten that men's violence is men's behavior. As such, it is not surprising that the more fruitful efforts to explain this behavior have focused on male characteristics. What is surprising is the enormous effort to explain male behavior by examining characteristics of women. It is hoped that future research will show more about the factors that promote violent male behavior and that stronger theory will be developed to explain it. (120)

CHAPTER FIVE

Children as Collateral Victims of Separation/Divorce Woman Abuse

In 2003, while a Family Court Judge, I made a devastating error . . .
I relied on other judges who taught me that I should be suspicious
of any woman who makes an abuse allegation during a divorce proceeding.
I implemented the policy of the court and as a result I made a horrific and
devastating decision. It is too late for me to correct the mistake. Nor can
I correct the harm that I caused J.M.

> Judge Salcido[1]

As the preceding chapters of this book show, separation does not end men's violence and abuse against female intimate partners. Indeed, separation is frequently the catalyst for an escalation of violence and diversification of abusive tactics. As abusers see they are losing control of their partners, they often up the ante to force them back into the relationship, punish them for disclosing violence, or exert the ultimate form of abuse by killing their partner, children, or pets (Johnson 2006; O'Hagan 2014; Sillito and Salari 2011). Threats by abusive men to kill and take children are common post-separation (Arendell 1995; Harrison 2008; Shalansky, Ericksen, and Henderson 1999; Varcoe and Irwin 2004), just as they are pre-separation (McFarlane et al. 1999). In fact, Hayes (2015) found that separated women were four times more likely to experience threats to take and harm children than nonseparated mothers. As the aunt of one mother whose partner murdered her two children explained it:

> He was losing power. He was gentle until he couldn't get his own way. He was obsessed with her and would never let her go, although she tried to get away.

Once she left him and moved into an upstairs unit. He came to the place where she was staying and climbed up the wall like a spider, he started to smash the window to break in and so she let him in. He said he would never let her or the kids go. So she returned. (Johnson 2005, 53)

Thus far, the chapters in this book have focused on the physical and non-physical risks to women from male partners at separation. Attention to the impact of separation/divorce abuse on *children* is also essential to understanding the dynamics and impact of woman abuse. This chapter draws together diverse sources in order to show how children are involved in abuse at separation and divorce. It also reviews some of the cultural and structural reasons that woman abuse and child abuse are not handled appropriately in the family law context. This research is extremely important because many professionals who are involved with families at separation and divorce believe that abuse ends at separation and that child abuse and woman abuse are discrete phenomena (Dallam and Silberg 2006). This is a misconception that is due in part to the greater emphasis in divorce research on the harms to children of family dissolution than the impact of violence and abuse (Arditti 1999; Bancroft and Silverman 2002; Fleury-Steiner et al. 2016; Harrison 2008). This chapter explains some key issues for children as collateral victims of woman abuse.

ABUSIVE FATHERS AT SEPARATION AND DIVORCE

There is a growing body of research on the tactics that abusers use in the context of child custody exchange, access visits, and family law disputes (Bancroft and Silverman 2002; Beeble, Bybee, and Sullivan 2007; Crossman, Hardesty, and Raffaelli 2016; Fleury-Steiner et al. 2016; Hardesty 2002; Harrison 2008; Toews, McKenry, and Catlett 2003; Zeoli et al. 2013). Some antifeminists and legal practitioners assume that the adversarial structure of the family court is what causes post-separation conflict. However, conflict often precedes the involvement of the family court; violence and abuse are common reasons for the separation and divorce in the first place. Similarly, much of the "conflict" that happens after separation is because of abuse. Among those families involved in disputes after separation, Moloney and colleagues (2016) found that 23 percent of mothers and 6 percent of fathers reported that their ongoing dispute was about violence or the safety of children. Actually, most parents settle child custody without disputes that require family court intervention. In Australia, which has the most comprehensive records on family court cases, only about 11 percent of child custody cases require court intervention (Qu and Weston 2010). In Norway, that figure is about 10 percent (Skjørten 2013). Since most parents come to agreement about child custody without requiring court intervention, the statistics on children's residence, which is primarily with mothers, reflects the agreement of the parents. It is based on past patterns of care rather than gender bias against men, as some antifeminists allege. The majority of the cases that require the court to come to a decision involve reported child or partner abuse (Kaspiew et al. 2009).

One of the reasons for family court disputes is that batterers are more likely to contest or seek custody than non-abusers. They drag out proceedings as a way to drain their partner of funds (Liss and Stahly 1993), regain control over their partners (Arendell 1995; Bancroft, Silverman, and Ritchie 2011), avoid paying child support, and negotiate unfair financial settlements with women who just want closure (Hardesty 2002; Kurz 1995; Pagelow 1993; Sev'er 1997; Slote et al. 2005). When joint custody is granted, batterers may use custody and access exchanges as opportunities to continue to abuse women (Arendell 1995; Fleury-Steiner et al. 2016; Hardesty 2002; Reihing 1999; Shalansky, Ericksen, and Henderson 1999; Zeoli et al. 2013).

In the rare instances where supervised visitation is recommended, there are minimal considerations to safety, such as staggered drop-off and pick-up times so the parents do not meet (Davis et al. 2011; Fleury-Steiner et al. 2016; O'Sullivan et al. 2006). This lack of protection for battered women may provide an ongoing, long-term opportunity for abusers to stalk, attack, and harass the women trying to leave them (Fleury-Steiner et al. 2016). One woman recounted her fear around access visits despite having a "safe" public drop-off point:

[W]hat he is doing now is he is walking with the kids towards my house. . . . And he does not know my address or my phone number, and he wants to know. . . . Up until now he has waited for me in the car at the corner where we meet. . . . And I said to him once, if I were seven minutes late, would you just keep walking and have the kids lead you to our door? Because, that is what he is doing. He's getting too close for comfort. (Shalansky, Ericksen, and Henderson 1999, 420)

This account illustrates how shallow the illusion of safety can be around post-separation child contact practices. It also highlights one of the problems associated with co-parenting with an abuser: the combination of ongoing fear and practical difficulties in maintaining safety.

In addition to the abusive tactics mentioned above, batterers use multiple forms of "paper abuse" post-separation (Miller and Smolter 2011). This means that abusers use courts and child protection systems as tools to extend abusive patterns of behavior post-separation. This might include making multiple court motions that take time and money to fight, false allegations, or retaliatory counter-accusations. Some abusers make false reports of child abuse against mothers, claim that the mother is unfit as a parent, or make false complaints of interference with or denial of visitation. When children themselves resist contact with abusers, they complain that the resistance is caused by the mother "alienating" the child rather than the children's own personal experiences of abuse (Miller and Smolter 2011; Przekop 2011). Batterers may undermine mothers' authority post-separation by being very lenient with children during visitation or allowing them to engage in unsafe or age inappropriate activities (Bancroft, Silverman, and Ritchie 2011; Zeoli et al. 2013). In addition to these indirect forms of abuse, which upset mothers and can undermine their relationship with children, there is a risk of ongoing violence post-separation.

FILICIDE: THE MURDER OF CHILDREN

Separation is a key risk factor for child murders, homicide-suicides, and familicides. It is estimated that one-third to half of victims of homicides following separation in the United States and Canada are children killed by their fathers (Cooper and Eaves 1996; Malphurs and Cohen 2002). Wilson, Daly, and Daniele (1995) identified two situations where children are at increased risk of death in the context of woman abuse: when a child is defending one parent from the other, and when "a child is assaulted or killed to spite or terrorize a spouse who will also be attacked" (278). In Australia, filicides (the killing of a child by a parent) constitute 17 percent of all family homicides, with the most common type being children killed by fathers in the context of parental separation and divorce (Mouzos and Rushforth 2003, 3). These murders are often accompanied by violence against the mothers, but this may be overlooked when the focus of the investigation is on the death of a child. In the most comprehensive study in Australia, Johnson (2005) identified risk factors for separation/divorce filicide in Western Australia. These include a history of domestic violence in the relationship, the abuser's refusal to accept the end of the relationship, self-centeredness, controlling behavior, extreme jealousy, past threats of harm, escalation of mental health problems after separation, and stalking (109).

Kirkwood's (2012) review of cases across Australia from 1997 to 2008 found that gendered institutional failures to consider the risk to children from violent men and protect their mothers post-separation exacerbated children's risks of filicide. In Box 5, Dragiewicz and Burgess (2016) describe a recent Australian example that garnered much nation-wide attention.

O'Hagan (2014) reported similar findings from the United Kingdom, identifying relationship breakdown, disputes over custody and access, and histories of domestic violence as central contexts for filicides. Holland et al.'s (2015) analysis of U.S. data on homicide-suicides involving child victims found that "intimate partner problems" including violence, separation, arguments, and custody problems were present in 61 percent of cases. They note, "In most cases, couples who were already experiencing chronic conflict also experienced acute stressors of separation, divorce, and child custody issues" (14). In their Canadian study, Varcoe and Irwin (2004) found that custody and access were the most serious concerns for abused mothers. All of the mothers in their study reported that their abuser had used the children as part of the abuse during the relationships; most also said their abusers had threatened to harm or kill the kids or take them away from their mothers.

CHILD EXPOSURE TO LETHAL AND NONLETHAL SEPARATION ASSAULT

The research on the overlap between child abuse and woman abuse draws from two primary literatures: violence studies with mothers who have experienced abuse, and research on child abuse that also records domestic violence (Edleson 1999). These studies demonstrate that violence against adults and children are not mutually exclusive and often co-occur before and after separation (Campo 2015). The Australian Bureau of Statistics' (2014) Personal Safety Survey (Australia's primary crime victimization survey) found that, in 2012, former partners were the most common perpetrators of violence against women, and 1,158,700 or 15 percent of women reported having experienced violence since they were 15 years old from a former partner. Of these women, 61 percent had children in their care at the time the incident took place. Forty-eight percent of these women said the children had heard or seen the violence. The Australian Institute of Family Studies' Survey of

Recently Separated Parents found that parents reported "1,011 children had witnessed violence before or during separation, 402 had witnessed violence since separation, and 1,389 had witnessed violence before, during and since separation" (De Maio et al. 2013, 93).

A limited number of studies directly investigate the nature of children's involvement in men's abuse of their mothers. This research finds that children are involved as they step in to assist their mothers, are drawn into joining in the abuse, or become targets of abuse themselves (Edleson et al. 2003). Another, larger group of studies looks at the impact of exposure to domestic violence on children. These studies find that exposure to abuse can contribute to problems with homelessness, trauma, learning, behavior, health, and well-being (Campo 2015; DeMaio et al. 2013; Edleson et al. 2003). In fact, Schwartz (1989) makes the argument that such children are often adjudicated as delinquent and punished for their aggressive behavior. He makes the direct link between the battering of adult women and the problem of juvenile delinquency in America: criminal justice scholars have decried the high level of juvenile delinquency and worried about various causative factors, while psychologists have argued that a significant number of physically (and criminally) aggressive youth are themselves victims of child abuse or were witnesses to their mothers being physically abused. Of course, all witnesses to violence do not become criminals. The effects of exposure to violence against a parent are moderated by resiliency factors such as support from a non-abusive adult (Wolfe et al. 2003).

Most of the literature on children's exposure to men's violence against women is focused on sub-lethal violence and abuse. However, children are also witnesses to femicide in the context of woman abuse. As we discussed in Chapter 2, murder is the most serious form of separation assault. Until recently, the studies on children affected by the killing of a parent were mostly limited to psychological case studies (see, e.g., Alisic et al. 2015; Black and Kaplan 1988; Burman and Allen-Meares 1994). As Black and Kaplan explain, children whose mothers are killed by their father may have been exposed to the killing and directly traumatized by it. But they also immediately lose both parents. In addition, they bear the stigma of being the child of a murderer (1998, 624). Although there has never been a comprehensive study of child custody following femicide, we know anecdotally that children whose father kills their mother are sometimes placed in the custody of the killer's family members, who may denigrate the mother. Custody can also revert to the man who killed their mother following his release (Black and Kaplan 1988).

Homicide data collection in many countries fails to systematically record histories of spousal violence. Although information about the relationship between perpetrator and victim may be recorded, classification based on marital status may or may not include former boyfriends or girlfriends. In addition, estrangement or separation is not systematically noted. However, Lewandowski and colleagues (2004, 212) used U.S. Uniform Crime Report data to estimate that about 3,300 children a year would be affected by domestic violence homicides; in addition, they estimate that there are roughly three times more attempted than completed femicides each year. It is rarely discussed, but children are more likely to witness intimate partner homicide-suicides than to be absent from the scene or killed in these incidents (Sillito and Salari 2011, 285).

Lewandowski and colleagues (2004, 215) found that about two-thirds of femicide victims in ten cities had children who were affected by the killing. These killings and threats to kill were closely linked to separation. In at least 13 percent of the cases, the father had threatened to harm the children if the mother left, and in at least 14.5 percent of the cases, the perpetrator had previously threatened to take the children if she left. In 35 percent of the femicides, one or more children had directly witnessed the murder. The pattern is similar in attempted femicide, where 68 percent of households included children, and in 71 percent there was a history of physical violence toward the mother. Seventeen percent of perpetrators of attempted femicide had threatened to take the children if the mother left, and 12 percent had threatened to harm the children if the mother left. In 62 percent of the attempted femicide cases, the children witnessed the perpetrator's attempt to kill their mother and an additional 28 percent found their mother after the attempted femicide. In an early study of child witnesses to murder, Pynoos and Eth (1984) found that 10 percent of homicides in Los Angeles (200 of 2,000 cases) had a dependent child as a witness. As Lewandowski and colleagues (2004) note, "The murder or attempted murder of one parent by the other carries profound and often lifelong consequences" (212), as the trauma of witnessing a killing is exacerbated when the perpetrator is another person with a significant relationship to the child.

Surviving children and their caregivers face significant challenges in the aftermath of femicide. In one of the first qualitative studies in this area, Hardesty and colleagues (2007) interviewed ten caregivers of surviving children. Six of the ten children in their study had witnessed the murder of their mother or found their mother's body. The caregivers reported that the children had significant overlapping mental health, behavior, and academic problems. Seven of the ten caregivers reported serious mental health issues, including depression, anxiety, prolonged grief, post-traumatic stress, and suicide attempts by the children. The caregivers also noted sleep disturbances and somatic concerns like stomach problems and headaches. The majority of the children also demonstrated behavioral and school problems. Significantly, Hardesty and colleagues took care to note that the children in the study had been exposed to domestic violence against their mothers before the femicide. Two of the cases had previous reports of sexual and physical abuse of the children, in some cases months beforehand. The children had witnessed abuse of other family members as well.

Death does not always end the abuse. Surviving children are exposed to the continuation of pre-femicide abuse and conflict after the murder, with abusers and their families fighting over custody of the children and abusers continuing abuse while incarcerated. One caregiver reported that the killer sent abusive letters from jail threatening to "take care of" the children who had testified against him (Hardesty et al. 2007). Astonishingly, some scholars and court staff show more concern about continuing the father's relationship with the children than the impact on the children of living with the killer's family members. In Box 6, Chereb (2008) provides a salient example of such concern.

This quote illustrates the family court's emphasis on equitable sharing of children moving forward and disregard for risks to children even in the most extreme cases of violence. These cases are traumatizing for children even if their mothers survive the attempts on their lives. Given the ongoing risks to children post-separation, it is important to consider why abuse is not taken seriously in the current family court climate.

BOX 6. CHARLA MACK

From Chereb 2008, 1

Darren Mack murdered his wife at a child custody exchange in Reno, Nevada, in 2006. He then shot the family court judge involved in his case. Charla Mack had previously told friends that she was afraid he would kill her. Darren Mack showed no remorse for killing his wife or shooting the judge. In a particularly graphic example of the way that courts prioritize father contact over histories of abuse, the judge in Mack's homicide case tearfully pleaded for the family of the convicted killer and the family of the murdered woman to share custody of the surviving daughter. Judge Herndon said, "You all can either choose to raise her, disparaging her parents on each side," he said, "or you can try to get past the court cases, the criminal proceedings . . . and teach her good things about both these parents."

CONTRIBUTING FACTORS TO CHILDREN'S AND WOMEN'S UNSAFETY IN FAMILY LAW

Criminal and civil legal responses to men's violence against women have changed and in many cases improved since the 1970s. Organizations have been developed to support safe separation from abusers, facilitated by new streams of government and nonprofit funding to support their work. Battered women's shelters, legal support for divorce, and support for transitional housing assist women in leaving their abusers without becoming homeless. Civil no-contact orders and criminal charges are intended to institutionalize support for efforts to separate from abusers. Although these measures are imperfect and unevenly applied, many women find such resources useful. However, resistance to women's efforts to effectively separate from abusers has intensified in other contexts, including family law (Dragiewicz 2014).

Given that woman abuse may continue after separation, it should not be surprising that children's exposure to violence—such as a parent being attacked, or a child's victimization at the hands of a parent—can also continue after separation. What is surprising is that this risk is not recognized by so many people, and that many of those who fail to recognize this are scholars, judges, lawyers, and child custody evaluators. Many of these important figures operate on the assumption that "everything changes at divorce"—that, with the termination of a legal relationship, the problem of violence has automatically ended.

As a result of this assumption, mothers often experience significant pressure to forget about the past and move forward cooperatively in joint custody and visitation with their batterers. Practitioners also often dismiss histories of violence as being in the past and therefore irrelevant to future parenting or safety (Macdonald 2015). This may be a nice idea where there is a history of co-parenting, but it is espoused even in cases where there is a history of abuse. Worse, this pressure is often present even when there is a statutory presumption against abusers receiving custody of children (Fleury-Steiner et al. 2016; Harrison 2008; Jaffe, Crooks, and Poisson 2003). Mothers may internalize the belief that not having a father in the picture will be bad for their kids. As a result, they may agree to co-parenting arrangements because they think it is in the best interest of the child. Other mothers agree to co-parent early on after separation because they hope it will appease their abuser or they want to avoid antagonizing him. Nonetheless, the co-parenting context is of special concern to abused mothers (Sev'er 1997). As mothers attempt to separate from abusive partners, the specific context of family law and child custody provides a series of specific challenges for mothers (Dragiewicz 2014; Harrison 2008). Shalansky, Ericksen, and Henderson (1999) documented women's feelings of being pressured by mediators into agreeing to joint custody and their clear impression that they would be punished if they did not go along. Mediation, which is based on an assumption of two equal partners needing to come to an agreement, can work to the detriment of battered women. When one partner is more powerful than the other, mediation may turn into an imposition of the more powerful person's will as approved by the State. In other words, it is a fairly popular view that mediation is less adversarial than court, but mediation is not necessarily experienced as nonadversarial by abused women. As Davis (1988) noted, despite growing recognition of the traumatic effects on children of exposure to abuse in other contexts, when physical violence is not specifically and directly aimed at the children, a history of serious ongoing physical violence within the family is often ignored in family law systems.

Although it is widely recognized that woman abuse is a common reason for divorce, research on abused mothers' experiences post-divorce is just beginning to grow (Hardesty 2002). Somewhat paradoxically, in the family law context patriarchal family norms have been reinforced just as resources for women to escape abuse and the prospect of criminal liability for batterers have emerged (Dragiewicz 2014). An important change from earlier years is that women are now frequently encouraged to separate from abusers. Psychologists today typically recognize the harm to children from exposure to abuse. But mothers can also lose custody of their children or face criminal charges if they fail to protect their children from their batterers' violence (Dunlap 2004; Jacobs 1998).

There is a disjuncture here. Women are often held accountable for protecting children from abusive partners during marriage. However, as soon as a mother separates from an abuser, she is vulnerable to being coerced into shared parenting with the same violent person, who is now considered an essential partner in the development of the child. If she *now* resists, attempting to protect her child from potential abuse, she can be punished by losing custody or can be barred from contact with her children. The issue extends to nonmarital relationships as well. In many jurisdictions, men who have never been caregivers for their children, fathers who were never married to the mothers they abuse, and men convicted of domestic violence and child abuse have rights to ongoing contact with, and often legal control over, their biological children.

In contested custody cases with a history of abuse, it is more common than not for children to be placed into joint custody with their mother and the father who abused her (Davis et al. 2011; Kernic et al. 2005; Macdonald 2015; Morrill et al. 2005; O'Sullivan et al. 2006; Rosen and O'Sullivan 2005). Even killing the mother does not preclude custody by the abusive father or his family. Lewandowski and colleagues (2004) found that 47 percent of children of femicide victims lived with the mother's family, 12 percent lived with the perpetrator's family, and 10 percent had shared custody between the victim and perpetrators' families. In attempted femicide cases, 47.5 percent of children lived with their mothers following their fathers' unsuccessful attempt to kill her, and 5 percent of the children lived with the perpetrator's family. Holland and colleagues (2015) argue that "separation, revenge, divorce, and child custody issues are risk factors in homicide-suicides involving children. Given these findings, system-level programs that better monitor and moderate the unique circumstances and stressors associated with these changes in family life might help reduce tensions and conflicts that could lead to fatal violence" (14–15). One challenge to making these changes is the very strong emphasis on co-parenting post-separation that has become a dominant theme in family law in the United States, Canada, the United Kingdom, and Australia.

Post-separation joint physical and legal custody, rebranded as "shared parenting" at the behest of antifeminist men's groups, has become increasingly conflated with the best interest of the child, even in contested custody and abuse cases (Barker 2013; Elizabeth, Gavey, and Tolmie 2012; Kurki-Suonio 2000; Rhoades 2002, 2008; Rhoades and Boyd 2004). Although scholars, legislators, courts, and advocates have dedicated significant attention to violence and abuse, divorce, and children's well-being, the scholarly literatures in these fields are poorly integrated with one another (Dragiewicz 2014; Hardesty 2002; Fineman 1987; Graycar 2000, 2012; Rathus 2014). This is perhaps especially true of the literatures relevant to contested child custody in the context of domestic violence and child abuse. Family court staff, politicians, scholars, lawyers, and advocates make frequent, presumably research-based references to best practices for promoting the best interest of the child following divorce. However, the scholarship on which these claims are ostensibly based often fails to consider violence against women or children as key contexts of divorce. This leads to the creation of laws that are focused on non-abusive family contexts, despite the over-representation of abuse in contested family law cases. Although family courts in the United States, the United Kingdom, and Australia are required to consider domestic violence in contested child custody cases, this is one of many factors. In practice, powerful social norms promoting joint custody shape outcomes of abuse cases even where they may pose risks to children and abused mothers.

Brinig, Frederick, and Drozd (2014) explain that custody statutes can either assume that there should be a rebuttable presumption against joint custody in domestic violence cases or they can assume that joint legal custody or physical custody is in the best interests of the child. They argue that the second type of statute is based less on the evidence in the case than an assumption about what kind of family structure is best for children. In addition, "Such presumptions shift the burden of proof in order to make it far less likely that a family will end up with any different arrangement than the statute presumes is in their interest" (272). In other words, the assumption that joint custody following divorce is "what children need" is derived from patriarchal ideology rather than research or case-specific evidence. Neither legal presumptions nor social science research support the joint custody preference in contested custody cases where there is a history of abuse. And yet it continues to be the law in many jurisdictions, and an implicit goal in many others. This is a symptom of pervasive implicit patriarchal family norms.

PATRIARCHAL FAMILY NORMS

Some violence scholars avoid discussions of gender inequality, sexism, and patriarchy in an effort to position themselves as objective researchers outside of politics. However, patriarchy is highly relevant to child custody determinations with and without violence against women (Elizabeth, Gavey, and Tolmie 2012). Walby (1990, 21) explains that patriarchy operates via structures including the household and family, paid employment, the state, male violence, and sexuality. Patriarchy is one form of social stratification that operates concurrently with other forms like racism and capitalism. Patriarchy is not monolithic or unchanging. Instead, patriarchy is manifested differently in different locations, and definitions of patriarchy have changed over time (Dragiewicz 2008). For example, Smart (2013) explains how the laws governing familial patriarchy have changed over the years such that the family is one site where persistent inequality is obscured. Smart argues that, though family law now appears to regulate relationships between equals, women continue to bear the disproportionate burden of care work. In other words, the mechanisms of enforcement and ways of talking about them have changed, but patriarchal family norms persist. As Boyd (2007) argues:

> The fraught area of post-separation parenting disputes has shown that the field of parenting remains gendered even in the face of an increasingly formalistic, gender neutral stance in the field. The status of fathers in relation to children has been strengthened, whereas the caregiving labour and

responsibility of mothers is often, and possibly increasingly, undervalued or rendered invisible. It is not clear that the best interests of children are served under this trend. (67; internal citation omitted)

One manner in which patriarchal family norms persist is through the prioritization of fathers' rights to legal or physical custody of children regardless of previous child care patterns and family dynamics. Although joint legal and physical custody may sound equitable or child-focused on their face, some of the arguments in favor of presumptive joint custody include providing an incentive for the payment of child support. The focus on equitable division of time can de-prioritize the central aims of parenting: responsibly providing nurturance, love, and guidance to children (Ver Steegh and Davis 2015, 280).

Children's interests can be sidelined when the focus shifts to fairness to parents or expediency for family law systems (Davis et al. 2010). Proposed starting points for custody negotiation such as 50/50 legal custody or a specific percentage of overnight physical custody,[2] often labelled as "shared parenting" or "co-parenting," shift attention to parents' interests with little regard for the impact on children or specific details of particular cases. It is significant that, despite sustained international pressure by "fathers' rights" groups to impose legal presumptions of 50/50 joint custody, family law reforms in multiple countries have repeatedly stopped short of this (Rhoades and Boyd 2004). As Ver Steegh and Davis (2015) explain, "In legal terms, presumptive parenting plans are problematic because they supplant consideration of the individual needs of children" (284). Still, patriarchal authority has not only remained important but also been reasserted with the imposition of shared legal custody and the ideologies of post-divorce shared parenting and friendly parenting. These doctrines, which will be explored further below, are based on assumptions about the nature and outcomes of divorce and its effect on children rather than evidence about the relationship between violence, abuse, and divorce.

ASSUMPTIONS ABOUT DIVORCE

The research on divorce and children is mostly composed of studies comparing families with married and divorced parents. Findings thought to indicate that families with married parents do better on some measures (such as income and children's adjustment) have gained the status of common knowledge despite contradictory research findings (Amato 2000). The increasing emphasis on the assumption that nuclear families with married parents are superior has resulted in changes to family law to promote joint custody, ostensibly in order to simulate intact families (Rhoades 2002). The research comparing children in different family structures is referenced to draw conclusions about what are termed "outcomes of divorce." However, it is not clear that the impact of the divorce is what is reflected in these studies. Most divorce studies fail to consider the reasons for the divorce or investigate the differential effects of divorce or various custody arrangements on abusive versus non-abusive families. For example, if families that divorce are more likely to be those marked by extensive discord, dysfunction, or unhealthy dynamics, it should be no surprise to find that children from these families have poorer outcomes on some measures. Joint custody may sound like it is mirroring happy, intact families. However, if one of the partners is an abuser, separation does not change the underlying abusive dynamics.

There is a shortage of research that investigates the benefits of divorce or factors that mediate the stress of divorce (Amato 2000; Arditti and Madden-Derdich 1995). However, a growing number of studies are separating out the outcomes of conflict from those of divorce (Cusimano and Riggs 2013; Kelly 2003), and some note the positive effects of divorce when negative family dynamics precede (Riggio 2004). These scholars call for researchers to disentangle the consequences of conflict from those of divorce. Although conflict is not the same as abuse, this is a potentially positive step toward separating out the effects of negative family dynamics, including violence and abuse pre-separation, from the effects of divorce itself. For example, Cusimano and Riggs (2013) found that college students' recollections of interparental conflict were correlated with psychological distress, a negative outcome often attributed to divorce. Riggio (2004) found that conflict was consistently correlated with negative outcomes to children and divorce was associated with lower quality father–child relationships. However, he also found that divorce was associated with significantly improved mother–child relationships, perceptions of social support, greater independence facilitated by both parents, and reduced anxiety in relationships (99). Macdonald

(2015) warns, nevertheless, that the conflict frame contributes to the minimization and distortion of the dynamics of abuse, leading practitioners to frame abuse as "mutual."

Studies that consider the quality of relationships between children and parents post-separation find that these are, in fact, significantly shaped by conflict and relationship quality pre-divorce (Booth and Amato 1994, 2001; Kalmijn 2015; Kelly 2003; Yu et al. 2010). Although much attention has been paid to research findings that ostensibly link divorce to negative outcomes for children, less attention has been paid to the research findings that indicate that children's exposure to conflict or violence is harmful to children. As Amato and Sobolewski (2001) put it, "Policymakers should keep in mind that restricting access to divorce will not address the central problem, as chronic marital discord between continuously married parents appears to be as detrimental as divorce" (918). In their recent review of the literature on children and divorce, McIntosh and colleagues (2009) note that, given the many changes that follow divorce, the emphasis on challenges for children is not surprising. However, the two predictors of children's adjustment most often found in the research are interparental conflict and the quality of children's relationships with their parents. In other words, they argue, it is not the divorce itself that is the problem, it is ongoing conflict between parents and poor parent-child relationships that are harmful to children. Family functioning is more important than family composition.

This is another example of divorce research not being well integrated with research in relevant fields. A significant body of research has documented the negative effects of exposure to men's violence against women and child abuse on children. However, to our knowledge, no divorce outcome study to date has investigated the impact of violence and abuse pre-divorce on children. Ultimately, assumptions about the negative outcomes of divorce harm women and children who are trying to separate from batterers. These assumptions fuel pressure to push children to spend time with abusive men, lead to formal requirements in family law to promote contact despite violence and abuse, and are influential in family law, mediation, and conciliation contexts.

ABUSE AS A REASON FOR DIVORCE

There has been significant research on the putative outcomes of divorce, but less attention has been paid to the reasons divorce happens in the first place. Nonetheless, there is consensus that women and men identify different reasons for divorce, with abuse constituting a significant reason for women to seek divorce. Amato and Previti (2003) found that 9.2 percent of women and no men in their sample reported that physical or mental abuse was the cause of their divorce. They also found that 53 percent of ex-husbands and 70 percent of ex-wives said the wife had wanted the divorce more (620). Amato and Previti found that "individuals with children were more likely to report abuse and substance use as causes of divorce. It seems likely that children increase the motivation of spouses (primarily wives) to leave abusive or substance-dependent spouses, perhaps to protect the children" (622–23). Research on the reasons for divorce sheds light on the reasons that many women report abuse in the family law context.

In Australia, Wolcott and Hughes (1999) conducted the most recent major study on reasons for divorce. They reported that 9.6 percent of women and .4 percent of men reported that "physical violence to you or your children" was the main reason for marriage breakdown. An additional 2.5 percent of women and 1.1 percent of men reported that emotional or verbal abuse was the reason for marriage breakdown. They also found that "Nearly two-thirds (64 percent) of women compared with one-fifth (21 percent) of men indicated that it was mostly themselves who had made the decision to separate. Conversely, more than half (53 percent) of men compared with 20 percent of women said that the decision had been mostly made by their former partner" (14).

The most recent study of reasons for separation is from Britain. Lampard (2014) compared the reasons for relationship dissolution in married and cohabiting couples. He found that 21.5 percent of women and 3 percent of men cited domestic violence as the cause of the separation (320). Married people were more likely (17 percent) to report domestic violence as the reason for separation than cohabiting people (10 percent).

In another fairly recent study from the Netherlands, de Graaf and Kalmijn (2006, 494) found that 26 percent of women and 6 percent of men identified domestic violence as the motive for divorce. Although results were not disaggregated by sex, 15 percent of adults with children reported that physical violence was the reason for the divorce. The authors noted that "[d]ivorce is less common if there are children living at home, but if it does occur, there is more wrong with the marriage" (503). What the few studies on reasons for divorce and separation tell us is that violence and abuse are the reason for separation in 9–26 percent of relationships. If violence and abuse are in fact the cause of a significant number of divorces, then violence and abuse are important to consider in relation to child custody determination in the family law context.

BEST INTEREST OF THE CHILD

The Best Interest of the Child is a legal principle central to determining child custody in contested cases at separation and divorce. In the United States until the 1900s, a belief in the importance of patriarchal property rights to children meant that fathers normally automatically received custody of children. Legal decisions in the late 1800s began to prioritize children's welfare over patriarchal property rights (Crippen 1990), which meant that it became more likely for mothers to receive custody of children. For about sixty years, many American courts applied a "tender years doctrine" that placed young children in the care of their mothers at divorce, reflecting pre-divorce care patterns. By 1970, the tender years doctrine was largely abolished and replaced with a range of gender-blind factors that de-prioritized continuity of caregiving for children. By the 1990s, new shared parenting norms prioritizing fairness to parents were in place in the United States, Canada, Australia, and the United Kingdom. The prioritization of shared care post-separation contributed to a widespread assumption that joint custody is in the best interest of the child (Macdonald 2015; Rhoades 2002; Rhoades and Boyd 2004).

As we discussed above, shared parenting norms are based on the assumption that children are harmed when there is inequitable allocation of parenting time and authority post-separation, but they may have negative consequences for women and children when the issue at hand is separation and divorce from abusers (Macdonald 2015; Rhoades 2002; Ver Steegh and Davis 2015). Although there may not be a legal presumption of 50/50 shared physical custody or right to equal contact, the assumption that 50/50 power over children is best in most cases has effectively made it more difficult for abused mothers to separate from abusers. As Laing (1999) explains:

> The father-child bond is idealized and replaces an archaic and now unacceptable principle of paternal preference and ownership of children. Thus, fathers' claims are cloaked in a rhetoric of children's rights and of male victimization. In the context of this "reality," women's claims of male sexual and physical violence, widely documented by empirical research, are held to be suspect or are dismissed as self-serving and false. (237)

The dismissal of concerns about abuse is accomplished via prioritization of protecting children from the risk of presumably harmful outcomes of divorce rather than the harms of abuse in the family. Current norms favoring joint custody and maximum contact with fathers have been manifested in calls to forget the past and move forward into the future as friendly parents.

FRIENDLY PARENT

The friendly parent concept presumes that custody should be awarded to the parent who is most likely to foster the child's relationship with the other parent. Formal laws and policies that encourage maximum contact with both parents and punish resistance to contact with the other parent are referred to as friendly parent provisions (Dore 2004). Although "friendly parents" certainly sound nice, such provisions can be harmful to abuse victims and serve to empower the perpetrator in families where one parent is abusive. For example, where mothers resist contact between children and abusive fathers, the mothers are sometimes punished with loss of custody and access to their children (Zorza 2007). The friendly parent ethos has resulted in a climate that actively discourages reporting of abuse in the context of contested custody cases. In fact, Australian family law was changed in 2006 following publication of research documenting increased risk and harms to women and children from abusive men post-separation due to an earlier 1995 reform promoting friendly parenting via joint custody:

> Many [parent] respondents who accessed services post-2006 said they did not disclose violence to the court for fear that if their allegations were unproven they would be viewed as an "unfriendly parent" and the children they were trying to protect would be exposed to the perpetrator for longer

periods. Only 34 percent of women and 19 percent of men who reported violence felt that their reports were believed. (Bagshaw et al. 2011)

PARENTAL ALIENATION

The most extreme manifestation of friendly parent norms and systematic invalidation of women's concerns about abuse is parental alienation theory. American psychiatrist Richard Gardner invented "Parental Alienation Syndrome" (PAS) to explain reports of child sexual abuse at separation. According to his conceptualization of PAS, one parent invents false allegations of abuse and then brainwashes children into resisting contact. Gardner's focus was on discrediting children's reasons for denying contact with one parent rather than investigating children's reasons for resisting contact (Bruch 2001). Use of PAS was later adapted to defend against requests for sole custody by abused mothers, but the National Council of Juvenile and Family Court Judges rejected PAS in 2008. Some key problems with PAS are presented in Box 7.

Since 2008, practitioners who use PAS in their paid testimony in contested child custody cases have worked to produce a body of scholarly publications on what they have rebranded as parental alienation. However, as a recent book chapter argues, there is little credible research basis for the reformulated definition of alienation. Saini and colleagues (2012) reviewed the thirty-nine published articles and unpublished student papers about alienation and concluded that the empirical studies were weak and that there was too little valid research on it to make claims about parental alienation. Most significantly for this chapter on violence against women and children, the authors noted that "[t]here is a virtual absence of empirical studies on the differential diagnosis of alienation in children from other conditions that share similar features with PA, especially child estrangement in response to parental abuse and witness to intimate partner violence" (435).

Nonetheless, practitioners continue to market themselves as experts in parental alienation, providing mediation, arbitration, parenting coordination, case consultation to child protection agencies and other professionals, expert court testimony, camps, reunification interventions,[3] and other programs designed to overcome children's resistance to contact with a parent. Despite the absence of credible research evidence, adherents of parental

BOX 7. A WORD OF CAUTION ABOUT PARENTAL
ALIENATION

*From Bowles et al. 2008, 12–13;
internal citations omitted*

Under relevant evidentiary standards, the court should not accept testimony regarding parental alienation syndrome, or "PAS." The theory positing the existence of PAS has been discredited by the scientific community. In *Kumho Tire v. Carmichael,* 526 US 137 (1999), the Supreme Court ruled that even expert testimony based in the "soft sciences" must meet the standard set in the *Daubert* case. *Daubert,* in which the court re-examined the standard it had earlier articulated in the *Frye* case, requires application of a multi-factor test, including peer review, publication, testability, rate of error, and general acceptance. PAS does not pass this test. Any testimony that a party to a custody case suffers from the syndrome or "parental alienation" should therefore be ruled inadmissible and stricken from the evaluation report under both the standard established in *Daubert* and the earlier *Frye* standard.

The discredited "diagnosis" of PAS (or an allegation of "parental alienation"), quite apart from its scientific invalidity, inappropriately asks the court to assume that the child's behaviors and attitudes toward the parent who claims to be "alienated" have no grounding in reality. It also diverts attention away from the behaviors of the abusive parent, who may have directly influenced the child's responses by acting in violent, disrespectful, intimidating, humiliating, or discrediting ways toward the child or the other parent. The task for the court is to distinguish between situations in which the child is critical of one parent because they have been inappropriately manipulated by the other (taking care not to rely solely on subtle indications), and situations in which the child has his or her own legitimate grounds for criticism or fear of a parent, which will likely be the case when that parent has perpetrated domestic violence. Those grounds do not become less legitimate because the abused parent shares them, and seeks to advocate for the child by voicing his or her concerns.

alienation theory continue to provide expert testimony and family reports about parental alienation, including recommendations to terminate the custody and access of parents (usually mothers) accused of being alienators. This is likely because, despite the lack of research evidence, "Surveys of mental health and legal professionals indicate that as a group they consider themselves knowledgeable about PA/PAS and its clinical manifestations, consider it important to assess in custody matters, and are aware of its limited empirical research basis" (Saini et al. 2012, 436). Recent research on child custody evaluation and evaluators has also found that, though the evaluators are very confident in their knowledge regardless of their education levels about domestic violence (Bow and Boxer 2003), their practice is often shaped by ideologies that harm abused women and their children. We discuss some key findings from recent research below.

CHILD CUSTODY EVALUATION IN ABUSE CASES

Family courts rely heavily on child custody evaluations and family reports from third parties in contested child custody cases. Unfortunately, these reports are often deeply problematic when there is a history of domestic violence in the case. Fortunately, there is an emerging body of research on child custody evaluation and evaluators. In the United States, the Department of Justice has funded multiple major studies in this area (e.g., Davis et al. 2011; O'Sullivan et al. 2006; Saunders, Faller, and Tolman 2013, 2015). The Office on Violence Against Women also funded a National Child Custody Project to improve practice (see Battered Women's Justice Project n.d., 2012; Praxis International 2011). In addition, the Association of Family and Conciliation Courts and the National Council of Juvenile and Family Court Judges convened a Domestic Violence and Family Courts Project to address persistent and serious problems with the identification of domestic violence in custody cases and failures to protect victims (Ver Steegh and Dalton 2008). In Australia, the Australian Institute of Family Studies has conducted numerous large studies as part of their planning and assessment of recent family law reforms (Kaspiew et al. 2009; Kaspiew et al. 2015; Moloney et al. 2016). In the United Kingdom, the Family Justice Council funded a study to examine the quality of expert reports provided to family courts and their admissibility (Ireland 2012).

The emerging research on child custody evaluation has identified numerous serious problems. Many evaluators fail to screen consistently and appropriately for violence and abuse (Bow and Boxer 2003; Ireland 2012; Pence et al. 2012; Saunders 2015). Inadequate screening can result in failure to recognize ongoing risk, identify the primary aggressor, or assess for coercive controlling behavior. Even when violence is detected, it appears to have little effect on court-ordered outcomes in custody cases (Pence et al. 2012; Johnson, Saccuzzo, and Koen 2005; Kernic et al. 2005; Macdonald 2015; Rosen and O'Sullivan 2005; Saunders 2015). Another finding is that many family law practitioners lack knowledge about the dynamics of relationships where there is a history of abuse. Despite reporting high levels of confidence with their skills, many report writers lack formal education about domestic violence (Bow and Boxer 2003; Ireland 2012; Saunders 2015). Given this dearth of formal education, it is not surprising that minimization and obfuscation of violence and abuse are also problems.

Pence and colleagues (2012) examined how U.S. family court evaluators approached domestic violence in eighteen contested child custody cases where domestic violence was reported. They found that evaluators inconsistently explained the nature of the violence in their reports, such that it was difficult to know who was doing what to whom. They found that the reports obscured domestic violence rather than assisting in understanding it. Furthermore, they identified six key contexts for this obfuscation: not receiving clear instructions from the court about what to evaluate; using a narrow incident-based approach to domestic violence; focusing only on physical violence; making subjective decisions about what information was important to include; subsuming violence into other frameworks including "high conflict," mental illness, and parental alienation; and substituting their own personal ideologies, values, and assumptions for investigation of facts in the case. They also found that the reports did not connect domestic violence to future parenting capacity or discuss the impact of violence on children. Macdonald (2015) had similar findings in the United Kingdom, including frequent framing of violence as mutual "conflict" or irrelevant to future arrangements and prioritization of father access over safety concerns.

These results are less surprising when we consider that another key finding of the research in this area is that personal beliefs and ideologies drive evaluator understandings of abuse and the resulting recommendations about custody (Haselschwerdt, Hardesty, and Hans 2011; Saunders, Faller, and Tolman 2013, 2015). Saunders, Faller, and Tolman (2015) studied the relationship between child custody evaluator beliefs, training, and custody recommendations and found that, for 465 custody evaluators, measured sexist beliefs correlated positively with recommendations for sole or joint custody to the perpetrator, and unsupervised visits. A belief in stereotypes that discredit reports of abuse and mirror abusers' minimization of abuse lead evaluators to favor joint parenting arrangements that trump considerations of safety and impede accurate assessment of risks in individual cases despite requirements in most states for family courts to consider domestic violence (Kernic et al. 2005; Morrill et al. 2005; Rhoades 2002). Brinig, Frederick, and Drozd (2014) argue that legal presumptions in favor of joint custody further discourage individualized assessment of violence and abuse, contributing to the likelihood of ongoing abuse and violence against battered mothers and their children.

One of the features of powerful cultural beliefs is that they are not just the preserve of a few extremists. A key characteristic of patriarchy is that it establishes people's commonsense views of what is natural and best. In the area of child custody, patriarchal cultural norms identify post-separation fathering as essential to children's well-being. Many battered women have internalized this belief system as well and seek to preserve contact with their batterers for the sake of the children until or even after it becomes clear that the children are also direct targets of abuse. For all parties, then, inside and outside the relationship, this framework normalizes fathers' rights to access post-separation regardless of abuse. Reports of abuse are systematically discredited and minimized when introduced in this context (Barker 2013; Dragiewicz 2014; Hardesty 2002; Hardesty and Chung 2006; Hardesty and Ganong 2006; Miller and Smolter 2011; Parkinson 2013; Rathus 2014; Rhoades 2008; Saunders 1994).

SUMMARY

As Hardesty (2002) argued, the failure to consider the dynamics of abuse as part of a holistic picture that includes post-separation parenting prevents a comprehensive understanding of the problem. The impact of abuse on children at separation is one of the most important concerns for abused mothers. Research on child custody disputes and systems responses to them supports feminist theories of woman abuse (Haselschwerdt, Hardesty, and Hans 2011). Patriarchal family structures, cultural norms, institutions, and structural inequalities not only are all related to woman abuse but can in many situations also be seen as a direct contributor to the abuse of women (Sev'er 1997). Abuse and violence are profoundly gendered, with structural gender inequality deeply affecting efforts to intervene in and prevent violence (Dragiewicz and Lindgren 2009). There is much to be done to ensure that violence and abuse are taken seriously at separation and divorce and that children are protected from abusers despite pervasive patriarchal norms enshrined in family law.

There is plenty of research to do in this area. Despite an emerging body of research on abused women's experiences with child contact post-separation, family courts and child custody are largely neglected areas of study outside of law. There is a need to study what is actually happening in the courtroom in woman abuse cases where custody is at stake. There is also a great need for research that considers children's perspectives on contact with abusers post-separation. The existing research on parenting, divorce, child custody, and abuse need to be better integrated to synthesize scattered findings into a more coherent whole (Dragiewicz 2014). Most importantly, men's violence against women cannot be separated from their parenting before or after separation. Parenting concerns are central to women's successful separation from abusers (Wuest and Merritt-Gray 1999). Not only does shared custody and access provide a possible context for batterers to continue their abuse post-separation, but family law and affiliated institutions actively enforce this contact. As a result, mothers may be unable to extricate themselves from abusive relationships to achieve safe separation from their batterers. In addition, the coerced ongoing contact prevents women and children from healing following abuse (Bancroft and Silverman 2002). Children and parenting at separation and divorce are central factors to consider if we want to understand woman abuse.

CHAPTER SIX

What Is to Be Done about Separation/Divorce Violence against Women?

You left an abusive situation and your confidence level is certainly not at its highest and you're going to these people to seek help and you're reaching out and then when they come and say to you there is nothing they can do. So you know basically that they're not there to help you. So, you suck it all up and minimize what's happened and I can see why so many women will go back.

> A female survivor of separation/divorce abuse who participated in a focus group conducted by staff affiliated with Luke's Place in 2007[1]

A central theme of this book has been to portray the process of exiting intimate relationships as potentially dangerous. The next step is to discuss what initiatives can reduce this danger. The above quote and the lack of help may not be typical of shelters, but it is true of many agencies to which women reach out. This chapter emphasizes the importance of avoiding simplistic solutions and the value of engaging in a multi pronged approach. No individual policy will substantially improve the well-being of women leaving abusive men. Moreover, a single strategy will not end the atrocities committed by men who were not abusive during an ongoing relationship but who became so after their partners left them. The solutions we advance here cover a broad range of approaches: legal reforms, social services, feminist men's efforts, and new electronic technologies. There are, of course, many more initiatives that could be discussed here.[2]

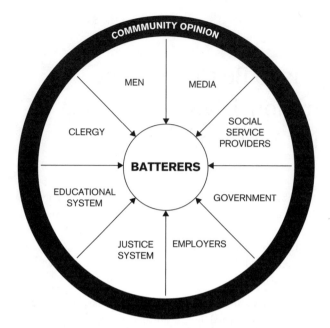

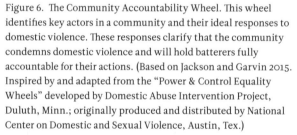

Figure 6. The Community Accountability Wheel. This wheel identifies key actors in a community and their ideal responses to domestic violence. These responses clarify that the community condemns domestic violence and will hold batterers fully accountable for their actions. (Based on Jackson and Garvin 2015. Inspired by and adapted from the "Power & Control Equality Wheels" developed by Domestic Abuse Intervention Project, Duluth, Minn.; originally produced and distributed by National Center on Domestic and Sexual Violence, Austin, Tex.)

Figure 6 is one potentially successful model for such an approach. Referred to as the Community Accountability Wheel (Jackson and Garvin 2015), it is the "ideal community response" to woman abuse and is inspired by and adapted from the Power and Control Wheel (figure 7), which is a way of visually representing the tactics typically used by men who batter. By batter, we mean the ongoing pattern of violence, coercion, intimidation, and abuse in an intimate relationship. The graphic was created in 1982 by Ellen Pence, Coral McDonnell, and Michael Paymar as part of a curriculum for a court-ordered program for men who batter. It was developed out of the experiences of women who were battered and attending support and educational groups in Duluth, Minnesota. The wheel is not a theory. It is a

What Is to Be Done?

Figure 6. (continued).

MEDIA WILL:

Educate the community about the epidemic of violence against women.

Prioritize safety, equal opportunity, and justice for women and children over profit, popularity, and advantage.

Expose and condemn patriarchal privilege, abuse, secrecy, and chauvinism.

Cease the glorification of violence against women and children.

SOCIAL SERVICE PROVIDERS WILL:

Become social change advocates for battered women.

Refer batterers to accountable intervention programs.

Stop blaming batterers' behavior on myths such as drugs and alcohol, family history, anger, provocation, "loss of control," etc.

Design and deliver services that are sensitive to women and children's safety needs.

Minimize how batterers use them to continue battering their families.

GOVERNMENT WILL:

Pass laws that define battering by men as criminal behavior without exception.

Vigorously and progressively sanction men's battering behavior.

Create standards for accountable batterer-intervention programs.

Require coordinated systems of intervention in domestic violence.

Provide ample funding to accomplish the goal of eradicating domestic violence.

EMPLOYERS WILL:

Condition batterers' continuing employment on remaining nonviolent.

Actively intervene against men's stalking in the workplace.

Support, financially and otherwise, advocacy and services for battered women and children.

Continually educate and dialogue about domestic violence issues through personnel services.

JUSTICE SYSTEM WILL:

Adopt mandatory arrest policy for men who batter.

Refer batterers exclusively to intervention programs that meet state or federal standards.

Never offer delayed or deferred sentence options to batterers.

Provide easily accessible protection orders and back them up.

Incarcerate batterers for noncompliance with any aspect of their adjudication.

EDUCATION SYSTEM WILL:

Dialogue with students about violence in their homes, the dynamics of domestic violence, and how it is founded on the oppression of women and the worship of men.

Provide a leadership role in research and theoretical development that prioritizes gender justice, equal opportunity, and peace.

Intervene in harassment, abuse, violence, and intimidation of girls and women in the educational system.

CLERGY WILL:

Conduct outreach within the congregation regarding domestic violence and provide a safe environment for women to discuss their experiences.

Develop internal policies for responding to domestic violence.

Speak out against domestic violence from the pulpit. Organize multi-faith coalitions to educate the religious community.

Interact with the existing domestic violence intervention community.

MEN WILL:

Acknowledge that all men benefit from men's violence.

Actively oppose men's violence.

Use peer pressure to stop violence against women and children.

Make peace, justice, and equality masculine virtues.

Vigorously confront men who indulge in misogynistic behavior.

Seek out and accept the leadership of women.

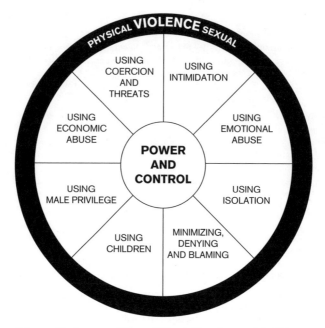

Figure 7. The Power and Control Wheel. (Based on work by Ellen Pence and others.)

conceptual tool. It helps people see the patterns in behavior and their significance. It is not intended to capture every tactic of control, just primary tactics. Nor will all empirical cases correspond exactly to the wheel. The wheel was based on women's experience in heterosexual intimate-partner relationships. The battered women did not identify a desire for power or control as motivating their partners to engage in these behaviors. Rather, men who batter gained power and control in the relationship as an outcome of those behaviors.

LEGAL REFORMS

For reasons described in Chapter 4, many abused women, regardless of whether their victimization occurs in ongoing relationships or during or after separation/divorce, are, to say the least, dissatisfied with the criminal justice system's responses to their plight. As discussed, law enforcement involvement can actually make matters worse. In fact, some of the key risk factors associated with separation/divorce violence may be found in settings

Figure 7. (continued).

USING INTIMIDATION:

Making her/him afraid by using looks, actions, gestures.
Smashing things.
Destroying her/his property.
Abusing pets.
Displaying weapons.

USING EMOTIONAL ABUSE:

Putting him/her down.
Making her/him feel bad about herself/himself.
Calling her/him names.
Making her/him think she's/he's crazy.
Playing mind games.
Humiliating her/him.
Making her/him feel guilty.

USING ISOLATION:

Controlling what she/he does, who she/he see and talks to, what she/he reads, where she/he goes.
Limiting her/his outside involvement.
Using jealousy to justify actions.

MINIMIZING, DENYING, AND BLAMING:

Making light of the abuse and not taking her/his concerns about it seriously.
Saying the abuse did not happen.
Shifting responsibility for abusive behavior.
Saying she/he caused it.

USING CHILDREN:

Making her/him feel guilty about the children.
Using the children to relay messages.
Using visitation to harass her/him.
Threatening to take the children away.

USING MALE PRIVILEGE:

Treating her/him like a servant.
Making all the big decisions.
Acting like the "master of the castle".
Being the one to define men's and women's roles.

USING ECONOMIC ABUSE:

Preventing her/him from getting or keeping a job.
Making her/him ask for money.
Giving her/him an allowance.
Taking her/his money.
Not letting her/him know about or have access to family income.

USING COERCION AND THREATS:

Making and/or carrying out threats to do something to hurt her/him.
Threatening to leave her/him, to commit suicide, to report her/him to welfare.
Making her/him drop charges.
Making her/him do illegal things.

adopted by criminal justice officials as measures to stop violence. Consider what happened to this rural Ohio survivor interviewed by DeKeseredy and Schwartz (2009):

> He had to go to domestic violence counseling every Monday for six months, but sending him to that counseling meant that I got beat every Monday night for six months. Because he would come home madder than hell because he had to go to that place. It was just the most horrible thing I could have done to him and it wasn't me. I told the judge, "I don't care what you do to him, but don't send him to counseling." And she sent him back there anyway. So every Monday for six more months I got beaten because he had to go for three hours and sit in class. . . . And then we meet up with a few of the guys from his class and I think they all did it. Because they were all mad every Monday night and a few of the women I talked to, they're like, "Yep, they come in extra mad because it's your fault we have to be there." I was like, For what? I don't hit you. So it was just the worst help ever. (90–91)

In other courtrooms, judges are slightly more vigilant in preventing physical abuse. In those batterer programs, many women have said, they may not be physically abused, but they become the object of a terroristic household, suffering psychological, emotional, and economic abuse, which we have suggested in the past might be worse (DeKeseredy and Schwartz 2013).

These problems with mandatory counseling do not mean that we should completely abandon any hope of improving the criminal justice system. Still, without effective changes, the criminal justice system alone cannot prevent the harms covered in this book. Further, family law mechanisms alone are inadequate. Empirical evidence demonstrates that "interagency cooperation and coordination" are essential (Hamby 2014). In other words, the police and courts need to develop strong, positive, collaborative relationships with other service agencies in the same community.

Evaluating New Programs and Legislation

In this chapter, we will discuss several new laws and initiatives. Unfortunately, whenever progressive legislation is proposed or enacted in any area of domestic abuse, one can anticipate claims that its value cannot be proven according to the principles of a conservative-oriented "evidence-based practice." Our preference, like many feminist scholars and practitioners (e.g., Gondolf 2012), is for a careful and fair evaluation through a gendered lens. However, there is no question that there is a growing popularity of evidence-based practice, which embraces an approach to knowledge production that idealizes systemic reviews, experimental research, evaluation studies, and quantitative meta-analysis as the path to criminological truth. This is not to say that there is no use for such reviews, which have been an important part of our own research for many years. However, without a theoretical core and often a gendered lens, such research can be used to undercut progressive policies.

To date, critiques of the conceptualization and implementation of evidence-based practice are concentrated in the research on education (Clegg 2005), and medicine (Goldenberg 2006). Scholars in these areas have excavated and critiqued the underlying assumptions of efforts to promote evidence-based practice, and they have pointed out how "evidence-based practices maintain an antiquated understanding of evidence as 'facts' about the world in the assumption that scientific beliefs stand or fall in light of the evidence" (Goldenberg 2006, 2622). These critics are concerned about a standard topic in criminological theory, which is the problem of nineteenth-century positivism that prioritized a "scientific" view of offenders as biologically or psychologically damaged and in need of therapy and repair. Critics of evidence-based criminology see it as heralding a return to a neo-positivist ethic that rejects all of the methodological advances of social science research (Goldenberg 2006) and particularly of the gendered-lens approach of feminist research.

Calls for evidence-based practice focus on an arbitrarily limited array of acts and measures, in particular those that can be reliably counted. We learned from the first proponents of positivism, such as Cesere Lombroso, that it is possible to spend years very carefully and very scientifically measuring what he could (in his case, nose length, eyebrow and forehead width, etc.), develop strong correlations, and still be completely and totally wrong (Lilly, Cullen, and Ball 2015). Recent publications supportive of evidence-based practice have selectively attacked laws, programs, and services that fall outside a narrow set of survey research, especially around woman abuse (DeKeseredy and Dragiewicz 2013; Gondolf 2012). This approach is used to target feminist theories as political rather than scientific. Instead of the gender-conscious, collaborative community initiatives supported by advocates for abused women, proponents of evidence-based practice call for individual-level treatments, interventions, and therapies for offenders (see Dutton 2006, 2010; Dutton and Corvo 2007). However, these "alternative approaches do not appear to be any more justified as 'evidence-based practice' than the gender-based cognitive-behavioral batterer programs" (Gondolf 2011, 351).

The journal *Partner Abuse* provides another example. The journal website claims that:

> [I]ts purpose is to advance knowledge, practice and policies through a commitment to rigorous, objective research and evidence-based solutions . . . A basic premise of the journal is that partner abuse is a human problem, and that the particular role of gender in the etiology, perpetration and consequences of emotional and physical partner abuse cannot be assumed, but rather must be subjected to the same empirical scrutiny as any other factor. (Hamel 2012)

While touting itself as scientific and apolitical, this approach emerges from and promotes a particular political position. As Goldenberg (2006) warns, "The appeal to the authority of evidence that characterizes evidence-based practice does not *increase* objectivity but rather *obscures* the subjective elements that inescapably enter all forms of human inquiry" (2621, emphasis in original). In other words, calls for evidence-based policy pose as atheoretical but obscure implicit theoretical assumptions. In the case of *Partner Abuse*, the editor assumes that the importance of gender needs to be proved, rather than disproved. Worldwide data on persistent gender inequality in areas such as health, income, and political representation would seem to suggest the opposite starting point (DeKeseredy and Dragiewicz 2013).

To date, calls for evidence-based practice focus on micro- or individual-level variables. As Sampson (2010) points out, the valorization of randomized clinical trials as the "gold standard" for knowledge production is especially problematic because the policies to be guided by the evidence are, by definition, implemented at the macro-level. It is worth stressing that critiquing evidence-based practice is not the same as eschewing evidence. Instead, as we show in this book, criminologists can use a variety of data-gathering techniques and a broad understanding of evidence to improve our understanding of various types of woman abuse.

This chapter, then, will look at a variety of polices and practices that include a gender-based approach, in line with our assumption throughout the book that the largest proportion of separation and divorce mechanisms of violence are perpetrated by men against women. That being the case, it would be foolish to ignore what kinds of society promote such a state of affairs, by ignoring the effects of gender.

Rather than repeat legal and criminal justice reforms described in other sources, such as breaking up the "good ol' boy network" that protects abusers (see DeKeseredy and Schwartz 2009) and collaborative conflict resolution proceedings (Ellis, Stuckless, and Smith 2015), we turn readers' attention to some timely issues. One, in particular, is gun control.

Stricter Gun Control

This section is, of course, more relevant to U.S. residents than to those living in other advanced industrial countries.[3] For example, women and children experience separation/divorce violence in Finland (Nikupeteri and Laitinen 2015), but they are far less likely to be killed by guns—due, in large part, to that country's stricter gun control legislation. The same can be said about survivors of separation/divorce violence in Sweden, Norway, and even in Canada, which has very high rates of nonlethal woman abuse (Alaggia and Vine 2012; DeKeseredy 2011; Johnson and Dawson 2011). Indeed, the U.S. "neo-liberal homeland" is characterized by a unique type of "exceptionalism" (Squires 2014). It is a nation characterized by a high level of gun ownership, and the "role of firearms in domestic violence is immense and indisputable" (Hall-Sanchez 2014, 497). Even when there are calls for stricter gun legislation, or just for current laws to be enforced, as President Barack Obama announced near the end of his tenure, these proposals are based heavily on reactions to mass shootings rather than on the more common types of gun murders that result in the death of a great many more victims (Levinson King 2015).

Undoubtedly, murders committed by people such as Elliot Rodger (see Chapter 1) are terrifying, and some of them, like his, are grounded in misogyny. At first glance, Obama's emphasis on mass shootings makes sense because there were 325 such U.S. killings in 2015, or nearly one a day that year (Levinson King 2015). Yet there were more than three times as many women murdered in that year by current or former partners. Overall, actually, mass shootings "produce a tiny fraction, less than two per cent, of America's gun deaths and injuries. . . . It's the little-noticed local tragedies . . . that make tighter gun laws a critical and immediate necessity" (Dale 2016, 1). Certainly, gun-related murders of women are among the highest number of these "little-noticed local tragedies." In 2013, for instance, 1,615 women were murdered by men in the United States. Of these victims, 94 percent were killed by someone they knew, and 53 percent were killed by a man with a gun. Of that 94 percent, 62 percent were the wives or other intimate partner of the killer (Violence Policy Center 2015). In other words, as mentioned, about three times as many women were killed by intimate partners as were killed in all of the mass shootings.

Obviously, the most common proposal to reduce this gun violence is to find a way to regulate guns more closely. On January 5, 2016, President Obama unveiled a strategy to use executive office powers to stiffen background-check requirements on gun purchases. A central feature of his plan was a "clarification" that people who sell guns regularly over the Internet as private collectors will have to operate as licensed federal dealers, which means that they must conduct background checks on their potential buyers. Although he said very little about violence against intimate partners, many people, including those belonging to gun safety or anti-gun coalitions, asserted that it would reduce the number of male-to-female homicides. For example, Allison Anderman, staff attorney at the Law Center to Prevent Gun Violence, claimed, "It means that more people will have to get a dealer license. . . . Those people are more likely to catch domestic abusers who try to buy guns, and it will limit the number of domestic abusers who will be able to buy guns without a background check" (cited in Jeltsen 2016, 1). Similarly, Ron Le Grand, vice president of public policy at the National Network to End Domestic Violence, responded to Obama's efforts by stating, "We need to know who is out there, and if they are convicted of a domestic violence act. If we don't know that, the background check is not as effective and efficient as it needs to be. . . . It is not going to save everybody, but it is a step in the right direction" (cited in ibid., 1).

There is some evidence that background checks work. Jeltsen (2016) claims that Le Grand has data showing that 38 percent fewer women are shot to death by intimate male partners in states where background checks are required for all handgun sales. Similarly, the U.S. Violence Against Women Act includes provisions that, when an order of protection (also referred to as a restraining order) is granted, it leads to the person being restrained losing any gun permits and/or permission to keep guns at home. This, in turn, leads to a reduction in intimate femicide (Hamby 2014). A number of states have gone further than the federal law, extending gun possession bans to people under temporary (not just permanent) restraining orders. Such bans have further reduced intimate partner homicide, with a best estimate of 8 percent. In general, these measures are often cited as one of the reasons why, since 1993, intimate partner homicide has decreased by one-third, since the reduction in gun homicides have been a major part of that drop (Cook and Goss 2014, 146).

Stricter gun control provisions are likely to reduce the rate not only of intimate femicide but also of the murder of children and assorted bystanders and relatives. In fact, when one is talking about mass shootings and intimate femicide, one is often talking about the same events. David Conley, as was discussed in Box 2, killed his former girlfriend Valerie Jackson, her six children, and her husband in August 2015. As reported in Box 8, murders like these make up the majority of mass killings in the United States. We do not recognize this because media coverage of them pales in comparison to mass murders like the one the same summer discussed in Chapter 1: Dylann Roof shot nine people inside the Emanuel African Methodist Episcopal Church in Charleston, South Carolina. That event generated hundreds of thousands of newspaper stories, editorials, and blogs around the entire world, and, of course, politicians postured to take advantage of the tragedy to argue for capital punishment, mercy, gun control, the banning of Confederate battle flags, or any of a variety of other causes.

One can argue that Dylann Roof's crimes are more "newsworthy" than David Conley's because interracial and racist shootings in church are an unusual event in America, whereas the deaths of Valerie Jackson and her children were more commonplace. Still, the argument that the shooting deaths of eight people in one family by an outsider is less newsworthy, less shocking, and less worth national hand-wringing because the killer was a former boyfriend of one of the victims tells us a great deal about both

BOX 8. MASS SHOOTINGS TARGET WOMEN
AND CHILDREN

Mass shootings in the United States get a lot of media coverage worldwide. When a white man gunned down black churchgoers in Charleston, South Carolina, or a man opened fire in a movie theater in Lafayette, Louisiana, these events were trumpeted throughout the world. However, they are not typical of mass shootings. Much more representative would be the case presented in Box 2, where David Conley killed his former girlfriend, her husband, and her six children by executing them one at a time. The typical mass shooting takes place not in a shopping mall but at home behind closed doors. The majority of victims are women and children. Such shootings involve men killing their former wives or girlfriends, and their families. These are men going out to kill not random strangers but people they know well.

The *Huffington Post* recently published an analysis of five years of mass shootings, defined as an event where at least four people were killed by a gun. Jeltsen (2015) summarizes the data: "We found that in 57% of mass shootings, the shooter targeted either a family member or an intimate partner. According to HuffPost's analysis, 64% of mass shooting victims were women and children. That's startling, since women typically make up only 15% of total gun violence homicide victims, and children only 7%. Mass shootings account for only a tiny fraction of gun deaths each year, but it's clear who overwhelmingly pays the price: women and children" (1).

American culture and the commonplace nature of the killing of women (and children, and bystanders) after separation.

Gun control legislation in the United States will be very difficult if not impossible to implement, given the sharp political opposition, including fierce resistance from the National Rifle Association. Still, a ban on the possession, purchase, sale, and transfer of handguns would make an enormous difference. For example, although there was no question that many criminals continued to obtain guns, including purchasing them legally at nearby Virginia gun shops, Loftin and colleagues' (1991) evaluation of the effects of Washington, D.C.'s 1976 handgun ban showed that gun homicides and suicides declined by roughly 25 percent in the years after the legislation was passed.

One point of opposition to handgun control is the argument that such bans will simply lead people to substitute more lethal long guns (Cook and Ludwig 2000), such as the Bushmaster AR-15 assault rifle that Adam Lanza used at Sandy Hook Elementary School in Newtown, Connecticut, in 2012. Of course, one answer to this problem is to ban assault rifles too. In Australia in 1996, certain rapid-fire long guns were banned under the National Firearms Agreement. This legislation led to the buyback of 650,000 guns and to stricter rules for licensing and safe storage. This law did not end gun ownership, but the chances of an individual being murdered with a firearm in Australia have dropped 72 percent. Most criminologists agree that curbing violent crime of all sorts, not just intimate femicide, cannot effectively be done without eliminating easy access to guns. In the words of Reiman and Leighton (2010), "Trying to fight crime while allowing such easy access to guns is like trying to teach a child to walk and then tripping him each time he stands up. In its most charitable light, it is hypocrisy. Less charitably, it is complicity in murder" (201).

Ironically, there are strict U.S. regulations in place for the sale of many things, such as ladders, that kill far fewer people than guns (Kristof 2012). Moreover, *toy* guns are regulated in the United States. The road to change did not look particularly hopeful when virtually all candidates for the presidency in 2016, on all political fronts, attacked gun control legislation.

Criminalizing Coercive Control

Chapter 1 makes explicit that coercive control by men is an integral component of the problem of separation/divorce violence against women.[4] Thus, any attempt to deal with this problem must include an effective legal response. As Stark observes in his path-breaking book *Coercive Control* (2007), this failure to take into account coercive control has made virtually all interventions that have been developed largely ineffective. The problem, he reports, is that traditional laws and programs are designed to deal with "the traditional forms of domestic violence," but coercive control is much more devastating. It is an attack on human liberty that is social, personal, and political at the same time, which means that responses need to speak to all three levels simultaneously. Legal changes, social services, and political action are all needed, he argues.

One example of a needed change occurred recently in England and Wales with the creation of the Serious Crime Act (2015). This act created the new offense of controlling or coercive behavior in intimate or familial relationships. Although the law has mechanisms for violent acts like simple or aggravated assault, it tries to fill a gap by criminalizing perpetrator behavior that involves psychological or emotional torment taking place repeatedly or continuously and that has a "serious effect" on the victims. This serious effect is defined as meaning that it has caused the victims to fear violence will be used against them on at least two occasions or has had a substantial adverse effect on the victims' daily activities. The law has provisions that try to draw a line between reasonable actions and coercive attempts to control a partner's life. The act also applies to men who control or who try to control women through surveillance apps, or try to keep them from socializing (Home Office 2015). Of course, it remains to be seen how the law operates in practice. In the same way that women who fought back or defended themselves from attack found themselves in some states being arrested either as part of a dual arrest or as a primary aggressor, there is reason to worry that a loosely worded law could be used to arrest women who yell at or argue loudly with their partners.

Women's Aid (2015) and other feminist organizations in the United Kingdom energetically campaigned to develop this law, and they view it as a landmark moment in the U.K. approach to violence against women. Even so, echoing Stark's concerns, Women's Aid recognizes that this law is not enough; it must be accompanied by efforts to raise public awareness and training for service providers in the field. The problem is that, as in North America, service providers and criminal justice officials are too often fooled by men who engage in coercive control. First responders like the police, in particular, are commonly faced with offenders who seem to be rational and calm when talking to the police, but with victims who are extremely upset and not calm at all (Fontes 2015). Because of this comparison of a calm man with an upset woman, many controlling men succeed in convincing responders that the badly frightened and upset women are unstable and are presumably exaggerating their descriptions of what was happening

(Bancroft 2002). Training first responders and judicial figures on this dynamic, many feel, will at minimum make them aware that this happens and encourage them to look deeper into the circumstances.

Criminalizing Image-Based Sexual Abuse

As discussed in Chapter 3, image-based sexual abuse—or what many refer to as online revenge porn—is now common and even normalized (Edwards 2014), but the criminal justice system's response has, thus far, been woefully inadequate (Stebnar 2013). In 2016, twenty-six U.S. states had revenge-porn laws, some making it a felony and some a lesser gravity misdemeanor. Among those without a specific law on revenge porn, states claim that they can respond through other criminal statutes such as those forbidding harassment, extortion, and stalking. Yet there remains considerable resistance to criminalization by groups who claim that the pain and suffering experienced by victims is "self-inflicted" because they allowed themselves to be photographed or recorded. Other opponents assert that criminalization is unnecessary because victims have other resources available to them, such as Digital Millennium Copyright Act takedown notices, which were designed to be used mainly on websites that allow the streaming of copyrighted video or music. The notion is that victims can obtain an order under that law to force a website to take down video of them that they did not authorize. Indeed, if one site is publishing a nude selfie, often obtained by a hacker or former friend, then a threat of a copyright suit may suffice to get it removed. Sites like Reddit may have no interest in ethics or concepts of right and wrong, but they do seem to worry about lawsuits for copyright violation (since the person who takes a selfie retains copyright) (Dewey 2014). Of course, when one's image has been posted to a variety of sites, or a video taken by a former boyfriend is what is posted, the solution in a state without a law might be a complex, highly expensive, and years-long lawsuit. Finally, there are opponents to revenge-porn laws who contend that such laws violate the First Amendment (Hoffmeister 2016).

Perhaps opponents to criminalization of revenge porn have little to worry about, because prosecutions and convictions are quite rare (Salter and Crofts 2015). A milestone was reached in December 2014 when Noe Iniguez, 36, of Los Angeles, became the first person to be convicted under California's revenge-porn law (and perhaps the first person in the United States). He posted nude photos of his ex-girlfriend without her consent on her employer's Facebook page. Consequently, he was sentenced to one year in jail and thirty-six months of probation, and he was required to attend domestic violence counseling for violating both the state's revenge-porn statute and two restraining orders (DeKeseredy and Corsianos 2016). It should be noted in passing that California was the first state to adopt revenge-porn legislation in October 2013 (O'Connor 2014). The other conviction of note in California came in April 2015, when Kevin Bollaert was convicted of operating an extraordinary website that posted over 10,000 images along with what amounted to invitations to harass the women (posting names and contact information) and then extorting women later for money to get the picture taken down. He was given eighteen years in prison after a parade of women testified (Zabala and Stickney 2015). Whether authorities will get convictions on less notorious and infamous cases remains to be seen.

We favor this criminalization of revenge porn for several reasons. First, not all speech is subject to the protection of the First Amendment. Perhaps the most obvious example is child pornography, which is illegal pretty much everywhere, and other forms of pornography have been more or less regulated by the government. Other speech is also regulated, including fraud, defamation, slander, true threats, incitement, and speech integral to criminal conduct (Hoffmeister 2016). U.S. Supreme Court Justice Oliver Wendall Holmes Jr. rather famously said in *Schenck v. United States* (249 U.S. 47, 1919) that "[t]he most stringent protection of free speech would not protect a man falsely shouting fire in a theater and causing a panic." Although the *Schenck* case itself is no longer U.S. case law, the basic value of the metaphor remains valid for noting that constitutional claims to free speech do have limits.

More importantly, revenge porn is a "ritualized element" specifically designed to publicly defile victims. Thus, Salter and Crofts (2015) assert that "the creation of offences that specifically target revenge porn may both deter perpetrators and operate symbolically to restore and reaffirm the dignity of victims" (255). As with other parts of the criminal law, there are practical benefits in terms of effectively stopping or reducing the amount of the proscribed behavior, and there are symbolic benefits from using the law to make a public stand on what is right and what is wrong (Schwartz 2012). One symbolic benefit of such laws is that image-based sexual abuse is a crime that is essentially a crime against separated and divorced women. Although there are other victims (such as by hacked or stolen videos), the crime was mostly conceived and carried out as a crime against former intimate partners, often to get even with a woman for breaking up with an entitled man.

Family Law

The research on family law and child custody evaluations indicates that minor legal changes alone, such as directives to judges dealing with child custody to prioritize safety over access, or instructions to inquire about violence before making a ruling, are inadequate to significantly change practice in family law (Kaspiew et al. 2015). Things tend to continue along the same lines as before. Of course, this is not a surprise, given the pervasive and powerful patriarchal norms in family law that assume that shared care after the breakdown of a relationship is almost always in the best interest of the child. In order to make major changes, more than directives are needed to overturn deep-seated gender bias. Rather, significant cultural and structural changes will be required.

However, steps can be taken now to improve research, practice, and law. These include prioritizing safety, integration of the abuse and family research, mandatory violence education for family law professionals, use of specific, detailed screening tools, compulsory accounting for abuse in custody and access reports and recommendations, presumptions against custody to abusers, accounting for pre-separation patterns of care, and taking children's views into account.

Foremost among these steps is that research on families and woman and child abuse needs to be better integrated. What is already known about the nature of violence and abuse, especially the likelihood of abuse continuing or escalating after separation, must be incorporated into the general research on families and divorce. In addition, this broader literature must take into account the risks associated with nonphysical forms of abuse like stalking, the significant overlap of woman and child abuse, and the effects of exposure to woman abuse on children. We need to better understand exactly how often there is a history or pattern of abuse in cases that come to family court. Studies on divorce outcomes should be critically evaluated, given their widespread failure to consider the impact of violence and abuse. Surprisingly, claims about the effects of divorce are prominent in contested child custody cases, where they are irrelevant to the issues at hand; the court is not deciding whether there will be a divorce at all, but what to do with the children. The prominence of discussions about outcomes of divorce in conversations about the best interest of the child is actually quite telling. It reveals more about cultural pressure to preserve patriarchal families than the best custody arrangements for kids and moms when there is a history of woman abuse.

More research is needed to better understand what is actually happening in family law cases where there is a history of violence or abuse, including developing research on actual child custody evaluations. Many attorneys in the field are convinced that abusers are able to use family law as a mechanism to continue to exercise coercive control over former partners and children post-separation. Solid information on this subject could affect many outcomes. Research is also sorely needed on the impact of disruptive joint custody regimes that include frequent transitions between residences for children. Finally, research should speak to the children affected by violence in the home about their needs and preferences. There has been virtually no research that asks children with an abusive parent what arrangements they want post-separation to make them feel safe, or perhaps querying adolescents on what they would have wanted if they had been asked. The needs of children with an abusive parent are not the same as the needs of children with non-abusive parents, and we should not assume that research on one group applies to the other. This research should be part of compulsory education for all family law practitioners, from judges to mediators and family report writers.

Practice recommendations include requirements for substantial education about violence and abuse for all family law professionals. This education should be based on research, even if that means challenging long-held beliefs. For example, practitioners should learn that it is not uncommon at all for custody cases that make it to family court to include histories of abuse; in fact, many believe that this is true in the majority of such cases. The evidence on how harmful exposure to abusive fathers is for children and women should be researched and presented. Another topic sorely needed is material on how it is common for violence not only to continue but also to escalate after separation. Practitioners should be required to use standard assessment tools consistently, such as those being developed by the Battered Women's Justice Project in Minneapolis, and to act to protect children and women where there is a history of abuse.

One sorely needed legal change is for rules to prioritize rights to safety and well-being over rights to equitable contact. For example, jurisdictions could institute rebuttable presumptions against joint custody where there is a history of abuse, with judges required to explain and defend any movement away from this presumption. Another very useful legal change would be to curtail sharply the involvement of so-called experts in the decision-making processes of family court. Once again, sponsored research could scrutinize the extent to which experts introduce bias that drives evaluation practice, along with an examination of whether the experts used have appropriate training and education. Likewise, some theories should be banned from use in family court, such as the invalid "parental alienation" theory that was created to discredit reports of abuse, dismiss children's fear of a parent, and pathologize a woman's efforts to seek safety.

Consideration of continuity of care before separation would serve to put into the foreground children's interests over parents' interests in an equitable division of children's time. One of the only legal changes that has had significant effects on custody outcomes to date is in Norway, where, since 2004, children older than seven have had a right to be heard about their preferences for residence. This legal change was based on the United Nations Convention on the Rights of the Child. Norway's law reform appears to have gone some way toward shifting the center of custody determination away from ideologically derived value judgments about parents' rights and moving it toward children's actual interests. Foregrounding children's voices could diminish any influence of bias introduced by third-party evaluators and judges. Although children's wishes are one of several factors considered, they have a greater influence in residence outcomes in Norway than in many other countries (Skjørten 2013). However, it is important that safety and welfare considerations are also applied. As Macdonald (2015) noted, U.K. evaluators tended to support children's wishes when they were aligned with their pro-contact ideologies.

In sum, family law is one of the most important contexts for abused women and their children. Abusers commonly use the family law context as an avenue to continue abuse after separation. Survivors forced into ongoing contact with their abusers experience hopelessness and fear when they are prevented by the state from protecting themselves and their children. Abusers are empowered when they see the family court enforcing ongoing control and access against the will of their partner. As the number of femicides and familicides in the context of family law disputes indicates, this should be among our highest priorities. Abused women and their children should not be forced into ongoing contact with abusers. There needs to be significant improvements in family law processes if we are to protect women and children from abuse post-separation.

SOCIAL SERVICES

Preventing abuse that occurs during and after "dangerous exits" requires much more than legal and criminal justice reforms; the other initiatives listed at the start of this chapter, such as social services, are also necessary. Years ago, Goetting (1999) saluted improved conditions by observing that, "[c]learly, today is a better time than a hundred years ago, or even twenty years ago, for a woman to leave a batterer" (279). Unfortunately, the entire point of this book is that there are still many major problems for such women. Celebration is not in order when there is still so much more that we can do. The first step to improve social services is to increase funding. At first glance, this recommendation may seem rather naive in a neo-liberal climate dominated by calls to reduce government spending. The trend in government today, supported by the mainstream media and by an increasing number of voters, is to cut social services to save money—but also, at least until recently, to dramatically increase spending on the military and on prisons. Much of the reason that people support these notions is because they assume that cuts in services will not affect them but will mainly affect visible minorities and the poor.

Many are quick to say that we cannot afford to help people in need. The complaints against what has been termed "Obamacare" in the United States have been loud and unending. The argument is that the United States, often proclaimed the richest nation on Earth with some of the world's lowest taxes, cannot afford to provide medical care to its poor at even a level lower than every other industrialized democracy. Yet we have been able to find the money in federal and state budgets to engage in a colossal project of mass incarceration. For example, a major federal report has documented that, from 1980 to 2013, state and local governments increased spending on prisons at a rate more than three times the increase on public education over the same period (Brown and Douglas-Gabriel 2016). State prison budgets have generally increased by at least 400 percent, and Congress has had little trouble with ever-increasing federal prisoner populations, as the Federal Bureau of Prisons budget has increased its population of inmates by about 3.3 times between 1990 and 2014 (Federal Bureau of Prisons 2016). If one goes a bit further back, the budget for federal prisons has ballooned from $333 million in 1980 to nearly $8.5 billion today (James 2014). The U.S. Department of Education has suggested that this money could be much better invested in reducing crime; diverting money from prisons to education could result in moving large numbers of people away from crime and imprisonment. Thus, if the government can find the will to lock up an increasing number of prisoners in ineffective penal institutions, then a similar force of will could fund programs to prevent many of these people from being imprisoned in the first place and to deal with some of the victims of their criminal acts.

If, by chance, widespread political will to fund social services emerges in the near future, how should funds be allocated to help curb separation/ divorce violence against women? We could easily write an entire chapter with answers to this question, but we will limit our discussion to a few important resources. First, we know that many women emotionally separate from their partners but are unable to leave because of what Matlow and DePrince (2015) refer to as *contextual factors*. Two of the most important such factors identified in their longitudinal study of women's readiness to leave a relationship following abuse are financial dependence on perpetrators and greater numbers of children in the home. Their research reveals that there is a major need for child-care assistance and emergency loans. Keep in mind this woman's account of why she was unable to leave an abusive man: "Time flies . . . hours, days, months, and many more years of being paralyzed in fear. Fear of leaving and knowing the threat of what could happen to my children. Fear of being able to raise my children on my own financially. Fear of our safety. Fear of the ultimate violence . . . death" (cited in Community Initiatives Against Family Violence [CIAFV] 2015, 13).

A vital resource is subsidized housing, which is occasionally available but very difficult to acquire, especially in rural communities. Jenny, a rural Ohio survivor of separation/divorce assault, explains that women like her need money for food, essential living expenses, safe housing, and even a car in rural areas to access stores and services:

> They have all of these subsidized housing developments all over the country. You know, but it is hard to get in as a woman because they don't want a single woman with children especially. They want income verification. They want employment history. They want deposits that women, in my situation at least, didn't have. So, there's no place to go, so you have to go back home to the guy because usually he's taken all your money. Mine always took mine. He even took my son's savings—we didn't even know. So make it possible for a woman who has literally nothing but the clothes on her back and interest in protecting herself and her children, make it possible for them to have somewhere to go that has a door with a lock, you know, that's hers and not his. (DeKeseredy and Schwartz 2009, 109–10)

Shelters constitute another example of a social service. Chapter 4 made it clear that shelters do not solve the problem of economic insecurity. To pick one example, in 2016 Washington, D.C. was legally committed to getting all homeless women with children off the streets. Many of these women had been forced into the streets to escape from an abusive man. To accomplish this, more than 250 families with about 600 children were housed at the old abandoned D.C. General Hospital. This building was condemned as a hospital in 2001 but has been "temporarily" used ever since as a shelter for homeless families. In addition, more than 730 homeless families including 1,300 children were living in single motel rooms, usually on busy commercial strips near the edge of the city (Brown 2016). These temporary, overcrowded rooms do not, as noted in Chapter 4, solve the problem of economic insecurity (Hamby 2014), but there are some innovative exceptions, such as the program in the Canadian province of Alberta, where women were provided with extensive programming to recover from abuse and to become an advocate for themselves and others. A dozen of these graduates eventually put together a program to provide emergency loans and furniture to allow women to immediately leave abusive situations. The program ran for years until the provincial government began a similar program (CIAFV 2015, 30–31).

Another Canadian federal government initiative helps to lighten the financial burden carried by abuse survivors. If women are able to set up an Individual Development Account, the federal government will match the funds they set aside. With this assistance, one woman quoted extensively by the CIAFV (2015) ended up purchasing a condominium and now works as a licensed financial professional coaching other women to reach their financial goals. Such positive stories are important, because the bulk of this book focuses on terrifying examples of what happens to these women. Still, though they endure the harms that were listed in Figure 7, most survivors of separation/divorce violence are "battered, but not beaten" (MacLeod 1987). They are survivors with plans for the future, and many of them eventually triumph against all odds.

The policy literature on separation/divorce assault is filled with calls for other state-sponsored services, such as job training and education. Of course, such opportunities would certainly lead to an increased number of survivors' success stories. What is less discussed is that similar opportunities would also prevent many men from victimizing the women who are trying to leave them. For example, rural men who lost their farms or jobs in lost industries such as shoe manufacturing would be less likely to spend time drinking, doing drugs, or engaging in hunting-culture activities with their friends if they were given opportunities to achieve meaningful employment. In some cases, their relationships would more likely remain intact, whereas in others the men would be less likely to seek to repair their damaged masculinity by engaging in the harms described in this book (Donnermeyer and DeKeseredy 2014).

There are other state-sponsored social services that could help make a difference in the lives of these women, such as increased income eligibility for legal aid (Dragiewicz and DeKeseredy 2008). Still, regardless of which and how many services are provided, government-sponsored "one size fits all" methods are not likely to help many women with special needs or circumstances. As Logan and colleagues (2004) observe, "[C]reative solutions must be developed in order to serve women with victimization histories within the context of the specific communities" (58). The most obvious example is the high numbers of abused women who cannot speak the official languages of the country where they live. Commonly, any help available to stop their abuse is culturally foreign to them, and it may be available only in a language in which they are not fluent. MacLeod and Shin (1994) point out that public services that are available, such as short-term welfare payments, are interpreted in some communities as robbing women of dignity by taking away their pride in self-sufficiency. Even if the language barriers are crossed, counseling about feelings (rather than on substantive solutions) may be interpreted as inappropriate and patronizing interference in their private lives by outsiders and strangers (Perilla et al. 2011).

There are many other challenges that have been identified by and for immigrant and refugee women across the globe that keep them from seeking services to stop battering: economic dependence on their husband; a lack of familiarity with laws; social isolation; fear of discrimination and racism; particularly for some women a fear of the police; the loss of social supports they might have earlier had; and being cut off from extended family and their home cultural community (Alaggia, Regehr, and Rishchynski 2009; Baobaid et al. 2015; Merchant 2000). In addition to these hurdles, immigration status is a common and frightening control mechanism used by abusive men to force their female partners to stay with them (Dutton, Orloff, and Hass 2000). Immigrant women who do not speak English have commonly reported being told by their husbands that, if they leave the home, they will be deported back to a country they fled. If they left those countries for good reasons, this can be a powerful threat (Raj and Silverman 2002).

Often missing in North American and Australian discussions about the intersections between woman abuse, race/ethnicity, class, gender, and sexuality are the concerns of Native, Indigenous, or Aboriginal people. Numerous members of these communities have unresolved grief and historical trauma as consequences of European domination, genocide, cultural genocide, and forced assimilation. To many members of the majority population, this is ancient history, but to people taken from their homes, sent to special schools, forced to stop using their Native names, and often victimized by enforced assimilation, these are current events.

Furthermore, many Native and Indigenous women and women from other minority cultures reject a strictly secular or individualistic approach to intervention or prevention and insist that their spiritual needs and faith traditions be woven into holistic and collectivist responses that address their needs and uphold their strengths (Baobaid et al. 2015; DeKeseredy 2011; Malley-Morrison and Hines 2004). In sum, then, when participating in group meetings about the creation and administration of effective social services, or any anti-violence initiative for that matter, "[W]e should always be conscious of who is not there and that we are not hearing those perspectives" (Gilfus et al. 1999, 1207).

FEMINIST MEN'S EFFORTS

Most men are not abusive, and an unknown but sizeable portion of men who were abusive eventually become nonviolent.[5] However, abusive men who embark on a process to end violence rarely succeed on their own (Acker 2013). For example, batterer intervention programs have been widely used throughout the United States, especially in court-ordered programs operated in conjunction with probation conditions for men convicted of violence against intimate partners. These programs have been widely studied for over twenty years. For a number of reasons, they seem to have only a modest impact, at best, on ending abuse (Chung 2015; Tolman and Edleson 2011). Why is this?

A variety of answers have been proposed, but perhaps the most important is that violence against women is a complex problem. This complexity means that it is unlikely that a single approach can be used in isolation to achieve major change in society and people's individual beliefs, attitudes, and orientations. Most men who are sentenced to take part in intervention progams, for example, are engaging in behavior that results from strongly held beliefs that were inculcated and absorbed over many years. The abuse of women may be only one of a series of complex problems (Chung 2015). Furthermore, few of these men enter such programs voluntarily and with a genuine desire to change; most typically, they have been sentenced as a condition of remaining on probation—and yet psychologists have long argued that any change is particularly difficult unless the patient enters therapy with a strong desire to change. These men, convicted of violent acts against intimate partners and sentenced to intervention classes, generally are not people who just need to hear some new ideas in order to change their behavior. More likely, they are desperate and out of options. They have to attend in order to save their marriages, stay out of jail, or get social workers out of their lives. Rarely are these reasons good enough to convince men to do the hard work of change (Acker 2013).

Although change is possible, it is particularly difficult for one therapist, working an hour or two a week, to effect it. For most men, a variety of other, nonviolent men have to get involved in the change process. Sometimes family and friends can band together to provide such role models and motivation, but unfortunately these people have usually been around throughout the batterer's life and have not been effective before. It is going to require different men to step forward and provide influence and guidance. These men do exist: over the past forty years, there has been considerable growth in the number of progressive male allies in the feminist movement to end woman abuse (Messner, Greenberg, and Peretz 2015). Still, we have a long way to go until we can turn many more caring, law-abiding males into active participants in the ongoing struggle to end these many forms of violence that prevent gender equality in so many parts of society. The problem is not that these males, who Porter (2006) refers to as "well-meaning men," sit on the sidelines praising themselves for being kind to women and children, but rather that they do not recognize that their silence itself supports abusive behavior (Bunch 2006; DeKeseredy and Schwartz 2013).

How do we get more men to acknowledge that ending the harms covered in this book is men's work (Messner, Greenberg, and Peretz 2015)? In other words, the problem has been caused by men, and men are going to need to be involved in any solutions to it. How do we, in the words of feminist male activist and educator Jackson Katz (2006), "increase dramatically the number of men who make these issues a priority in their person and professional lives" (254)? A growing number of nonprofit and other organizations, such as the White Ribbon Campaign and A Call to Men, have answers to these important questions, but it is beyond the objective of this chapter to cover them in depth. Rather, our intent is to offer examples of the type of work that feminist male violence preventionists do today. The goal is for this information to stimulate male readers to follow suit and to read more about the work of Katz (2006, 2015), Funk (2006), Messner, Greenberg, and Peretz (2015), and the other men who work tirelessly to end violence against women and other injurious symptoms of patriarchy.

There are variations in what is labeled either the feminist or the profeminist men's movement, but the general point of agreement is that men must take an active role in stopping woman abuse and eliminating other forms of patriarchal control and domination throughout society. In fact, it is more than an active role. Feminist men place the responsibility for woman abuse squarely on men. One widely cited assertion is that "since it is men who are the offenders, it should be men—not women—who change their behavior" (Thorne-Finch 1992, 236).

Feminist men are involved in an ongoing process of changing themselves, self-examination, and self-discovery (DeKeseredy, Schwartz, and Alvi 2000; Messner, Greenberg, and Peretz 2015), with the ultimate goals of shedding their "patriarchal baggage" (Thorne-Finch 1992). Godenzi (1999) refers to this process as anti-sexist men seeking gender democracy. Though a relatively small but growing group, these men work individually and collectively to change other men. Of course, staying within the level of microdynamics (changing yourself or small groups) will do little to generate fundamental social transformation. So, together with feminist women, feminist men begin the process of broadening awareness by critiquing the broader social and economic structure and institutions like the pornography industry, the military, the mainstream media, professional sports, and the justice system (DeKeseredy and Corsianos 2016; Katz 2015).

Depending on their time and energy, some men are able to work on the dual level of changing individual people and social institutions. Others have more limited goals. Most limited of all are those who only privately support the principles of feminism and restrict their efforts to creating and maintaining egalitarian relationships (Christian 1994), and many "well-meaning men" fall under this category. This separation of private and public attempts to eliminate patriarchy continues to be one of the most central challenges for feminist men (DeKeseredy and Schwartz 2013).

Feminist men and men's groups are scattered throughout the United States, the United Kingdom, Australia, Canada, and many other countries, and most of their work involves stopping woman abuse. Individually, feminist men engage in strategies such as the following suggested by DeKeseredy and Corsianos (2016), Thorne-Finch (1992), the University of Kentucky Violence Intervention and Prevention Center (2012), Warshaw (1988), and Funk (2006):

Put a sticker on your office door declaring your workplace a woman abuse-free zone.

Confront male friends, classmates, coworkers, teachers, and others who make sexist jokes or who engage in sexist conversations.

Confront the above people and others who speak about violent and dehumanizing pornography in an approving manner.

Ask women in your life what you can do to help take a stand against violence.

Have a conversation with a younger man or boy who looks up to you about how important it is for men to help end violence.

Support and participate in woman abuse awareness programs.

What should a feminist man do if he discovers that another male (neighbor, relative, coworker) is abusing his current or former partner? It is certainly not easy to directly confront such a person, but these strategies suggested by the Ontario Women's Directorate (2006) should be considered:

Choose the right time and place to have a full discussion.
Approach him when he is calm.
Be direct and clear about what you have seen.
Tell him that his behavior is his responsibility. Avoid making judgmental comments about him as a person. Don't validate his attempt to blame others for his behavior.
Inform him that his behavior needs to stop.
Don't try to force him to change or to seek help.
Tell him that you are concerned about the safety of his partner and children.
Never argue with his abusive actions. Recognize that confrontational argumentative approaches may make the situation worse and put her at higher risk.
Call the police if the woman's safety is in jeopardy. (7–8)

Teaming up with other men to implement collective strategies is another vital step. DeKeseredy (2011) suggests that a good place to start is to get involved with a feminist men's organization, such as the aforementioned White Ribbon Campaign. It is now an international feminist men's movement that was initiated in Canada in October 1991 by the Men's Network for Change in Toronto, Ottawa, London, Kingston, and Montreal in response to a mass shooting on December 6, 1989. That day, Marc Lepine shot and killed fourteen female students at the University of Montreal, in what is now known as the Montreal Massacre. He repeatedly stated that he hated women and feminists, a sentiment shared by many serial and mass killers (DeKeseredy, Fabricius, and Hall-Sanchez 2015), especially those like Elliot Rodger (see Chapter 1) who feel entitled to sex and who experience rejection.

In response to Lepine's outburst against women being allowed to study engineering, the Men's Network for Change drafted a document stating that violence against women is a major social problem, that male silence about violence against women is complicity, and that men can be part of the solution (Sluser and Kaufman 1992). The campaign's goals are to get men involved in the struggle to end violence against women, to raise public awareness of this problem, and to support organizations that deal with the types of harms covered in this book. Each year, for one week prior to the anniversary of the massacre, men are encouraged to wear a white ribbon that symbolizes a call for men to stop being violent to women. The idea has caught on, attracting much attention throughout Canada, Australia, and, to some degree, the United States and other countries. However, even without this particular movement, men are organizing across the globe to work together to try to end gender-based violence everywhere (Kimball et al. 2012).

There are major advantages to working with groups such as the White Ribbon Campaign. One is that it helps feminist men avoid "reinventing the wheel" because, just like many women involved in the struggle to end woman abuse, they are at risk of "burning out" or wasting their time and energy if they simply duplicate the work done by other progressive organizations (Thorne-Finch 1992, 257). Yet the ultimate question for many people is, "Do the individual and collective efforts of feminist men really make a difference?" They do. Consider these indicators of success:

Research shows that campaigns that encourage men to hold other men accountable for their abuse are likely to be much more effective than those that simply blame all men.

Male friends and relatives of women abusers can have a major impact on their behavior by addressing the abuse directly and defining it as unacceptable.

Communicating with men about the importance of condemning abuse and providing them with some advice on how to confront abusers in a way that does not jeopardize their female partners will eventually create an environment in which woman abuse becomes socially unacceptable. (compiled from Katz 2015)

NEW ELECTRONIC TECHNOLOGIES

We do not have to remind our readers that we live in an era dominated by constant growth in new electronic technologies; some variations of the "dark side" of new technology were identified in Chapter 3.[6] Moreover, an increasing number of people are now spending more time communicating with each other electronically than they do face-to-face. This is especially the case with youth (J. Klein 2012). Whatever the value of lamenting the loss of interpersonal contact that characterized "the good old days," what is not up for dispute is the need for progressives to harness these new technologies to help promote peace and gender equality. There are a variety of ways of doing so, including using Facebook, Twitter, and other social media to send out antiviolence messages, motivating people to join antiviolence organizations, raising woman abuse awareness, sharing information, and providing support to survivors as well as to scholars, activists, and practitioners in the field. In fact, this campaign has already begun, with various groups now using electronic communication and social marketing campaigns in an attempt to speak out against women abuse (Flood 2015).

In the previous section, we mentioned the importance of avoiding "reinventing the wheel." Indeed, there are many useful websites that individuals and organizations can share with allies in the struggle to end woman abuse, with survivors, and with offenders seeking help to end their abusive behavior and to eliminate their sexist attitudes and beliefs. Developed by Acker (2013, 196), Box 9 includes a list of such sites and the organizations that maintain them. There are certainly many more, and new ones continue to arrive, but these are an excellent starting point. Box 9 includes sites that are beneficial to members of various ethnic/racial groups, such as Latinas and Indigenous women, and a section on groups by and for men trying to end violence.

Although many readers may already be familiar with some, or maybe most, of the organizations listed in Box 9, it has been our experience that most people know very few of them. In fact, after up to forty years of working with organizations devoted to stopping violence against women, we were unfamiliar with some of the ones listed. This is actually a good thing. It is a sign that people today are continuing to join hands in the international struggle to stop gender violence. On top of this transformation, the social scientific literature on violence against women has mushroomed over the past four decades, and it is very difficult, even for experts in the field, to keep up to date on all the new and important developments.

The three authors of this book have worked closely with some of the groups listed in Box 9. What we have learned is that their dedication and commitment is inspiring; the work they have done has saved many lives and will continue to do so. Please share Box 9 with others, because this might make a big difference in someone's life.

Another aspect of new electronic technologies can also make a difference: music. Although music and songs have been a part of social justice struggles for as long as we know, it first became a widespread social phenomenon with the development of folk music, records, and radio, through artists such as Woody Guthrie, Lead Belly, and Pete Seeger and the Weavers. By the early 1960s, the civil rights and feminist revolutions solidified the use of folk music in progressive struggles (Denisoff 1971). Awareness of the anti–Vietnam War movement was spread and to some degree popularized in the late 1960s and early 1970s through such artists as Country Joe MacDonald, Phil Ochs, Barry Sadler, Melanie Safka, Grand Funk Railroad, and the Doors (Kauzlarich and Awsumb 2012). In fact, music has been a part of virtually every antiwar effort, from Eric Bogle's extraordinarily powerful ballad about the futility of Australia's participation in World War I ("And the Band Played Waltzing Matilda") to songs about the Iraq War released by Iron Maiden, Pink, and Neil Young. Since electronic media were invented (vinyl records, radio), labor organizations, civil rights groups, feminist collectives, and other organizations have also benefited from music, and there is no reason to believe that activists

BOX 9. ORGANIZATIONS ADDRESSING VIOLENCE AGAINST WOMEN

From Acker 2013, 195–97

RESOURCE CENTERS AND COALITIONS

> Asian and Pacific Islander Institute on Domestic Violence:
> www.apiidv.org

> Australian Institute of Family Studies, Children and Young People in
> Separated Families Project: https://aifs.gov.au/projects
> /children–and–young–people–separated–families

> Battered Women's Justice Project, Criminal and Civil Justice Center:
> www.bwjp.org

> Courageous Kids Network: www.courageouskids.net

> DV LEAP Custody and Abuse Project: www.dvleap.org/Programs
> /CustodyAbuseProject.aspx

> Family Court of Australia, Family Violence page: www.familycourt.gov
> .au/wps/wcm/connect/fcoaweb/family–law–matters/family–
> violence

> Futures Without Violence (formerly the Family Violence Prevention
> Fund): www.futureswithoutviolence.org, and the youth site,
> https://thatsnotcool.com

> National Center on Domestic Violence, Trauma, and Mental Health:
> www.nationalcenterdvtraumamh.org

> National Clearinghouse for the Defense of Battered Women:
> www.ncdbw.org

> National Council of Juvenile and Family Court Judges, Family Violence
> and Domestic Relations Project: www.ncjfcj.org/our–work
> /domestic–violence

> National Health Resource Center on Domestic Violence:
> www.futureswithoutviolence.org

> National Indigenous Women's Resource Center: www.niwrc.org

> National Latino Network for Healthy Families and Communities:
> www.nationallatinonetwork.org

National Network to End Domestic Violence: www.nnedv.org

National Resource Center on Domestic Violence: www.nrcdv.org

V Day: www.vday.org

MEN'S GROUPS OR COALITIONS

A Call to Men: www.acalltomen.com

Men Against Violence Against Women: www.mavaw.org

Men Can Stop Rape: www.mencanstoprape.org

MenEngage Alliance: www.menengage.org

Men's Resources International: www.mensresourcesinternational.org

Mentors in Violence Prevention: www.mvpnational.org

White Ribbon Campaign: www.whiteribbon.ca

working to end woman abuse cannot do the same. Certainly, music has been used to send out powerful messages to large audiences about the pain and suffering caused by patriarchal men. One might consider, for example, Tracy Chapman's song "Behind the Walls," which is about a battered woman and the lack of attention given to her by the police.

Scores of readers could suggest other transformative ways of using new technologies. The main point to consider here is that communication technology is constantly changing, and scholars, practitioners, and activists committed to raising awareness about woman abuse must stay on top of it and harness it for their causes. Some of these media have been extremely important politically, such as Black Twitter, which is a cluster of Twitter users interested in race issues and black culture who have formed a high-density and prestigious network of users. It has been influential in several specific instances and, more broadly, with the #BlackLivesMatter hashtag. There have been debates as to what Black Twitter really is and what it stands for, but there is no question that it is a prime example of how a group of active Twitter users can both engage internally in up-to-the-minute political debate and influence culture and politics outside of itself.

All of this is not to say, of course, that using the Internet should be a substitute for other political action, including many of the policies recommended in this book and elsewhere. New technologies should be part of a multi-pronged effort to curb patriarchal practices of all sorts (Corsianos 2009).

SUMMARY

A key objective of this book has been to broaden the focus of separation and divorce violence against women theory and research. Still, for women who are abused during and/or after exiting a relationship, social scientific scholarship is of little, if any, value unless it informs policies and practices that prevent them and their children from being victimized. We concur, which is why this chapter was written. It is not the first, nor will it be the last, document outlining initiatives aimed at enhancing the health and well-being of women and children like those featured in this book. Yet, regardless of what solutions are proposed in the future, it is always necessary to keep in mind this point raised by Renate Klein (2012): "Ending abuse is not only about specialized services delivered by trained professionals. It is perhaps more importantly about 'humdrum' cultural change in which everyone does things a little differently every day" (127). What part will you choose to play in the struggle to end men's abuse of women and children?

All too often, people think of ending violence as an event simple enough to fit on a bumper sticker or the side of a coffee mug. Just leave, and then it will be over. Unfortunately, for a large number of women and children, it is necessary to remember that leaving and ending up in a safe place is a complex, ongoing process, and for some women and children it is one that never ends. It is definitely not a single event (LaViolette and Barnett 2014). Rather, as one women who left an angry, violent man some time ago explains: "It's not just about the leaving. . . . It has taken hours, days, months and many years for my children and I to recover from the violence" (cited in CIAFV 2015, 17). This woman is a survivor, and, like numerous women who had similar experiences and successfully escaped, she now has high hopes for the future. Hence, perhaps it is best to end this book with these words: "The story of battered women is not a story of empty efforts. It is a story of perseverance, endurance, strength, and protection" (Hamby 2014, 187).

CHAPTER ONE. CONCEPTUALIZING SEPARATION/
DIVORCE VIOLENCE AGAINST WOMEN

1. This section includes revised portions of work published previously in DeKeseredy 2014; DeKeseredy et al. 2016; DeKeseredy and Rennison 2013a, 2013b.

2. For reviews of key definitional issues in the field of violence against women, see DeKeseredy and Schwartz 2011 and 2013.

3. For reviews of these studies, see DeKeseredy 2014; DeKeseredy, Rogness, and Schwartz 2004; DeKeseredy and Schwartz 2009.

4. This section includes modified portions of work published earlier in DeKeseredy and Rennison 2013a, 2013b.

5. For reviews of the North American social scientific literature on woman abuse in dating relationships, see Basile and Black 2011; DeKeseredy 2011; DeKeseredy and Schwartz 2013.

6. This section includes revised portions of material published previously in DeKeseredy, Fabricius, and Hall-Sanchez 2015; DeKeseredy and MacLeod 1997; DeKeseredy and Schwartz 1998; Dragiewicz and DeKeseredy 2008.

7. This play has been widely anthologized in the form of a short story entitled "A Jury of Her Peers," particularly in Women's Studies texts.

8. Personal communication, 1992.

9. Some government agencies and community groups prefer the term *intimate partner violence* because they claim that it addresses the fact that there is also abuse in same-sex relationships (Denham and Gillespie 1999; Sinclair 2004).

10. For reviews of studies that debunk the myth that women's and men's violence is symmetrical and mutual, see DeKeseredy 2011; DeKeseredy and Schwartz 2011 and 2013; Dragiewicz and DeKeseredy 2012.

11. See www.nydailynews.com/news/national/elliot-rodger-retribution-santa-barbara-shooter-sick-words-article-1.1804761.

CHAPTER TWO. THE EXTENT AND DISTRIBUTION OF SEPARATION/DIVORCE ASSAULT

1. See Marshall and Summers 2013; Smit, de Jong, and Bijleveld 2013.

2. For in-depth reviews of the extant literature on the extent and distribution of nonlethal forms of woman abuse in intimate relationships, theoretical perspectives on such harms, and debates about whether or not woman abuse is a gendered social problem, see DeKeseredy 2011; DeKeseredy and Schwartz 2011 and 2013.

3. See Auchter 2010; Adams 2007; Campbell et al. 2003; Dobash and Dobash 2015; Dobash et al. 2004; Ellis, Stuckless, and Smith 2015; Walker et al. 2004; Websdale 1999; Wilson and Daly 1993.

4. This section includes revised sections of work published previously in DeKeseredy and Schwartz 2013.

5. This section includes modified portions of work published previously in DeKeseredy and Hall-Sanchez in press; DeKeseredy and Schwartz 2009; DeKeseredy et al. 2006.

6. For more detailed information on the relationship between all-male sexist conversations, alcohol consumption, and sexual assault on college campuses, see DeKeseredy and Schwartz 2013; Schwartz and DeKeseredy 1997; Schwartz et al. 2001.

7. To the best of our knowledge, Ellis, Stuckless, and Smith (2015) are the only experienced separation/divorce assault researchers who do not view patriarchal control as a key risk factor, and they do not view "patriarchy theory" as a sound explanation for the link between separation and femicide.

8. For more information about the nature of the pornography industry and data about consumption and production, see DeKeseredy and Corsianos 2016; Dines 2010; Jensen 2007.

9. For reviews of the extant literature, see, e.g., Brownridge 2009; DeKeseredy and Schwartz 2009.

10. Parts of this section include modified excerpts of work published previously in DeKeseredy and Rennison 2013a; Donnermeyer and DeKeseredy 2014; Rennison, DeKeseredy, and Dragiewicz 2012 and 2013.

11. For more information on this survey, see Black et al. 2011.

CHAPTER THREE. NEW TECHNOLOGIES AND SEPARATION/DIVORCE VIOLENCE AGAINST WOMEN

1. Reddit is an entertainment, social media, and news website.

2. This involves supervising women's phone calls and using caller ID screens to call targets of low-tech stalking (Navarro 2016; Southworth et al. 2007).

3. Amazon is singled out only because it is so widely known and available. Such devices are available easily around the world.

4. Cited in www.returnofkings.com.

5. For an in-depth review of the extant social scientific literature on the relationship between pornography and violence against women, see DeKeseredy and Corsianos 2016.

6. This section includes small, revised portions of work published previously in DeKeseredy and Corsianos 2016; DeKeseredy and Schwartz 2013.

7. This quotation was on www.endrevengeporn.org/my-letter-to-legislators.html. This page, however, no longer exists.

CHAPTER FOUR. EXPLAINING SEPARATION/DIVORCE VIOLENCE AGAINST WOMEN

1. This section includes modified segments of work published previously in DeKeseredy and MacLeod 1997; DeKeseredy, Rogness, and Schwartz 2004; DeKeseredy and Schwartz 2009; Ellis and DeKeseredy 1997.

2. For reviews of the empirical literature on this correlation, see Adams 2007; Brownridge 2009; Dobash and Dobash 2015; Ellis, Stuckless, and Smith 2015.

3. This section includes modified portions of work published previously in Ellis and DeKeseredy 1997.

4. See, e.g., research published in Browne 1987; Crawford and Gartner 1992; DeKeseredy and Schwartz 2009; Ellis, Stuckless, and Smith 2015; Mercy and Saltzman 1989.

5. For example, the men are also violent toward their children and other family members.

6. In his study of thirty-one men who killed their intimate female partners, Adams (2007) found that, next to jealous men, the largest group of murderers was composed of those who were also substance abusers.

7. Tolman and Edleson (2011) do, however, make explicit that "the promise of typologies has not yet been thoroughly tested" (356).

8. Hamby (2014) correctly points out that orders of protection reduce physical violence more than sexual violence and psychological abuse.

9. This section includes revised sections of theoretical work published earlier in DeKeseredy, Rogness, and Schwartz 2004; DeKeseredy and Schwartz 2009 and 2013.

10. Familial patriarchy refers to male control in domestic or intimate settings (Barrett 1980; DeKeseredy and Schwartz 1998; Eisenstein 1980; Ursel 1986).

11. For in-depth reviews of this literature, see DeKeseredy and Schwartz 2009; Hardesty 2002; Ellis, Stuckless, and Smith 2015.

12. This section includes modified portions of work published previously in DeKeseredy et al. 2007.

13. Theories like these have in common the notion that urban ecological variables (e.g., neighborhood structural density) influence crime and delinquency via their impact on formal and informal processes of social control. Lee (2008) points out that these theories rely on a very narrow conception of neighborhoods and that this "analysis is extremely problematic for the rural context given that conventional urban-type neighborhoods are few and far between so that in many places the nearest neighbors actually live miles apart" (468).

14. This section includes revised sections of work published previously in DeKeseredy, Alvi, Schwartz, and Tomaszewski 2003; DeKeseredy, Schwartz, and Alvi 2008.

15. Ecological models address multiple levels of influence and maintain that violence against women should be examined within a nested set of environmental contexts or systems (Graham-Bermann and Gross 2008; Dragiewicz 2011).

CHAPTER FIVE. CHILDREN AS COLLATERAL VICTIMS OF SEPARATION/DIVORCE WOMAN ABUSE

1. This quote is from a judge who awarded unsupervised overnight visits to a father who was sexually abusing his daughter. The protective mother then fled interstate with her daughter to protect her from the abuse but was caught, charged with a felony, and placed on probation. Custody of the daughter was returned to the abusive father until he was arrested six years later for sexually abusing two other children and manufacturing child pornography (cited in Silberg and Dallam 2014).

2. In many jurisdictions, child support is calculated based on the percentage of "overnights," or nights spent in each parent's home. Child support is reduced if a certain percentage of overnights are spent with the non-primary parent. Not surprisingly, activism to promote presumptive joint custody coincided with this change to the calculation of child support. Companies have developed commercial software to calculate overnights to change the amount of support paid. See, e.g., www.custodyxchange.com/florida/child-support-calculations.php.

3. See, e.g., www.familysolutionstoronto.ca/fidler.html and www.warshak.com/services/family-bridges.html. These programs assess whether parents whose children do not want to have contact with the other parent are sufficiently "friendly" to the parent the child fears.

CHAPTER SIX. WHAT IS TO BE DONE ABOUT
SEPARATION/DIVORCE VIOLENCE AGAINST WOMEN?

1. Luke's Place, in Oshawa, Ontario, Canada, is a family law resource center for women and children.

2. See, e.g., DeKeseredy and Schwartz 2009; Ellis, Stuckless, and Smith 2015.

3. This section includes modified portions of work published previously in Donnermeyer and DeKeseredy 2014.

4. This section includes revised parts of work published earlier in DeKeseredy and Dragiewicz 2013.

5. This section includes revised portions of material published previously in DeKeseredy 2011; DeKeseredy, Schwartz, and Alvi 2000.

6. This section includes revised portions of work published previously in DeKeseredy and Corsianos 2016.

Acker, S. E. (2013). *Unclenching Our Fists: Abusive Men on the Journey to Nonviolence.* Nashville, Tenn.: Vanderbilt University Press.

Adams, D. (2007). *Why Do They Kill? Men Who Murder Their Intimate Partners.* Nashville, Tenn.: Vanderbilt University Press.

Alaggia, R., C. Regehr, and G. Rishchynski (2009). Intimate partner violence and immigration laws in Canada: How far have we come? *International Journal of Law and Psychiatry* 23: 335–41.

Alaggia, R., and C. Vine, eds. (2012). *Cruel but Not Unusual: Violence in Canadian Families.* 2d ed. Waterloo, Canada: Wilfred Laurier University Press.

Aldarondo, E. (1996). Cessation and persistence of wife assault: A longitudinal analysis. *American Journal of Orthopsychiatry* 66: 141–60.

Alexander, M. (2012). *The New Jim Crow: Mass Incarceration in the Age of Colorblindness.* New York: The New Press.

Alisic, E., R. N. Krishna, A. Groot, and J. W. Frederick (2015). Children's mental health and well-being after parental intimate partner homicide: A systematic review. *Clinical Child and Family Psychology Review* 18: 328–45. http://doi .org/10.1007/s10567-015-0193-7.

Amato, P. R. (2000). The consequences of divorce for adults and children. *Journal of Marriage and Family* 62: 1269–87. http://doi.org/10.1111/j.1741-3737.2000 .01269.x.

Amato, P. R., and D. Previti (2003). People's reasons for divorcing: Gender, social class, the life course, and adjustment. *Journal of Family Issues* 24: 602–26. http://doi.org/10.1177/0192513X03254507.

Amato, P. R., and J. M. Sobolewski (2001). The effects of divorce and marital discord on adult children's psychological well-being. *American Sociological Review* 66: 900–921. http://doi.org/10.2307/3088878.

Anderson, D. K., D. G. Saunders, M. Yoshihama, D. L. Bybee, and C. M. Sullivan (2003). Long-term trends in depression among women separated from abusive partners. *Violence Against Women* 9: 807–38.

Anderson, N., S. Svurluga, and S. Clement (2015). Survey: 1 in 5 women in college sexually assaulted. *Washington Post*, Sept. 22, p. A3.

Arditti, J. A. (1999). Rethinking relationships between divorced mothers and their children: Capitalizing on family strengths. *Family Relations* 48: 109–19.

Arditti, J. A., and D. Madden-Derdich (1995). No regrets: Custodial mothers' accounts of the difficulties and benefits of divorce. *Contemporary Family Therapy* 17: 229–48. http://doi.org/10.1007/BF02252361.

Arendell, T. J. (1995). *Fathers and Divorce*. Thousand Oaks, Calif.: Sage.

Arnold, R. (2015). Accused killer David Conley speaks out in jailhouse interview with KPRC2. KPRC2, Aug. 11. *www.click2houston.com/news/local/harris-county/accused-killer-david-conley-speaks-out-in-jailhouse-interview-with-kprc-2*.

Ascione, F. R., C. V. Weber, T. M. Thompson, J. Heath, M. Maruyama, and K. Hayashi (2007). Battered pets and domestic violence: Animal abuse reported by women experiencing intimate violence and by nonabused women. *Violence Against Women* 13: 354–73. http://doi.org/10.1177/1077801207299201.

Auchter, B. (2010). Men who murder their families: What the research tells us. *NIJ Journal* 266. www.nij.gov/journals/266/murderfamilies.htm.

Australian Bureau of Statistics (2014). *Personal Safety Survey Australia*. Canberra: Australian Bureau of Statistics.

Bachman, R., and L. Saltzman (1995). *Violence against Women: Estimates from the Redesigned Survey*. Washington, D.C.: Bureau of Justice Statistics.

Bagshaw, D., T. Brown, S. Wendt, A. Campbell, E. McInnes, B. Tinning, and P. Fernandez Aria (2011). The effect of family violence on post-separation parenting arrangements: The experiences and views of children and adults from families who separated post-1995 and post-2006. https://aifs.gov.au/publications/family-matters/issue-86/effect-family-violence-post-separation-parenting-arrangements.

Ball, M. (2013). Heteronormativity, homonormativity and violence. In *Crime, Justice and Social Democracy*, edited by K. Carrington, M. Ball, E. O'Brien, & J. Tauri, 186–99. New York: Palgrave Macmillan.

Bancroft, L. (2002). *Why Does He Do That? Inside the Minds of Angry and Controlling Men*. New York: Penguin.

Bancroft, L., and J. G. Silverman (2002). Impeding recovery: The batterer in custody and visitation disputes. In *The Batterer as Parent*, edited by L. Bancroft and J. G. Silverman, 98–129. Thousand Oaks, Calif.: Sage.

Bancroft, L., J. G. Silverman, and D. Ritchie (2011). *The Batterer as Parent: Addressing the Impact of Domestic Violence on Family Dynamics.* 2d ed. Thousand Oaks, Calif.: Sage.

Baobaid, M., N. Kovacs, L. MacDiarmid, and E. Tremblay (2015). A culturally integrative model of domestic violence response for immigrant and newcomer families of collectivist backgrounds. In *Critical Issues on Violence against Women: International Perspectives and Promising Strategies,* edited by H. Johnson, B. S. Fisher, and V. Jaquier, 154–65). London: Routledge.

Barker, K. (2013). Children and contact in the context of parental separation and family violence: A practice perspective. *Children Australia* 38: 171–77. doi: 10.1017/cha.2013.29.

Barrett, M. (1980). *Women's Oppression Today: Problems in Marxist Feminist Analysis.* London: Verso.

Basile, K. C., and M. C. Black (2011). Intimate partner violence against women. In *Sourcebook on Violence against Women,* edited by C. M. Renzetti, J. L. Edleson, and R. Kennedy Bergen, 2d ed., 111–32. Thousand Oaks, Calif.: Sage.

Battered Women's Justice Project (n.d.). National Child Custody Project. www.bwjp.org/our-work/projects/national-child-custody-project.html.

Battered Women's Justice Project (2012). *OVW Child Custody Differentiation Project Progress Summary.* Minneapolis, Minn.: Battered Women's Justice Project. www.bwjp.org/assets/documents/pdfs/custody_project_history_and_future_directions.pdf.

Bauman, S., R. Toomey, and J. Walker (2013). Associations among bullying, cyberbullying, and suicide in high school students. *Journal of Adolescence* 36: 341–50.

BBC News (2016). Revenge porn: More than 200 prosecuted under new law. BBC News, Sept. 6. www.bbc.com/news/uk-37278264.

Beeble, M. L., D. Bybee, and C. M. Sullivan (2007). Abusive men's use of children to control their partners and ex-partners. *European Psychologist* 12: 54–61.

Belknap, J., A. T. Chu, and A. P. DePrince (2011). Roles of phones and computers in threatening and abusing women victims of male intimate partner abuse. *The Duke Journal of Gender, Law, and Policy* 19: 373.

Bennett, J. (2014). Yik Yak App spurs unease on university campuses. *The Hoya,* Oct. 3. www.thehoya.com/yik-yak-app-spurs-unease-on-university-campuses.

Bergen, R. K. (1996). *Wife Rape: Understanding the Response of Survivors and Service Providers.* Thousand Oaks, Calif.: Sage.

Bernstein, M. (2014). Portland man faced restraining and stalking orders for escalating threats before he killed ex-wife, then himself. *The Oregonian,* Nov. 10. www.oregonlive.com/portland/index.ssf/2014/11/portland_man_faced _restraining.html.

Bierstedt, R. (1957). *The Social Order*. New York: McGraw-Hill.

Biroscak, B. J., P. K. Smith, and L. A. Post (2006). A practical approach to public health surveillance of violent deaths related to intimate partner relationships. *Public Health Reports* 121: 393–99.

Black, D. (1983). Crime as social control. *American Sociological Review* 48: 34–45.

Black, D., and T. Kaplan (1988). Father kills mother: Issues and problems encountered by a child psychiatric team. *The British Journal of Psychiatry* 153: 624–30.

Black, M. C., K. C. Basile, M. J. Breiding, S. G. Smith, M. L. Walters, M. T. Merrick, J. Chen, and M. R. Stevens (2011). *The National Intimate Partner and Sexual Violence Survey (NISVS): 2010 Summary Report*. Atlanta, Ga.: National Center for Injury Prevention and Control, Centers for Disease Control and Prevention.

Block, C. R. (2000). *The Chicago Women's Health Risk Study*. Washington, D.C.: U.S. Department of Justice.

Block, C. R., and W. S. DeKeseredy (2007). Forced sex and leaving intimate relationships: Results of the Chicago women's health risk study. *Women's Health and Urban Life* 6: 6–23.

Booth, A., and P. R. Amato (1994). Parental marital quality, parental divorce, and relations with parents. *Journal of Marriage and Family* 56, no. 1: 21–34.

—— (2001). Parental predivorce relations and offspring postdivorce well-being. *Journal of Marriage and Family* 63, no. 1: 197–212.

Bourgois, P. (1995). *In Search of Respect: Selling Crack in El Barrio*. New York: Cambridge University Press.

Bow, J. N., and P. Boxer (2003). Assessing allegations of domestic violence in child custody evaluations. *Journal of Interpersonal Violence* 18: 1394–1410.

Bowker, L. H. (1983). *Beating Wife-beating*. Lexington, Mass.: Lexington Books.

Bowles, J. J., K. K. Christian, M. B. Drew, and K. L. Yetter (2008). *A Judicial Guide to Child Safety in Custody Cases*. Reno, Nev.: National Council of Juvenile and Family Court Judges. www.ncjfcj.org/sites/default/files/judicial%20guide_0_0.pdf.

Boyd, S. B. (2007). Gendering legal parenthood: Bio-genetic ties, intentionality and responsibility. *Windsor Yearbook of Access to Justice* 25: 63–94.

Bridges, A. J., and C. Anton (2013). Pornography and violence against women. In *Violence against Girls and Women: International Perspectives*, edited by J. A. Sigal and F. L. Denmark, 183–206. Santa Barbara, Calif.: Praeger.

Brinig, M. F., L. M. Frederick, and L. M. Drozd (2014). Perspectives on joint custody presumptions as applied to domestic violence cases. *Family Court Review* 52: 271–81.

Brogan, J. (2013). When teen dating turns dangerous: The scars from abusive teen dating relationships can last into adulthood. *The Boston Globe*, Apr. 1. www

.bostonglobe.com/lifestyle/health-wellness/2013/03/31/dangerous-dating
/BasnGkyWQG2UMTaEXdWR1I/story.html

Brown, D. L. (2016). DC has a long history of housing families in motels. *Washington Post*, Feb. 6. www.washingtonpost.com/news/local/wp/2016/02/06/d-c-has-a-long-history-of-housing-homeless-families-in-motels.

Brown, E., and D. Douglas-Gabriel (2016). Since 1980, spending on prisons has grown three times as much as spending on public education. *Washington Post*, July 7. www.washingtonpost.com/news/education/wp/2016/07/07/since-1980-spending-on-prisons-has-grown-three-times-faster-than-spending-on-public-education.

Brown, D. L., and K. A. Schafft (2011). *Rural People and Communities in the Twenty-first Century: Resilience and Transformation*. Boston: Polity Press.

Brown, J. D., S. Keller, and S. Stern (2009). Sex, sexuality, sexting, and sex ed: Adolescents and the media. *The Prevention Researcher* 26: 12–16.

Browne, A. (1987). *When Battered Women Kill*. New York: Free Press.

Browning, C. (2002). The span of collective efficacy: Extending social disorganization theory in partner violence. *Journal of Marriage and Family* 64: 833–50.

Brownridge, D. A. (2006). Violence against women post-separation. *Aggression and Violent Behavior* 11: 514–30.

—— (2009). *Violence against Women: Vulnerable Populations*. New York: Routledge.

Brownridge, D. A., and S. S. Halli (2001). *Explaining Violence against Women in Canada*. Lanham, Md.: Lexington Books.

Brownstein, H. H., T. M. Mulcahy, and J. Huessy (2014). *The Methamphetamine Industry in America*. New Brunswick, N.J.: Rutgers University Press.

Bruch, C. S. (2001). Parental alienation syndrome and parental alienation: Getting it wrong in child custody cases. *Family Law Quarterly* 35: 527–52.

Brunson, R. K., and J. Gau (2015). Officer race vs. macrolevel context: A test of competing hypotheses about black citizens' experiences with and perceptions of black police officers. *Crime and Delinquency* 61: 213–42.

Bunch, T. (2006). *Ending Men's Violence against Women*. New York: A Call to Men: National Association of Men and Women Committed to Ending Violence Against Women.

Burke, S. C., M. Wallen, K. Vail-Smith, and D. Knox (2011). Using technology to control intimate partners: An exploratory study of college undergraduates. *Computers in Human Behavior* 27: 1162–67.

Burleigh, N. (2014). Women against womyn. *New York Observer*, July 30. http://observer.com/2014/07/women-against-womyn-first-wave-second-wave-third-wave-and-now-three-steps-back.

Burman, S., and P. Allen-Meares (1994). Neglected victims of murder: Children's witness to parental homicide. *Social Work* 39: 28–34.

Byun, S., J.L. Meece, and M.J. Irvin (2011). Rural-nonrural disparities in post-secondary educational attainment revisited. *American Educational Research Journal* 49: 412–37.

Calvert, R. (1975). Criminal and civil liability in husband-wife assaults. In *Violence in the Family,* edited by S.K. Steinmetz and M.A. Straus, 88–91. New York: Dodd, Mead.

Campbell, H. (2000). The glass phallus: Pub(lic) masculinity and drinking in rural New Zealand. *Rural Sociology* 65: 532–36.

Campbell, J.C. (1989). Women's response to sexual abuse in intimate relationships. *Health Care for Women International* 10: 335–46.

—— (2007). *Assessing Dangerousness: Violence by Batterers and Child Abusers.* 2d ed. New York: Springer.

—— (2008). Femicide. In *Encyclopedia of Interpersonal Violence,* edited by C.M. Renzetti and J.L. Edleson, 265–67. Thousand Oaks, Calif.: Sage.

Campbell, J.C., J. Alhusen, J. Draughton, J. Kub, and B. Walton-Moss (2011). Vulnerability and protective factors for intimate partner violence. In *Violence against Women and Children: Mapping the Terrain,* edited by J.W. White, M.P. Koss, and A.E. Kazdin, 243–64. Washington, D.C.: American Psychological Association.

Campbell, J.C., N. Glass, P.W. Sharps, K. Laughon, and T. Bloom (2007). Intimate partner homicide: Review and implications of research and policy. *Trauma, Violence, and Abuse* 8: 246–69.

Campbell, J.C., P. Miller, M.M. Cardwell, and R.A. Belknap (1994). Relationship status of battered women over time. *Journal of Family Violence* 9: 99–111.

Campbell, J.C., L. Rose, J. Kub, and D. Nedd (1998). Voices of strength and resistance: A contextual and longitudinal analysis of women's responses to battering. *Journal of Interpersonal Violence* 13: 743–62.

Campbell, J.C., and K.L. Soeken (1999). Women's responses to battering over time: An analysis of change. *Journal of Interpersonal Violence* 14: 21–40.

Campbell, J.C., D. Webster, D.J. Koziol-McLain, C. Block, D. Campbell, M.A. Curry, F. Gary, et al. (2003). Risk factors for femicide in abusive relationships: Results from a multisite case control study. *American Journal of Public Health* 22: 1089–97.

Campo, M. (2015). *Children's Exposure to Domestic and Family Violence.* Melbourne: Australian Institute of Family Studies. https://aifs.gov.au/cfca/sites/default/files/publication-documents/cfca-36-children-exposure-fdv.pdf.

Cao, L. (2004). *Major Criminological Theories: Concepts and Measurement.* Belmont, Calif.: Wadsworth.

Caringella, S. (2009). *Addressing Rape Reform in Law and Practice*. New York: Columbia University Press.

Carrington, K. (2015). *Feminism and Global Justice*. London: Routledge.

Cavezza, C., and T. E. McEwan (2014). Cyberstalking versus off-line stalking in a forensic sample. *Psychology, Crime and Law* 20: 955–70.

CBS News (2015). Witnesses to fatal stabbing on DC Metro train didn't intervene. CBS News, July 10. www.cbsnews.com/news/witnesses-to-fatal-stabbing-on-d-c-metro-train-watched-it-unfold.

Chan, A., and J. Payne (2013). *Homicide in Australia: 2008–09 to 2009–10 National Homicide Monitoring Program Annual Report* (No. 21). Canberra: Copyright Australian Institute of Criminology. www.aic.gov.au/publications/current%20series/mr/21-40/mr21.html.

Chereb, S. (2008). Darren Mack gets maximum sentence for killing wife, shooting judge. *KOLO 8 News Now*. Reno, Nev. www.kolotv.com/home/headlines/15382516.html.

Christian, H. (1994). *The Making of Antisexist Men*. London: Routledge.

Chung, D. (2015). Behavior change programs for intimate partner violence abusers: A means to promote the safety of women and children. In *Critical Issues on Violence against Women: International Perspectives and Promising Strategies*, edited by H. Johnson, B. S. Fisher, and V. Jaquier, 171–82. London: Routledge.

Citron, D. K., and M. A. Franks (2014). Criminalizing revenge porn. *Wake Forest Law Review* 49: 345–91.

Clegg, S. (2005). Evidence-based practice in educational research: A critical realist critique of systematic review. *British Journal of Sociology of Education* 26: 415–28.

Clevenger, S., and C. D. Marcum (2016). The relationship between negative relationships and cybercrimes. In *The Intersection between Intimate Partner Abuse, Technology, and Cybercrime: Examining the Virtual Enemy*, edited by J. N. Navarro, S. Clevenger, and C. D. Marcum, 3–12. Durham, N.C.: Carolina Academic Press.

CoinDesk (2015). What is bitcoin? CoinDesk, Mar. 1. www.coindesk.com/information/what-is-bitcoin.

Collins, P. H. (2000). *Black Feminist Thought*. 2d ed. New York: Routledge.

Community Initiatives Against Family Violence (2015). *Moving Forward: Journeys of Strength and Hope*. Edmonton, Canada: CIAFV.

Cook, P. J., and K. A. Goss (2014). *The Gun Debate: What Everyone Needs to Know*. New York: Oxford University Press.

Cook, P. J., and J. Ludwig (2000). *Gun Violence: The Real Costs*. New York: Oxford University Press.

Cooper, A., and E. L. Smith (2011). *Homicide Trends in the United States, 1980-2008: Annual Rates for 2009 and 2010*. Washington, D.C.: U.S. Department of Justice, Bureau of Justice Statistics.

Cooper, M., and D. Eaves (1996). Suicide following homicide in the family. *Violence and Victims* 11: 99-112.

Corsianos, M. (2009). *Policing and Gendered Justice: Examining the Possibilities*. Toronto: University of Toronto Press.

Council of Economic Advisors (2012). *Strengthening the Rural Economy: The Current State of Rural America*. Washington, D.C.: CEA.

Crawford, M., and R. Gartner (1992). *Woman Killing: Intimate Femicide in Ontario, 1974-1990*. Toronto: Women We Honor Action Committee.

Crippen, G. (1990). Stumbling beyond best interests of the child: Reexamining child custody standard-setting in the wake of Minnesota's four year experiment with the primary caretaker preference. *Minnesota Law Review* 75: 427-503.

Crisafi, D. N., A. R. Mullins, and J. L. Jasinski (2016). The rise of the "virtual predator": Technology and the expanding reach of intimate partner abuse. In *The Intersection between Intimate Partner Abuse, Technology, and Cybercrime: Examining the Virtual Enemy*, edited by J. N. Navarro, S. Clevenger, and C. D. Marcum, 95-123. Durham, N.C.: Carolina Academic Press.

Cross, W. F. (1993). *Differentiation of Sexually Coercive and Noncoercive males*. Ph.D. diss., Ohio University, Athens.

Crossman, K. A., J. L. Hardesty, and M. Raffaelli (2016). "He could scare me without laying a hand on me": Mother's experiences of nonviolent coercive control during marriage and after separation. *Violence Against Women* 22: 454-73.

Curran, D. J., and C. M. Renzetti (2001). *Theories of Crime*. 2d ed. Boston: Allyn and Bacon.

Currie D., and B. D. MacLean (1993). Woman abuse in dating relationships: Rethinking women's safety on campus. *Journal of Human Justice* 4: 1-24.

Currie, E. (1993). *Reckoning: Drugs, the Cities and the American Future*. New York: Hill and Wang.

Cusimano, A. M., and S. A. Riggs (2013). Perceptions of interparental conflict, romantic attachment, and psychological distress in college students. *Couple and Family Psychology: Research and Practice* 2: 45-59.

Cussen, T., and W. Bryant (2015). *Domestic/Family Homicide in Australia* (No. 38). Canberra: Australian Institute of Criminology. www.aic.gov.au/media_library/publications/rip/rip38/rip38.pdf.

Cyber Civil Rights Initiative (2016). *34 states + DC have revenge porn laws*. www.cybercivilrights.org/revenge-porn-laws.

Dale, D. (2016). The faces of American gun violence. *Toronto Star*, Jan. 10. www
.thestar.com/news/world/2016/01/10/the-faces-of-american-gun-violence
.html.

Dallam, S., and J. L. Silberg (2006). Myths that place children at risk during custody litigation. *Sexual Assault Report* 9: 33–47.

Darvell, M., S. Walsh, and K. White (2011). Facebook tells me so: Applying the
theory of planned behavior to understand partner-monitoring behavior on
Facebook. *Cyberpsychology, Behavior, and Social Networking* 14: 717–22.

Dasgupta, S. D. (1999). Just like men? A critical review of violence by women. In
*Coordinating Community Response to Domestic Violence: Lessons from Duluth and
Beyond*, edited by M. F. Shephard and E. L. Pence, 195–222. Thousand Oaks,
Calif.: Sage.

Davies, J. (2011). Personal reflection. In *Sourcebook on Violence against Women*,
edited by C. M. Renzetti, J. L. Edleson, and R. Kennedy Bergen, 2d. ed., 188.
Thousand Oaks, Calif.: Sage.

Davies, J., E. Lyon, and D. Monti-Catania (1998). *Safety Planning with Battered
Women: Complex Lives/Difficult Choices*. Thousand Oaks, Calif.: Sage.

Davis, G., C. Lizdas, S. Tibbetts Murphy, and J. Yauch (2010). *The Dangers of Presumptive Joint Physical Custody*. Minneapolis, Minn.: Battered Women's Justice
Project. www.bwjp.org/resource-center/resource-results/the-dangers-of-
presumptive-joint-physical-custody.html.

Davis, K. E. (1988). Interparental violence: The children as victims. *Issues in Comprehensive Pediatric Nursing* 11: 291–302.

Davis, M. S., C. S. O'Sullivan, K. Susser, and M. D. Fields (2011). *Custody Evaluations When There Are Allegations of Domestic Violence: Practices, Beliefs, and Recommendations of Professional Evaluators*. Washington, D.C.: National Institute
of Justice.

Davis, R. C., D. Weisburd, and E. E. Hamilton (2010). Preventing repeat incidents
of family violence: A randomized field test of a second responder program.
Journal of Experimental Criminology 6: 297–418.

De Graaf, P. M., and M. Kalmijn (2006). Divorce motives in a period of rising
divorce evidence from a Dutch life-history survey. *Journal of Family Issues* 27:
483–505.

DeGue, S., and D. DiLillo (2008). Is animal cruelty a "red flag" for family violence? Investigating co-occurring violence toward children, partners, and
pets. *Journal of Interpersonal Violence* 24: 1036–56.

DeKeseredy, W. S. (1988). Woman abuse in dating relationships: The relevance of
social support theory. *Journal of Family Violence* 3: 1–13.

——— (1995). Enhancing the quality of survey data on woman abuse: Examples
from a Canadian national study. *Violence Against Women* 1: 158–73.

—— (2011). *Violence against Women: Myths, Facts, Controversies.* Toronto: University of Toronto Press.

—— (2014). Separation/divorce assault. In *Intimate Partner Sexual Violence: A Multidisciplinary Guide to Improving Services and Support for Survivors of Rape and Abuse,* edited by L. McOrmond-Plummer, P. Easteal AM, and J. Y. Levy-Peck, 65–75. London: Jessica Kinsley Publishers.

DeKeseredy, W. S., S. Alvi, and M. D. Schwartz (2006). An economic exclusion/male peer support model looks at "wedfare" and woman abuse. *Critical Criminology* 14: 23–41.

DeKeseredy, W. S., S. Alvi, M. D. Schwartz, and E. A. Tomaszewski (2003). *Under Siege: Poverty and Crime in a Public Housing Community.* Lanham, Md.: Lexington Books.

DeKeseredy, W. S., and M. Corsianos (2016). *Violence against Women in Pornography.* New York: Routledge.

DeKeseredy, W. S., J. F. Donnermeyer, M. D. Schwartz, K. D. Tunnell, and M. Hall (2007). Thinking critically about rural gender relations: Toward a rural masculinity crisis/male peer support model of separation/divorce sexual assault. *Critical Criminology* 15: 295–311.

DeKeseredy W. S., and M. Dragiewicz (2007). Understanding the complexities of feminist perspectives on woman abuse: A commentary on Donald G. Dutton's rethinking domestic violence. *Violence Against Women* 13: 874–84.

—— (2013). Gaps in knowledge and emerging areas in gender and crime studies. In *Routledge International Handbook of Crime and Gender Studies,* edited by C. M. Renzetti, S. L. Miller, and A. R. Gover, 297–307. London: Routledge.

—— (2014). Woman abuse in Canada: Sociological reflections on the past, suggestions for the future. *Violence Against Women* 20: 228–44.

DeKeseredy, W. S., A. Fabricius, and A. Hall-Sanchez (2015). Fueling aggrieved entitlement: The contribution of women against feminism postings. In W. S. DeKeseredy & L. Leonard (Eds.), *Crimsoc Report 4: Gender, Victimology and Restorative Justice.* Sherfield Gables, England: Waterside Press.

DeKeseredy, W. S., and A. Hall-Sanchez (2016). Adult pornography and violence against women in the heartland: Results from a rural southeast Ohio study. *Violence Against Women:* 1–20. doi: 10.1177/1077801216648795.

DeKeseredy, W. S., A. Hall-Sanchez, M. Dragiewicz, and C. M. Rennison (2016). Intimate violence against women in rural communities. In *Routledge International Handbook of Rural Criminology,* edited by J. F. Donnermeyer, 171–80. London: Routledge.

DeKeseredy, W. S., and C. Joseph (2006). Separation/divorce sexual assault in rural Ohio: Preliminary results from an exploratory study. *Violence Against Women* 12: 301–11.

DeKeseredy, W.S., and K. Kelly (1993). The incidence and prevalence of woman abuse in Canadian university and college dating relationships. *Canadian Journal of Sociology* 18: 137–59.

DeKeseredy, W.S., and L. MacLeod (1997). *Woman Abuse: A Sociological Story.* Toronto: Harcourt Brace.

DeKeseredy, W.S., and C.M. Rennison (2013a). Comparing female victims of male perpetrated separation/divorce assault across geographical regions: Results from the national crime victimization survey. *International Journal for Crime, Justice and Social Democracy* 2: 65–81.

—— (2013b). New directions in the social scientific study of separation/divorce assault. In *Crime, Justice and Social Democracy: Proceedings of the 2nd International Conference, 2013, volume 1*, edited by K. Richards and J. Tauri, 47–57. Brisbane, Australia: Crime and Justice Research Center, Faculty of Law, Queensland University of Technology.

DeKeseredy, W.S., M. Rogness, and M.D. Schwartz (2004). Separation/divorce sexual assault: The current state of social scientific knowledge. *Aggression and Violent Behavior* 9: 675–91.

DeKeseredy, W.S., and M.D. Schwartz (1993). Male peer support and woman abuse: An expansion of DeKeseredy's model. *Sociological Spectrum* 13: 394–414.

—— (1998). *Woman Abuse on Campus: Results from the Canadian National Survey.* Thousand Oaks, Calif.: Sage.

—— (2002). Theorizing public housing woman abuse as a function of economic exclusion and male peer support. *Women's Health and Urban Life* 1: 26–45.

—— (2005). Masculinities and interpersonal violence. In *Handbook of Studies on Men and Masculinities*, edited by M. Kimmel, J. Hearn, and R.W. Connell, 313–25. Thousand Oaks, Calif.: Sage.

—— (2008). Separation/divorce sexual assault in rural Ohio: Survivors' perceptions. *Journal of Prevention and Intervention in the Community* 36: 1–15.

—— (2009). *Dangerous Exits: Escaping Abusive Relationships in Rural America.* New Brunswick, N.J.: Rutgers University Press.

—— (2011). Theoretical and definitional issues in violence against women. In *Sourcebook on Violence against Women*, edited by C.M. Renzetti, J.L. Edleson, and R. Kennedy Bergen, 2d. ed., 3–21. Thousand Oaks, Calif.: Sage.

—— (2013). *Male Peer Support and Violence against Women: The History and Verification of a Theory.* Boston: Northeastern University Press.

DeKeseredy, W.S., M.D. Schwartz, and S. Alvi (2000). The role of profeminist men in dealing with woman abuse on the Canadian college campus. *Violence Against Women* 9: 918–35.

——— (2008). Which women are more likely to be abused? Public housing, cohabitation, and separated/divorced women. *Criminal Justice Studies* 21: 283–93.

DeKeseredy, W. S., M. D. Schwartz, D. Fagen, and M. Hall (2006). Separation/divorce sexual assault: The contribution of male support. *Feminist Criminology* 1: 228–50.

De Maio, J., R. Kaspiew, D. Smart, J. Dunstan, and S. Moore (2013). *Survey of Recently Separated Parents: A Study of Parents Who Separated Prior to the Implementation of the Family Law Amendment (Family Violence and Other Matters) Act 2011.* Melbourne: Australian Institute of Family Studies.

Denham, D., and J. Gillespie (1999). *Two Steps Forward . . . One Step Back: An Overview of Canadian Initiatives and Resources to End Woman Abuse 1989–1997.* Ottawa: Family Violence Prevention Unit, Health Canada.

Denisoff, R. S. (1971). *Great Day Coming: Folk Music and the American Left.* Urbana: University of Illinois Press.

Dewey, C. (2014). How copyright became the best defense against revenge porn. *Washington Post,* Sept. 8. www.washingtonpost.com/news/the-intersect /wp/2014/09/08/how-copyright-became-the-best-defense-against-revenge-porn/?tid=a_inl.

Dimond, J. P., C. Fiesler, and A. S. Bruckman (2011). Domestic violence and information communication technologies. *Interacting with Computers* 23: 413–21.

Dines, G. (2010). *Pornland: How Porn Has Hijacked Our Sexuality.* Boston: Beacon Press.

Dobash, R. E., and R. P. Dobash (1979). *Violence against Wives: A Case against the Patriarchy.* New York: Free Press.

——— (2015). *When Men Murder Women.* New York: Oxford University Press.

Dobash, R. E., R. P. Dobash, K. Cavanaugh, and R. Lewis (1998). Separate and intersecting realities: A comparison of men's and women's accounts of violence against women. *Violence Against Women* 4: 382–414.

——— (2004). Not an ordinary killer—just an ordinary guy: When men murder an intimate woman partner. *Violence Against Women* 10: 577–605.

Donnermeyer, J. F., and W. S. DeKeseredy (2014). *Rural Criminology.* London: Routledge.

Donnermeyer, J. F., P. Jobes, and E. Barclay (2006). Rural crime, poverty, and community. In *Advancing Critical Criminology: Theory and Application,* edited by W. S. DeKeseredy and B. Perry, 199–218. Lanham, Md.: Lexington Books.

Dore, M. K. (2004). The friendly parent concept: A flawed factor for child custody. *Loyola Journal of Public Interest Law* 6: 41–56.

DPost.com (2014). Friends, family remember Jody Hunt. *DPost.com*. http://thedpost.com/Friends,-family-remember-Jody.

Dragiewicz, M. (2008). Patriarchy reasserted: Fathers' rights and anti-VAWA activism. *Feminist Criminology* 3: 121–44.

—— (2011). *Equality with a Vengeance: Men's Rights, Battered Women, and Antifeminist Backlash*. Boston: Northeastern University Press.

—— (2012). Antifeminist backlash and critical criminology. In *Routledge Handbook of Critical Criminology*, edited by W.S. DeKeseredy and M. Dragiewicz, 280–89. London: Routledge.

—— (2014). Domestic violence and family law: Criminological concerns. *International Journal for Crime, Justice and Social Democracy* 3: 121–34.

Dragiewicz, M., and J. Burgess (2016). Domestic violence on #qanda: The "man" question in live Twitter discussion on the Australian Broadcasting Corporation's Q&A. *Canadian Journal of Women and the Law* 28: 211–29.

Dragiewicz, M., and W.S. DeKeseredy (2008). *A Needs Gap Assessment Report on Abused Women without Legal Representation in the Family Courts*. Oshawa, Canada: Luke's Place Support and Resource Center.

—— (2012). Claims about women's use of non-fatal force in intimate relationships: A contextual review of the Canadian research. *Violence Against Women* 18: 1008–26.

Dragiewicz, M., and Y. Lindgren (2009). The gendered nature of domestic violence: Statistical data for lawyers considering equal protection analysis. *Journal of Gender, Social Policy and the Law* 17, no. 2: 229–68.

Dugan, L., D.S. Nagin, R. Rosenfeld (2003). Do domestic violence services save lives? *NIJ Journal* 250: 20–25.

Duggan, M., N.B. Ellison, C. Lampe, A. Lenhart, and M. Madden (2015). *Social Media Update 2014*. Pew Research Center. www.pewinternet.org/fact-sheets/social-networking-fact-sheet.

Dunlap, J.A. (2004). Sometimes I feel like a motherless child: The error of pursuing battered mothers for failure to protect. *Loyola Law Review* 50: 565–622.

Dutton, D.G. (2006). *Rethinking Domestic Violence*. Vancouver: University of British Columbia Press.

—— (2010). The gender paradigm and the architecture of antiscience. *Partner Abuse* 1: 5–25.

—— (2012). The cases against the role of gender in intimate partner violence. *Aggression and Violent Behavior* 17: 99–104.

Dutton, D.G., and K. Corvo (2007). The Duluth model: A data-impervious paradigm and a failed strategy. *Aggression and Violent Behavior* 12: 658–67.

Dutton, M.A., L. Orloff, and G.A. Hass (2000). Characteristics of help-seeking behaviors, resources, and service needs of battered immigrant Latinas: Legal and policy implications. *Georgetown Journal on Poverty Law and Policy* 7: 247–305.

Dutton, M. A., S. Ostoff, and M. Dichter (2009). *Update of the "Battered Woman Syndrome" Critique.* VAWNet Applied Research Forum. www.vawnet.org, p. 11.

Dvorak, P. (2014). #YesAllWomen: Elliot Rodger's misogynistic ravings inspire a powerful response on Twitter. *Washington Post*, May 26, p. B-1.

—— (2015). Passengers watched killing on Metro car. Should they have intervened? *Washington Post*, July 9, p. B-1.

Economist (2014). Misery merchants: Revenge porn. *The Economist*, July 5. www.economist.com/news/international/21606307-how-should-online-publication-explicit-images-without-their-subjects-consent-be.

Edleson, J. L. (1999). Children's witnessing of adult domestic violence. *Journal of Interpersonal Violence* 14: 839–70.

Edleson, J. L., L. F. Mbilinyi, S. K. Beeman, A. K. Hagemeister (2003). How children are involved in adult domestic violence: Results from a four-city telephone survey. *Journal of Interpersonal Violence* 18: 18–32.

Edwards, K. M., and C. A. Gidycz (2014). Stalking and psychological distress following the termination of an abusive relationship: A prospective analysis. *Violence Against Women* 20: 1383–97.

Edwards, L. (2014). Revenge porn: Why the right to be forgotten is the right remedy. *The Guardian*, July 29. www.theguardian.com/technology/2014/jul/29/revenge-porn-right-to-be-forgotten-house-of-lords.

Eisenstein, Z. (1980). *Capitalist Patriarchy and the Case for Socialist Feminism.* New York: Monthly Review Press.

Elizabeth, V., N. Gavey, and J. Tolmie (2012). The gendered dynamics of power in disputes over the postseparation care of children. *Violence Against Women* 18, no. 4: 459–81.

Ellis, D. (1988). Post-separation woman abuse: The contribution of social support. *Victimology* 14: 4–15.

—— (1994). *Family Mediation Project. Report Submitted to the Attorney General of Ontario.* Toronto: Attorney General's Office.

—— (2000). Safety, equity, and human agency. *Violence Against Women* 6: 1012–27.

Ellis, D., and W. S. DeKeseredy (1989). Marital status and woman abuse: The DAD model. *International Journal of Sociology of the Family* 19: 67–87.

—— (1997). Rethinking estrangement, intervention, and intimate femicide. *Violence Against Women* 3: 590–609.

Ellis, D., and G. Kerry (1994). *Life Course and Intimate Femicide: An Empirical Study of the Impact of Social Interventions.* Toronto: LaMarsh Research Center on Violence and Conflict Resolution, York University.

Ellis, D., and N. Stuckless (1996). *Mediating and Negotiating Marital Conflicts*. Thousand Oaks, Calif.: Sage.

Ellis, D., N. Stuckless, and C. Smith (2015). *Marital Separation and Lethal Domestic Violence*. London: Routledge.

Ellis, D., and L. Wight (1987). Post-separation woman abuse: The contribution of lawyers. *Victimology* 13: 420–29.

Estrich, S. (1987). *Real Rape: How the Legal System Victimizes Women Who Say No*. Cambridge, Mass.: Harvard University Press.

Fawcett, J. (2010). *Up to Us: Lessons Learned and Goals for Change after Thirteen Years of the Washington State Domestic Violence Fatality Review*. Seattle: Washington State Coalition Against Domestic Violence. https://fatalityreview.files.wordpress.com/2013/11/2010-dvfr-report.pdf.

Federal Bureau of Investigation (2012). Table 13: Murder circumstances. In *Crime in the United States: Uniform Crime Reports, Supplementary Homicide Reports*. Washington, D.C.: Government Printing Office.

Federal Bureau of Prisons (2016). *Statistics*. www.bop.gov/about/statistics/population_statistics.jsp.

Felson, R. B. (2002). *Violence and Gender Reexamined*. Washington, D.C.: American Psychological Association.

Fields, M. D. (2008). Getting beyond "What did she do to provoke him?": Comments by a retired judge on the special issue on child custody and domestic violence. *Violence Against Women* 14: 93–99.

Fineman, M. A. (1987). The uses of social science data in legal policymaking: Custody determinations at divorce. *Wisconsin Law Review* 1: 107–58.

Finkelhor, D., and K. Yllo (1985). *License to Rape: Sexual Abuse of Wives*. New York: Holt, Rinehart and Winston.

Fisher, B. S., L. E. Daigle, and F. T. Cullen (2010). *Unsafe in the Ivory Tower: The Sexual Victimization of College Women*. Thousand Oaks, Calif.: Sage.

Fleury, R. E., C. M. Sullivan, and D. I. Bybee (2000). When ending the relationship does not end the violence: Women's experiences of violence by former partners. *Violence Against Women* 6: 1363–83.

Fleury-Steiner, R. E., S. L. Miller, S. Maloney, and E. B. Postel (2016). "No contact, except . . .": Visitation decisions in protection orders for intimate partner abuse. *Feminist Criminology* 11: 3–22.

Flood, M. (2015). Current practices to preventing sexual and intimate partner violence. In *Critical Issues on Violence against Women: International Perspectives and Promising Strategies*, edited by H. Johnson, B. S. Fisher, and V. Jaquier, 209–20. London: Routledge.

Fontes, L. A. (2015). *Invisible Chains: Overcoming Coercive Control in Your Intimate Relationship*. New York: Guilford Press.

Franklin, C. A., L. A. Bouffard, and T. C. Pratt (2012). Sexual assault on the college campus: Fraternity affiliation, male peer support, and low self-control. *Criminal Justice and Behavior* 39: 1457–80.

Franklin, C. A., and T. A. Menaker (2014). Feminism, status inconsistency, and women's intimate partner victimization in heterosexual relationships. *Violence Against Women* 20: 825–45.

Franklin, D. L., and A. D. James (2015). *Ensuring Inequality: The Structural Transformation of the American Family.* Rev. ed. New York: Oxford University Press.

Franks, M. A. (2015). Drafting an effective "revenge porn" law: A guide for legislators. https://poseidon01.ssrn.com/delivery.php?ID=736013.

Frisina, A. (2006). Back-talk focus groups as a follow-up tool in qualitative migration research: The missing link? *Forum* 7: 12–25.

Funk, R. E. (2006). *Reaching Men: Strategies for Preventing Sexist Attitudes, Behaviors, and Violence.* Indianapolis, Ind.: Jist Life.

Funnell, N. (2011). Sexting and peer-to-peer porn. In *Big Porn Inc.: Exposing the Harms of the Global Pornography Industry,* edited by M. Tankard Reist and A. Bray, 34–40. Melbourne, Australia: Spinfex.

Gallup-Black, A. (2005). Twenty years of rural and urban trends in family and intimate partner homicide: Does place matter? *Homicide Studies* 9: 149–73.

Gannoni, A., and T. Cussen (2014). Same-sex intimate partner homicide in Australia. www.aic.gov.au/media_library/publications/tandi_pdf/tandi469.pdf.

Gedeon, K. (2013). Poll finds Fox News is the most watched news station in America. *Madame Noire,* July 9. http://madamenoire.com/285197/poll-finds-fox-news-is-the-most-watched-news-station-in-america.

Gelles, Richard J. (1980). Violence in the family: A review of research in the seventies. *Journal of Marriage and the Family* 42: 873–85.

Gilfus, M. E., S. Fineran, D. J. Cohan, S. A. Jensen, L. Hartwick, and R. Spath (1999). Research on violence against women: Creating survivor-informed collaborations. *Violence Against Women* 10: 1194–1212.

Godenzi, A. (1999). Style or substance: Men's response to feminist challenge. *Men and Masculinities* 1: 385–92.

Goetting, A. (1999). *Getting Out: Life Stories of Women Who Left Abusive Men.* New York: Columbia University Press.

Goldenberg, M. J. (2006). On evidence and evidence-based medicine: Lessons from the philosophy of science. *Social Science and Medicine* 62: 2621–32.

Goldstein, S. (2014). West Virginia gunman targeted tow company rival, ex-girlfriend and her two lovers before killing self, cops. *New York Daily News,* Dec 2. www.nydailynews.com/news/crime/wv-man-killed-tow-company-rival-lovers-cops-article-1.2030388.

Gondolf, E. W. (1999). MCMI-III results for batterer program participation in four cities: Less pathological than expected. *Journal of Family Violence* 14: 1-17.

—— (2011). The weak evidence for batterer program alternatives. *Aggression and Violent Behavior* 16: 347-53.

—— (2012). *The Future of Batterer Programs: Reassessing Evidence-based Practice.* Boston: Northeastern University Press.

Gondolf, E. W., and E. R. Fisher (1988). *Battered Women as Survivors: An Alternative to Treating Learned Helplessness.* New York: Lexington.

Goodkind, J. R., T. L. Gillum, D. I. Bybee, and C. M. Sullivan (2003). The impact of family and friends' reactions on the well-being of women with abusive behaviors. *Violence Against Women* 9: 347-73.

Goodmark, L. (2011). State, national, and international legal initiatives to address violence against women: A survey. In *Sourcebook on Violence against Women,* edited by C. M. Renzetti, J. L. Edleson, and R. Kennedy Bergen 2d ed., 191-208. Thousand Oaks, Calif.: Sage.

Gordon, L. (1988). *Heroes of Their Own Lives: The Politics and History of Family Violence.* New York: Viking.

Graham-Bermann, S., and M. Gross (2008). Ecological models of violence. In *Encyclopedia of Interpersonal Violence,* edited by C. M. Renzetti and J. L. Edleson, 212-15. Thousand Oaks, Calif.: Sage.

Graycar, R. (2000). Law reform by frozen chook: Family law reform for the new millennium? *Melbourne University Law Review* 24: 737.

—— (2012). Family law reform in Australia, or frozen chooks revisited again? *Theoretical Inquiries in Law* 13: 241-69.

Greeson, M. L., A. C. Kennedy, D. J. Bybee, M. Beeble, A. E. Adams, and C. Sullivan (2014). Beyond deficits: Intimate partner violence, maternal parenting, and child behavior over time. *American Journal of Community Psychology* 54: 46-58.

Grisso, J. A., D. F. Schwartz, C. G. Miles, and J. H. Holmes (1996). Injuries among inner-city minority women: A population-based longitudinal study. *American Journal of Public Health* 86: 67-70.

Hall, S., and S. Winlow (2015). *Revitalizing Criminological Theory: Towards a New Ultra-realism.* London: Routledge.

Hall-Sanchez, A. K. (2013). *Talking Back: Rural Ohio Women's Reflections on Violent Intimate Relationships.* Ph.D. diss., Department of Sociology, University of Hawaii, Manoa.

—— (2014). Male peer support, hunting, and separation/divorce sexual assault in rural Ohio. *Critical Criminology* 22: 495-510.

Hamby, S. (2014). *Battered Women's Protective Strategies: Stronger Than You Know.* New York: Oxford University Press.

Hamel, J., ed. (2012). *Partner Abuse: New Directions in Research, Intervention, and Policy*. www.springerpub.com/product/19466560#.TyHvoPmwXoK.

Hand, T., D. Chung, and M. Peters (2009). *The Use of Information and Communication Technologies to Coerce and Control in Domestic Violence and Following Separation*. Sydney: Australian Domestic and Family Violence Clearinghouse, University of New South Wales.

Hardesty, J. L. (2002). Separation assault in the context of postdivorce parenting: An integrative review of the literature. *Violence Against Women* 8: 597–625.

Hardesty, J. L., J. C. Campbell, J. M. McFarlane, and L. A. Lewandowski (2007). How children and their caregivers adjust after intimate partner femicide. *Journal of Family Issues* 29: 100–124.

Hardesty, J. L., and G. H. Chung (2006). Intimate partner violence, parental divorce, and child custody: Directions for intervention and future research. *Family Relations* 55: 200–210.

Hardesty, J. L., and L. H. Ganong (2006). How women make custody decisions and manage co-parenting with abusive former husbands. *Journal of Social and Personal Relationships* 23: 543–63.

Harrell, F. E. (2001). *Regression Modeling Strategies, with Applications to Linear Models, Logistic Regression and Survival Analysis*. New York: Springer-Verlag.

Harris, R., and R. Bologh (1985). The dark side of love: Blue and white collar wife abuse. *Victimology* 10: 242–52.

Harrison, C. (2008). Implacably hostile or appropriately protective? Women managing child contact in the context of domestic violence. *Violence Against Women* 14: 381–405.

Haselschwerdt, M. L., J. L. Hardesty, and J. D. Hans (2011). Custody evaluators' beliefs about domestic violence allegations during divorce: Feminist and family violence perspectives. *Journal of Interpersonal Violence* 26: 1694–1719.

Haselschwerdt, M. L., E. T. Mitchell, M. Raffaelli, and J. L. Hardesty (2016). Divorcing mothers' use of protective strategies: Differences over time and by violence experience. *Psychology of Violence* 6: 182–92.

Hayes, B. E. (2015). Indirect abuse involving children during the separation process. *Journal of Interpersonal Violence*, online first: 1–23. https://doi.org/10.1177/0886260515596533.

Healey, E. (2016). Jian Ghomeshi trial exposes troubling double-standard. *Toronto Star*, Feb. 15. www.thestar.com/opinion/commentary/2016/02/15/jian-ghomeshi-trial-exposes-troubling-double-standard.html.

Herbst, C. (2005). Shock and awe: Virtual females and the sexing of war. *Feminist Media Studies* 5, no. 3: 311–24. http://doi.org/10.1080/14680770500271446.

HG.org (2015). Divorce and legal separation in West Virginia. www.hg.org/divorce-law-westvirginia.html.

Hinduja, S., and J. W. Patchin (2010). Bullying, cyberbullying, and suicide. *Archives of Suicide Research* 14: 206–21.

Hirschel, D., and E. Buzawa (2002). Understanding the context of dual arrest with directions for future research. *Violence Against Women* 8: 1449–73.

Hirschman, A. O. (1970). *Exit, Voice and Loyalty*. Cambridge, Mass.: Harvard University Press.

Hoffmeister, T. (2016). Legislative reactions. In *The Intersection between Intimate Partner Abuse, Technology, and Cybercrime: Examining the Virtual Enemy*, edited by J. N. Navarro, S. Clevenger, and C. D. Marcum, 187–204. Durham, N.C.: Carolina Academic Press.

Hogg, R., and K. Carrington (2006). *Policing the Rural Crisis*. Sydney, Australia: Federation Press.

Holland, K. M., S. V. Brown, J. E. Hall, and J. E. Logan (2015). Circumstances preceding homicide-suicides involving child victims: A qualitative analysis. *Journal of Interpersonal Violence*. http://doi.org/10.1177/0886260515605124.

Holloway, P. (2014). *Living in Infamy: Felon Disfranchisement and the History of American Citizenship*. New York: Oxford University Press.

Holzman, H. R., R. A. Hyatt, and J. M. Dempster (2001). Patterns of aggravated assault in public housing: Mapping the nexus of offense, place, gender, and race. *Violence Against Women* 6: 662–84.

Home Office (2015). *Controlling or Coercive Behaviour in an Intimate or Family Relationship: Statutory Guidance Framework*. www.gov.uk/government/uploads/system/uploads/attachment_data/file/482528/Controlling_or_coercive_behaviour_-_statutory_guidance.pdf.

Hooks, B. (1989). *Talking Back: Thinking Feminist, Thinking Black*. Cambridge, Mass.: South End Press.

Hopper, J. (1993). The rhetoric of motives in divorce. *Journal of Marriage and Family* 55: 801–13.

Horton, A. L., and B. L. Johnson (1993). Profile and strategies of women who have ended abuse. *Families in Society* 74: 481–92.

Hotaling, G., and D. Sugarman (1986). An analysis of risk markers and husband to wife violence: The current state of knowledge. *Violence and Victims* 1: 102–24.

Ireland, J. L. (2012). Evaluating expert witness psychological reports: Exploring quality. Summary Report, University of Central Lancashire, Mercyside and Cheshire Family Justice Forum. www.mfjc.co.uk/home/mfjccou1/public_ftp/resources/FINALVERSIONFEB2012.pdf.

Jackson, M., and D. Garvin (2015). *Community Accountability Wheel*. Ann Arbor: Domestic Violence Institute of Michigan.

Jacobs, M. S. (1998). Requiring battered women die: Murder liability for mothers under failure to protect statutes. *The Journal of Criminal Law and Criminology* 88: 579–660.

Jacobson, N. S., J. M. Gottman, E. Gortner, S. Berns, and J. W. Shortt (1996). Psychological factors in the longitudinal course of battering: When do the couples split up? When does the abuse decrease? *Violence and Victims* 11: 371–92.

Jacquier, V., H. Johnson, and B. Fisher (2011). Research methods, measures, and ethics. In *Sourcebook on Violence against Women*, edited by C. M. Renzetti, J. L. Edleson, and R. K. Bergen, 2d ed., 23–45. Thousand Oaks, Calif.: Sage.

Jaffe, P. G., C. V. Crooks, and S. E. Poisson (2003). Common misconceptions in addressing domestic violence in child custody disputes. *Juvenile and Family Court Journal* (fall): 57–68.

Jaffe, P. G., N. K. Lemon, and S. E. Poisson (2003). *Child Custody and Domestic Violence: A Call for Safety and Accountability.* Thousand Oaks, Calif.: Sage.

Jaffe, P., K. Scott, A. Jenney, M. Dawson, A. L. Straatman, and M. Campbell (2014). *Risk Factors for Children in Situations of Family Violence in the Context of Separation and Divorce.* Ottawa: Department of Justice Canada.

Jaishankar, K. (2009). Sexting: A new form of victimless crime? *International Journal of Cybercriminology* 3: 21–25.

James, N. (2014). *The Bureau of Prisons (BOP): Operations and Budget.* Congressional Research Service. www.fas.org/sgp/crs/misc/R42486.pdf.

Jasinski, J. L. (2001). Theoretical explanations for violence against women. In *Sourcebook on Violence against Women*, edited by C. M. Renzetti, J. L. Edleson, and R. K. Bergen, 1st ed., 5–22. Thousand Oaks, Calif.: Sage.

—— (2004). Pregnancy and domestic violence: A review of the literature. *Trauma, Violence, and Abuse* 5: 47–64.

Jeltsen, M. (2015). We're missing the big picture on mass shootings. *Huffington Post*, Sept. 15. www.huffingtonpost.com/entry/mass-shootings-domestic-violence-women_us_55d3806ce4b07addcb44542a.

—— (2016). What Obama's new move on guns does for domestic violence survivors. *Huffington Post,* Jan. 6. www.huffingtonpost.com/entry/obama-gun-control-domestic-violence_us_568d5ff7e4b0c8beacf54c1c?ir.

Jensen, R. (2007). *Getting off: Pornography and the End of Masculinity.* Cambridge, Mass.: South End Press.

Jewkes, R., K. Dunkle, M. P. Koss, J. B. Levin, M. Nduna, N. Jama, and Y. Sikweyiya (2006). Rape perpetration by young rural South African men: Prevalence, patterns, and risk factors. *Social Science and Medicine* 63: 2949–61.

Johnson, C., and M. Sachmann (2014). Familicide-suicide: From myth to hypothesis and toward understanding. *Family Court Review* 52, no. 1: 100–113.

Johnson, C. H. (2005). *Come with Daddy: Child Murder-suicide after Family Breakdown*. Crawley: University of Western Australia Press.

—— (2006). Familicide and family law: A study of filicide-suicide following separation. *Family Court Review* 44: 448–63.

Johnson, H. (1996). *Dangerous Domains: Violence against Women in Canada*. Toronto: Nelson.

Johnson, H., and M. Dawson (2011). *Violence against Women in Canada: Research and Policy Perspectives*. Toronto: Oxford University Press.

Johnson, N. E., D. P. Saccuzzo, and W. J. Koen (2005). Child custody mediation in cases of domestic violence: Empirical evidence of a failure to protect. *Violence Against Women* 11: 1022–53.

Kalmijn, M. (2015). How childhood circumstances moderate the long-term impact of divorce on father-child relationships. *Journal of Marriage and Family* 77: 921–38.

Kaspiew, R., R. Carson, J. Dunstan, L. Qu, B. Horsfall, J. A. De Maio, L. Moloney, M. Coulson, and S. Tayton (2015). *Evaluation of the 2012 Family Violence Amendments: Synthesis Report*. Melbourne: Australian Institute of Family Studies. https://aifs.gov.au/publications/evaluation-2012-family-violence-amendments.

Kaspiew, R., M. Gray, R. Weston, L. Moloney, K. Hand, and L. Qu (2009). *Evaluation of the 2006 Family Law Reforms*. Melbourne: Australian Institute of Family Studies.

Katz, C. (2014). The dead end of domestic violence: Spotlight on children's narratives during forensic investigations following domestic homicide. *Child Abuse and Neglect* 38: 1976–84. http://doi.org/10.1016/j.chiabu.2014.05.016.

Katz, J. (2006). *The Macho Paradox: Why Some Men Hurt Women and How All Men Can Help*. Naperville, Ill.: Sourcebooks.

—— (2015). Engaging men in the prevention of violence against women. In *Critical Issues on Violence against Women: International Perspectives and Promising Strategies*, edited by H. Johnson, B. S. Fisher, and V. Jaquier, 233–43. London: Routledge.

Kauzlarich, D., and C. M. Awsumb (2012). Confronting state oppression: The role of music. In *Routledge Handbook of Critical Criminology*, edited by W. S. DeKeseredy and M. Dragiewicz, 501–12. London: Routledge.

Kelly, J. B. (2003). Changing perspectives on children's adjustment following divorce: A view from the United States. *Childhood* 10: 237–54.

Kelly, L. (2012). Preface: Standing the test of time? Reflections on the concept of the continuum of sexual violence. In *Handbook on Sexual Violence*, edited by J. M. Brown and S. L. Walklate, xvii–xxxvi. London: Routledge.

Kempe, C. H., F. N. Silverman, B. F. Steele, W. Droegemueller, and H. K. Silver (1962). The battered-child syndrome. *Journal of the American Medical Association (JAMA)* 181 (July 17): 17–24.

Kernic, M. A., D. J. Monary-Ernsdorff, J. K. Koepsell, and V. L. Holt (2005). Children in the crossfire: Child custody determinations among couples with a history of intimate partner violence. *Violence Against Women* 11, no. 8: 991–1021.

Kernsmith, P. (2008). Coercive control. In *Encyclopedia of Interpersonal Violence,* edited by C. M. Renzetti and J. L. Edleson, 133–34. Thousand Oaks, Calif.: Sage.

Kilpatrick, D. G. (2004). What is violence against women? Defining and measuring the problem. *Journal of Interpersonal Violence* 19: 1209–34.

Kim, Y., and B. Leventhal (2008). Bullying and suicide: A review. *International Journal of Adolescent Medicine and Health* 20: 133–54.

Kimball, E., J. L. Edleson, R. M. Tolman, T. Neugut, and J. Carlson (2012). Global efforts to engage men in violence prevention: An International Survey. *Violence Against Women* 19: 924–29.

Kimmel, M. (2002). Gender symmetry in domestic violence: A substantive and methodological review. *Violence Against Women* 8: 1336–67.

—— (2013). *Angry White Men: American Masculinity at the End of an Era.* New York: Nation Books.

Kingston Frontenac Anti-Violence Coordinating Committee (2015). Women/children murdered. http://kfacc.org/ontariofemicide.

Kirkwood, C. (1993). *Leaving Abusive Partners: From the Scars of Survival to the Wisdom for Change.* London: Sage.

Kirkwood, D. (2012). *"Just Say Goodbye": Parents Who Kill Their Children in the Context of Separation.* Victoria, Australia: Domestic Violence Resource Centre Victoria. www.dvrcv.org.au.

Klein, A., and B. Hart (2012). *Practical Implications of Current Domestic Violence Research for Victim Advocates and Service Providers.* Washington, D.C.: U.S. Department of Justice.

Klein, J. (2012). *The Bully Society: School Shootings and the Crisis of Bullying in America's Schools.* New York: New York University Press.

Klein, R. (2012). *Responding to Intimate Violence against Women: The Role of Informal Networks.* New York: Cambridge University Press.

Klomek, A., A. Sourander, and M. Gould (2011). Bullying and suicide: Detection and intervention. *Psychiatric Times* 28 (Feb. 10): 1–6.

Kowalski, R., G. Giumetti, and A. Schroeder (2014). Bullying in the digital age: A critical review and meta-analysis of cyberbullying research among youth. *Psychological Bulletin* 140: 1073–1137.

Kowalski, R., S. Limber, and P. Agatston (2012). *Cyberbullying: Bullying in the Digital Age.* 2d ed. Malden, Mass.: Wiley-Blackwell.

Krishnan, S. P., J. C. Hilbert, and M. Pase (2001). An examination of intimate partner violence in rural communities: Results from a hospital emergency department study from southwest United States. *Family Community Health* 24: 1–14.

Kristof, N. D. (2012). Do we have courage? *New York Times International Weekly,* Dec. 23, p. 15.

Kurki-Suonio, K. (2000). Joint custody as an interpretation of the best interests of the child in critical and comparative perspective. *International Journal of Law, Policy and the Family* 14: 183–205.

Kurz, D. (1995). *For Richer, for Poorer: Mothers Confront Divorce.* New York: Routledge.

LaCapria, K. (2016). Misandry mondays. *Scopes.com,* Feb. 1. www.snopes.com /roosh-v-43-countries.

LaFree, G., and G. Hunnicutt (2006). Female and male homicide victimization trends: A cross-national context. In *Gender and Crime: Patterns of Victimization and Offending,* edited by K. Heimer and C. Kruttschnitt, 195–229. New York: New York University Press.

Laing, M. (1999). For the sake of the children: Preventing reckless new laws. *Canadian Journal of Family Law* 16: 229–82.

Lampard, R. (2014). Stated reasons for relationship dissolution in Britain: Marriage and cohabitation compared. *European Sociological Review* 30: 315–28.

Lamphere, R. D., and K. T. Pikciunas (2016). Sexting, sextortion, and other Internet sexual offenses. In *The Intersection between Intimate Partner Abuse, Technology, and Cybercrime: Examining the Virtual Enemy,* edited by J. N. Navarro, S. Clevenger, and C. D. Marcum, 141–65. Durham, N.C.: Carolina Academic Press.

LaViolette, A. D., and O. W. Barnett (2014). *It Could Happen to Anyone: Why Battered Women Stay.* 3d ed. Thousand Oaks, Calif.: Sage.

Lee, M. R. (2008). Civic community in the hinterland: Toward a theory of rural social structure and violence. *Criminology* 46: 447–78.

Lehman, P. (2006). Introduction: "A dirty little secret"—Why teach and study pornography? In *Pornography: Film and Culture,* edited by P. Lehman, 1–24. New Brunswick, N.J.: Rutgers University Press.

Lentz, S. A. (1998). Revisiting the rule of thumb. *Women and Criminal Justice* 10: 9–27.

Levinson King, R. (2015). Where did the worst mass shootings take place in the U.S. in 2015? *Toronto Star,* Dec. 3. www.thestar.com/news/world/2015/12 /03/where-did-the-worst-mass-shootings-take-place-in-the-us-in-2015 .html.

Lewandowski, L. A., J. Mcfarlane, J. C. Campbell, F. Gary, and C. Barenski (2004). "He killed my mommy!" Murder or attempted murder of a child's mother. *Journal of Family Violence* 19: 211–20.

Lewis, S. H. (2003). *Unspoken Crimes: Sexual Assault in Rural America*. Enola, Pa.: National Sexual Violence Resource Center.

Licata, V., J. Fehrens, and E. Hoff (2014). Jody Hunt: A man with vengeful motives. *Mountaineer News Service*. http://mountaineernewsservice.com /jody-hunt-a-man-with-vengeful-motives.

Liem, M. C. A., and D. Oberwittler (2013). Homicide followed by suicide in Europe. In *Handbook of European Homicide Research: Patterns, Explanations, and Country Studies*, edited by M. C. A. Liem and W. A. Pridemore, 197–215. New York: Springer.

Lilly, J. R., F. T. Cullen, and R. A. Ball (2015). *Criminological Theory; Context and Consequences*. 6th ed. Thousand Oaks, Calif.: Sage.

Liss, M. B., and G. B. Stahly (1993). Domestic violence and child custody. In *Battering and Family Therapy: A Feminist Perspective*, edited by M. Hansen and M. Harway, 175–87. Thousand Oaks, Calif.: Sage.

Lobao, L. (2006). Gendered places and place-based gender identities: Reflections and refractions. In *Country Boys: Masculinity and Rural Life*, edited by H. Campbell, M. Mayerfeld Bell, and M. Finney, 267–76. University Park: Pennsylvania State University Press.

Lobao, L., and K. Meyer (2001). The great agricultural transition: Crisis, change, and social consequences of twentieth century US farming. *Annual Review of Sociology* 27: 103–24.

Loftin, C., D. McDowall, B. Wiersema, and T. Cottey (1991). Effects of restrictive licensing of handguns on homicide and suicide in the District of Columbia. *New England Journal of Medicine* 325: 1625–30.

Logan, T. K., J. Cole, L. Shannon, and R. Walker (2006). *Partner Stalking: How Women Respond, Cope, and Survive*. New York: Springer.

Logan, T. K., L. Evans, E. Stevenson, and C. E. Jordan (2005). Barriers to services for rural and urban survivors of rape. *Journal of Interpersonal Violence* 20: 591–616.

Logan, T. K., E. Stevenson, L. Evans, and C. Leukefeld (2004). Rural and urban women's perceptions of barriers to health, mental health, and criminal justice services: Implications for victim services. *Violence and Victims* 19: 37–62.

Lohmann, N., and R. A. Lohmann (2005). *Rural Social Work Practice*. New York: Columbia University Press.

Lyndon, A., J. Bonds-Raacke, and A. Cratty (2011). College students' Facebook stalking of ex-partners. *Cyberpsychology, Behavior, and Social Networking* 14: 711–16.

Macdonald, G. S. (2015). Domestic violence and private family court proceedings: Promoting child welfare or promoting contact? *Violence Against Women* 22: 832–52.

MacLean, B. D. (1991). In partial defense of socialist realism: Some theoretical and methodological concerns of the local crime survey. *Crime, Law and Social Change* 15: 213–54.

MacLeod, L. (1987). *Battered but Not Beaten: Preventing Wife Battering in Canada.* Ottawa: Advisory Council on the Status of Women.

MacLeod, L., and M. Shin (1994). *"Like a Wingless Bird": A Tribute to the Survival and Courage of Women Who Are Abused and Who Speak Neither English nor French.* Ottawa: Public Health Agency of Canada.

Macmillan, R., and C. Kruttschnitt (2005). *Patterns of Violence against Women: Risk Factors and Consequences.* Washington, D.C.: U.S. Department of Justice.

Mahler, J. (2015). Who spewed that abuse? Anonymous Yik Yak app isn't telling. *New York Times,* Mar. 8. www.nytimes.com/2015/03/09/technology/popular-yik-yak-app-confers-anonymity-and-delivers-abuse.html.

Mahoney, M. (1991). Legal issues of battered women: Redefining the issue of separation. *Michigan Law Review* 90: 1–94.

Mahoney, P., and L. M. Williams (1998). Sexual assault in marriage: Prevalence, consequences, and treatment of wife rape. In *Partner Violence: A Comprehensive Review of 20 Years of Research,* edited by J. L. Jasinski and L. M. Williams, 113–62. Thousand Oaks, Calif.: Sage.

Maier, S. L. (2014). *Rape, Victims, and Investigations: Experiences and Perceptions of Law Enforcement Officers Responding to Reported Rapes.* New York: Routledge.

Malecki, S. (2012). *Learning from the Enemy: The GUNMAN Project.* Fort Meade, Md.: Center for Cryptologic History, National Security Agency.

Malley-Morrison, K., and D. A. Hines (2004). *Family Violence in a Cultural Perspective: Defining, Understanding, and Combating Abuse.* Thousand Oaks, Calif.: Sage.

Malphurs, J. E., and D. Cohen (2002). A newspaper surveillance study of homicide-suicide in the United States. *American Journal of Forensic Medicine and Pathology* 23: 142–48.

Marcotte, A. (2012). Defense attorney blames 11-year-old victim because that's his job. *Slate,* Nov. 29. www.slate.com/blogs/xx_factor/2012/11/29/cleveland_texas_rape_case_defense_attorney_calls_pre_teen_victim_a_spider.html.

——— (2015). Why men kill is not a mystery. *XX factor,* Aug. 10. www.slate.com/blogs/xx_factor/2015/08/10/eight_people_dead_in_houston_domestic_homicide_it_s_a_tragedy_but_not_a.html.

Marriner, C. (2015). Revenge porn: Government urged to make it illegal. *The Sydney Morning Herald,* Oct. 4. www.smh.com.au/national/government-urged-to-outlaw-revenge-porn-20150926-gjvod5.html.

Marshall, I. H., and D. L. Summers (2013). Contemporary differences in rates and trends of homicide among European nations. In *Handbook of European*

Homicide Research: Patterns, Explanations, and Country Studies, edited by M. C. A. Liem and W. A. Pridemore, 39-69. New York: Springer.

Martin, M. E. (1997). Double your trouble: Dual arrest in family violence. *Journal of Family Violence* 12: 139-57.

Marwick, A. (2013). Donglegate: Why the tech community hates feminists. *Wired.com*, Mar. 29. www.wired.com/2013/03/richards-affair-and-misogyny-in-tech.

Matlow, R. B., and A. P. DePrince (2015). The impact of appraisals and context on readiness to leave a relationship following intimate partner abuse. *Violence Against Women* 21: 1043-64.

Mayo, B. (2014). Police say W. Va. shooter Jody Hunt held personal, professional grudges. *Pittsburgh's ActionNews*.www.wtae.com/news/police-say-west-virginia-shooter-jody-hunt-held-personal-grudges/30024628.

McAfee Security (2013). *Love, Relationships, and Technology Survey.* www .photoxels.com/mcafee-canada-2013-love-relationships-and-technology-survey-pitfalls-of-couples-sharing-personal-data-and-passwords.

McFarlane, J. M., J. C. Campbell, S. Wilt, C. J. Sachs, Y. Ulrich, and X. Xu (1999). Stalking and intimate partner femicide. *Homicide Studies* 3: 300-316.

McFarlane, J., and A. Malecha (2005). *Sexual Assault among Intimates: Frequency, Consequences, and Treatments.* Final Report, grant #2002-WG-BX-0020. Washington, D.C.: Department of Justice, National Institute of Justice.

McGlynn, C., and E. Rackley (2016). Not "revenge porn," but abuse: Let's call it image-based sexual abuse. *Inherently Human: Critical Perspectives on Law, Gender and Sexuality* 41 (Feb. 15). https://inherentlyhuman.wordpress.com /2016/02/15/not-revenge-porn-but-abuse-lets-call-it-image-based-sexual-abuse.

McIntosh, J., A. Burns, N. Dowd, and H. Gridley (2009). *Parenting after separation: A literature review prepared for the Australian Psychological Society.* Melbourne: The Australian Psychological Society.

McKinley, Jr., J. C. (2011). Vicious assault shakes Texas town. *New York Times*, Mar. 9, p. A13.

McMurray, A. M. (1997). Violence against ex-wives: Anger and advocacy. *Health Care for Women International* 18: 543-56.

McMurray, A. M., I. D. Froyland, D. G. Bell, and D. J. Curnow (2000). Post-separation violence: The male perspective. *Journal of Family Studies* 6: 89-105.

McNair, B. (2002). *Striptease Culture: Sex, Media, and the Democratisation of Desire.* London: Routledge.

McOrmond-Plummer, L., P. Easteal AM, and J. Y. Levy-Peck, eds. (2014). *Intimate Partner Sexual Violence: A Multidisciplinary Guide to Improving Services and Support for Survivors of Rape and Abuse.* London: Jessica Kingsley Publishers.

Mechanic, M. B., M. H. Uhlmansick, T. L. Weaver, and P. A. Resick (2000). The impact of severe stalking experienced by acutely battered women: An examination of violence, psychological symptoms, and strategic responses. *Violence and Victims* 15: 443–58.

Melander, L. A. (2010). College students' perceptions of intimate partner cyber harassment. *Cyberpsychology, Behavior, and Social Networking* 13: 263–68.

Meloy, M. L., and S. L. Miller (2011). *The Victimization of Women: Law, Policies, and Politics*. New York: Oxford University Press.

Melton, H. C. (2007a). Predicting the occurrence of stalking in relationships characterized by domestic violence. *Journal of Interpersonal Violence* 22: 3–25.

——— (2007b). Stalking in the context of intimate partner abuse: In the victim's words. *Feminist Criminology* 2: 347–63.

Merchant, M. (2000). A comparative study of agencies assisting domestic violence victims: Does the South Asian community have special needs? *Journal of Social Distress and the Homeless* 9: 249–59.

Mercy, J. A., and L. E. Saltzman (1989). Fatal violence among spouses in the United States. *American Journal of Public Health* 79: 595–99.

Merwin, E., A. Snyder, and E. Katz (2006). Differential access to quality rural healthcare: Professional and policy challenges. *Family and Community Health* 29: 186–94.

Messerschmidt, J. W. (1993). *Masculinities and Crime: Critique and Reconceptualization*. Lanham, Md.: Roman and Littlefield.

Messinger, A. M. (2014). Marking 35 years of research on same-sex intimate partner violence: Lessons and new directions. In *Handbook of LGBT Communities, Crime, and Justice*, edited by D. Peterson and V. Panfil, 65–85. New York: Springer.

Messner, M. A., M. A. Greenberg, and T. Peretz (2015). *Some Men: Feminist Allies and the Movement to End Violence against Women*. New York: Oxford University Press.

Miller, M. (2013). Revenge porn victim Holly Jacobs "ruined my life," ex says. *Miami New Times*, Oct. 17. www.miaminewtimes.com/news/revenge-porn-victim-holly-jacobs-ruined-my-life-ex-says-6393654.

Miller, S. L. (2005). *Victims as Offenders: The Paradox of Women's Violence in Relationships*. New Brunswick, N.J.: Rutgers University Press.

Miller, S. L., and E. Bonistall (2012). Gender and policing: Critical issues and analyses. In *Routledge Handbook of Critical Criminology*, edited by W. S. DeKeseredy and M. Dragiewicz, 316–27. London: Routledge.

Miller, S. L., L. Iovanni, and K. D. Kelley (2011). Violence against women and the criminal justice response. In *Sourcebook on Violence against Women*, edited by C. M. Renzetti, J. L. Edleson, and R. Kennedy Bergen, 2d ed., 267–86. Thousand Oaks, Calif.: Sage.

Miller, S. L., and N. L. Smolter (2011). "Paper abuse": When all else fails, batterers use procedural stalking. *Violence Against Women* 17: 637–50.

Mills, C. W. (1959). *The Sociological Imagination*. New York: Oxford University Press.

Moloney, L., B. Smyth, N. Richardson, and S. Capper (2016). *Understanding Parenting Disputes after Separation*. Melbourne: Australian Institute of Family Studies. https://aifs.gov.au/publications/understanding-parenting-disputes-after-separation.

Moloney, P. (2016). Supporters of anti-woman group Return of Kings to meet in Perth. *Sydney Morning Herald*, Feb. 1. www.smh.com.au/national/supporters-of-antiwoman-group-return-of-kings-to-meet-in-perth-20160201-gmir9o.html.

Monsebraaten, L. (2016). Anti-poverty advocates call for affordable Internet. *Toronto Star*, Feb. 2. www.thestar.com/news/gta/2016/02/02/anti-poverty-advocates-call-for-affordable-internet.html.

Moracco, K. E., C. W. Runyan, and J. D. Butts (1998). Femicide in North Carolina, 1991–1993: A statewide study of patterns and precursors. *Homicide Studies* 2: 422–46.

Morrill, A. C., J. Dai, S. Dunn, I. Sung, and K. Smith (2005). Child custody and visitation decisions when the father has perpetrated violence against the mother. *Violence Against Women* 11: 1076–1107.

Mouzos, J., and C. Rushforth (2003). *Family Homicide in Australia*. Canberra: Australian Institute of Criminology.

Mudaly, N., and C. Goddard (2006). *The Truth Is Longer than a Lie: Children's Experiences of Abuse and Professional Interventions*. London: Jessica Kingsley.

Mueller, K. J., and A. C. MacKinney (2006). Care across the continuum: Access to health care services in rural America. *Journal of Rural Health* 22: 43–49.

National Campaign to Prevent Teen and Unplanned Pregnancy and CosmoGirl. Com (2012). *Sex and Tech: Results from a Survey of Teens and Young Adults*. Retrieved July 23, 2012. www.thenationalcampaign.org/sextech/PDF/SexTech_Summary.pdf.

Navarro, J. N. (2016). Cyberabuse and cyberstalking. In *The Intersection between Intimate Partner Abuse, Technology, and Cybercrime: Examining the Virtual Enemy*, edited by J. N. Navarro, S. Clevenger, and C. D. Marcum, 125–39. Durham, N.C.: Carolina Academic Press.

Navarro, J. N., S. Clevenger, and C. D. Marcum, eds. (2016). *The Intersection between Intimate Partner Abuse, Technology, and Cybercrime: Examining the Virtual Enemy*. Durham, N.C.: Carolina Academic Press.

Newburn, T. (2013). *Criminology*. 2d ed. London: Routledge.

NiCarthy, G. (1986). *Getting Free: A Handbook for Women Who Left Abusive Relation-ships*. Seattle: Seal.

Niehaus, I. (2005). Masculine dominance in sexual violence: Interpreting accounts of three cases of rape in the South Africa Lowveld. In *Men Behaving Differently*, edited by G. Reid and L. Walker, 65–83. Cape Town, South Africa: Juta.

Nikupeteri, A., and M. Laitinen (2015). Children's everyday lives shadowed by stalking: Postseparation stalking narratives of Finnish children and women. *Violence and Victims* 30: 830–45.

NSW Domestic Violence Death Review Team (DVDRT) (2015). *SNW Domestic Vio-lence Death Review Team Annual Report 2012-2013*. Sydney, Australia: Justice and Attorney General, New South Wales Government. www.coroners .justice.nsw.gov.au/Documents/dvdrt_2013_annual_reportx.pdf.

O'Brien, J. E. (1971). Violence in divorce-prone families. *Journal of Marriage and the Family* 33: 692–98.

O'Connor, L. (2014). "Revenge porn" law sees first conviction in California. *Huff-ington Post*, Dec. 2. www.huffingtonpost.com/2014/12/02/revenge-porn-california-first-conviction_n_6258158.html.

Office of the State Coroner (2015). *Office of the State Coroner Annual report 2013-2014*. Brisbane: Queensland Courts.

O'Hagan, K. (2014). *Filicide-suicide: The Killing of Children in the Context of Separa-tion, Divorce and Custody Disputes*. London: Palgrave Macmillan.

Okun, L. (1986). *Woman Abuse: Facts Replacing Myths*. Albany: SUNY Press.

Olafson, E., D. L. Corwin, and R. C. Summit (1993). Modern history of child sexual abuse awareness: Cycles of discovery and suppression. *Child Abuse and Neglect* 17: 7–24.

Ontario Domestic Violence Death Review Committee (2009). *Seventh Annual Report of the Domestic Violence Death Review Committee–2009*. Toronto: Office of the Chief Coroner, Province of Ontario. www.crvawc.ca/documents /DVDRC2010.pdf.

Ontario Women's Directorate (2006). *Neighbors, Friends, and Families: How to Talk to Men Who Are Abusive*. Toronto: Government of Ontario.

O'Sullivan, C. S., L. A. King, K. Levin-Russell, and E. Horowitz (2006). *Supervised and Unsupervised Parental Access in Domestic Violence Cases: Court Orders and Consequences*. Washington, D.C.: National Institute of Justice. www.ncjrs .gov/pdffiles1/nij/grants/213712.pdf

Owen, S. (2012). *Integrated Response Policy to Domestic Violence in NSW: A Critical Analysis*. Ph.D. diss., Queensland University of Technology, School of Justice, Brisbane, Australia.

Pagelow, M. D. (1993). Commentary: Justice for victims of spouse abuse in divorce and child custody cases. *Violence and Victims* 8: 69–83.

Parkinson, P. (2013). Violence, abuse and the limits of shared parental responsibility. *Family Matters* 92: 7–17.

Parton, N. (1979). A natural history of child abuse: A study in social problem definition. *British Journal of Social Work* 9: 431–51.

Patterson, P. D. (2006). Emergency medical services and the federal government's evolving role: What rural and frontier emergency medical services advocates should know. *Journal of Rural Health* 22: 97–101.

Peek-Asa, C., A. Wallis, K. Harland, K. Beyer, P. Dickey, and S. Saftlas (2011). Rural disparity in domestic violence prevalence and access to resources. *Journal of Women's Health* 20: 1743–49.

Pence, E., G. Davis, C. Beardslee, and D. Gamache (2012). *Mind the Gap: Accounting for Domestic Abuse in Child Custody Evaluations*. Minneapolis, Minn.: Battered Women's Justice Project.

Perilla, J. L., C. Lippy, A. Rosales, and J. V. Serrata (2011). Prevalence of domestic violence. In *Violence against Women and Children: Mapping the Terrain, Volume 1*, edited by J. W. White, M. P. Koss, and A. E. Kazdin, 221–42. Washington, D.C.: American Psychological Association.

Perrault, S. (2011). *Violent Victimization of Aboriginal People in the Canadian Provinces*. Ottawa: Statistics Canada.

Peterson del Mar, D. (1996). *What Trouble I Have Seen: A History of Violence Against Wives*. Cambridge, Mass.: Harvard University Press.

Pfohl, S. J. (1977). The "discovery" of child abuse. *Social Problems* 24: 310–23.

Pleck, E. H. (1987). *Domestic Tyranny: The Making of American Social Policy against Family Violence from Colonial Times to the Present*. Urbana-Champaign: University of Illinois Press.

Polk, K. (1994). *When Men Kill: Scenarios of Masculine Violence*. Cambridge, Engl.: Cambridge University Press.

Porter, T. (2006). *Well Meaning Men: Breaking out of the Man Box*. Charlotte, N.C.: A Call to Men: National Association of Men and Women Committed to Ending Violence Against Women.

Potok, M., and E. Schlatter (2012). Men's rights movement spreads false claims about women. *Southern Poverty Law Center Intelligence Report* 145. www.splcenter.org/fighting-hate/intelligence-report/2012/men's-rights-movement-spreads-false-claims-about-women.

Potter, H. (2015). *Intersectionality and Criminology: Disrupting and Revolutionizing Studies of Crime*. London: Routledge.

Powell, A., and N. Henry (2015). *Digital Harassment and Abuse of Adult Australians: A Summary Report*. https://research.techandme.com.au/wp-content

/uploads/REPORT_AustraliansExperiencesofDigitalHarassmentandAbuse.
pdf.

Praxis International (2011). *Report of the Henry County, Ohio, Child Custody and Domestic Violence Safety and Accountability Audit.* Praxis International. www .bwjp.org/assets/documents/pdfs/ohio_custody_safety_assessment.pdf.

Przekop, M. (2011). One more battleground: Domestic violence, child custody, and the batterers' relentless pursuit of their victims through the courts. *Seattle Journal of Social Justice* 9: 1053–1106.

Ptacek, J. (1999). *Battered Women in the Courtroom: The Power of Judicial Responses.* Boston: Northeastern University Press.

Pynoos, R. S., and S. Eth (1984). The child as witness to homicide. *Journal of Social Issues* 40, no. 2: 87–108. http://doi.org/10.1111/j.1540-4560.1984 .tb01095.x.

Qu, L., and R. Weston (2010). *Parenting Dynamics after Separation: A Follow-up Study of Parents Who Separated after the 2006 Family Law Reforms.* Canberra, Australia: Attorney-General's Department.

Raj, A., and J. Silverman (2002). Violence against immigrant women: The roles of culture, context, and legal immigrant status on intimate partner violence. *Violence Against Women* 8: 367–98.

Raphael, J. (2001). Public housing and domestic violence. *Violence Against Women* 7: 699–706.

—— (2013). *Rape Is Rape: How Denial, Distortion, and Victim Blaming Are Fueling a Hidden Acquaintance Rape Crisis.* Chicago: Chicago Review Press.

Rathus, Z. (2014). The role of social science in Australian family law: Collaborator, usurper or infiltrator? *Family Court Review* 52: 69–89.

Reed, L. A., R. M. Tolman, and L. M. Ward (2016). Snooping and sexting: Digital media as a context for dating aggression and abuse among college students. *Violence Against Women* 22: 1556–76. doi: 10.1177/1077801216630143.

Reihing, K. M. (1999). Protecting victims of domestic violence and their children after divorce: The American Law Institute's model. *Family and Conciliation Courts Review* 37: 393–410.

Reiman, J., and P. Leighton (2010). *The Rich Get Richer and the Poor Get Prison.* 9th ed. Boston: Allyn and Bacon.

Rennison, C. M., W. S. DeKeseredy, and M. Dragiewicz (2012). Urban, suburban, and rural variations in separation/divorce rape/sexual assault: Results from the national crime victimization survey. *Feminist Criminology* 7: 282–97.

—— (2013). Intimate relationship status variations in violence against women: Urban, suburban, and rural differences. *Violence Against Women* 19: 1312–30.

Rentschler, C. A. (2014). Rape culture and the feminist politics of social media. *Girlhood Studies* 7: 65–82.

Renzetti, C. M. (2011). Economic issues and intimate partner violence. In *Source-book on Violence against Women*, edited by C. M. Renzetti, J. L. Edleson, and R. Kennedy Bergen, 2d. ed., 171–88. Thousand Oaks, Calif.: Sage.

—— (2013). *Feminist Criminology*. London: Routledge.

Renzetti, C. M, J. L. Edleson, and R. Kennedy Bergen (2011). Theoretical and methodological issues in researching violence against women. In *Sourcebook on Violence against Women*, edited by C. M. Renzetti, J. L. Edleson, and R. Kennedy Bergen, 2d ed., 1–2. Thousand Oaks, Calif.: Sage.

Renzetti, C. M., and S. L. Maier (2002). Private crime in public housing: Fear of crime and violent victimization among women public housing residents. *Women's Health and Urban Life* 1: 46–65.

Reyns, B. W., B. Henson, and T. J. Holt (2016). Theoretical explanations of personal forms of online victimization. In *The Intersection between Intimate Partner Abuse, Technology, and Cybercrime: Examining the Virtual Enemy*, edited by J. N. Navarro, S. Clevenger, and C. D. Marcum, 75–94. Durham, N.C.: Carolina Academic Press.

Rhoades, H. (2002). The rise and rise of shared parenting laws: A critical reflection. *Canadian Journal of Family Law* 19: 75–158.

—— (2008). The dangers of shared care legislation: Why Australia needs (yet more) family law reform. *Federal Law Review* 36: 279–99.

Rhoades, H., and S. B. Boyd (2004). Reforming custody laws: A comparative study. *International Journal of Law, Policy and the Family* 18: 119–46.

Richie, B. (1996). *Compelled to Crime: The Gender Entrapment of Battered Black Women*. New York: Routledge.

Riggio, H. R. (2004). Parental marital conflict and divorce, parent-child relationships, social support, and relationship anxiety in young adulthood. *Personal Relationships* 11: 99–114.

Rockell, B. A. (2013). Women and crime in the rural-urban fringe. *International Journal of Rural Criminology* 2: 24–45.

Rogness, M. (2002). Toward an integrated male peer support model of marital rape in the United States. Master's thesis, Department of Sociology and Anthropology, Ohio University, Athens.

Rosen, L. N., and C. S. O'Sullivan (2005). Outcomes of custody and visitation petitions when fathers are restrained by protection orders: The case of the New York family courts. *Violence Against Women* 11: 1054–75.

Rosenfeld, B. (2004). Violence risk factors in stalking and obsessional harassment: A review and preliminary meta-analysis. *Criminal Justice and Behavior* 31: 9–36.

Royal Canadian Mounted Police (2013). *Urban and Rural Firearm Deaths in Canada*. www.recmp-grc.gc.ca/cfp-pcaf/res-rec/urb-eng.htm.

RT (2015). Dylann Roof "manifesto": Massacre suspect explains why he "chose" Charleston. *RT News*, June 20. Retrieved June 23, 2015, https://www.rt.com /usa/268612-roof-racist-manifesto-shooting.

Russell, D. E. H. (1975). *The Politics of Rape: The Victim's Perspective*. New York: Stein and Day.

—— (1990). *Rape in Marriage*. New York: Macmillan.

—— (1993). *Against Pornography: The Evidence of Harm*. Berkeley: Russell Publications.

Saini, M. A., J. R. Johnston, B. J. Fidler, and N. Bala (2012). Parenting plan evaluations: Applied research for the family court. In *Parenting Plan Evaluations: Applied Research for the Family Court*, edited by K. Kuehnle, 399–441. New York: Oxford University Press.

Salter, M., and T. Crofts (2015). Responding to revenge porn: Challenging online legal immunity. In *New Views on Pornography: Sexuality, Politics and the Law*, edited by L. Comella and S. Tarrant, 233–54. Westport, Conn.: Praeger.

Sampson, R. J. (2010). Gold standard myths: Observations on the experimental turn in quantitative criminology. *Journal of Quantitative Criminology* 26: 489–500.

Saunders, D. G. (1994). Child custody decisions in families experiencing woman abuse. *Social Work* 39: 51–59.

—— (2015). Research based recommendations for child custody evaluation practices and policies in cases of intimate partner violence. *Journal of Child Custody* 12: 71–92.

Saunders, D. G., K. C. Faller, and R. M. Tolman (2013). Factors associated with child custody evaluators' recommendations in cases of intimate partner violence. *Journal of Family Psychology* 27: 473–83.

—— (2015). Beliefs and recommendations regarding child custody and visitation in cases involving domestic violence: A comparison of professionals in different roles. *Violence Against Women* 22: 722–44. http://doi.org/10.1177 /1077801215608845.

Schmidt, P. (2015). A new faculty challenge: Fending off abuse on Yik Yak. *Chronicle of Higher Education*, Jan. 29. http://chronicle.com/article/A-New-Faculty-Challenge-/151463.

Schulman, M. A. (1981). *A Survey of Spousal Violence against Women in Kentucky.*. New York: Garland Publishing.

Schwartz, M. D. (1982). The spousal exemption for criminal rape prosecution. *Vermont Law Review* 7: 33–57.

—— (1989). Family violence as a cause of crime: Rethinking our priorities. *Criminal Justice Policy Review* 3: 115–32.

—— (2000). Methodological issues in the use of survey data for measuring and characterizing violence against women. *Violence Against Women* 8: 815–38.

—— (2012). The myth that the best police response to domestic violence is to arrest the offender. In *Demystifying Crime and Criminal Justice*, edited by R. M. Bohm and J. T. Walker, 2d ed., 193–203. New York: Oxford University Press.

Schwartz, M. D., and H. Brownstein (2016). Critical criminology. In *Handbook of Criminology Theory*, edited by A. Piquero, 301–17. New York: Blackwell-Wiley.

Schwartz, M. D., and W. S. DeKeseredy (1994). "People without data" attacking rape: The Gilbertizing of Mary Koss. *Violence Update* 5: 5, 8, 11.

—— (1997). *Sexual Assault on the College Campus: The Role of Male Peer Support*. Thousand Oaks, Calif.: Sage.

Schwartz, M. D., W. S. DeKeseredy, D. Tait, and S. Alvi (2001). Male peer support and routine activities theory: Understanding sexual assault on the college campus. *Justice Quarterly* 18: 701–27.

Schwartz, M. D., and C. A. Nogrady (1996). Fraternity membership, rape myths, and sexual aggression on a college campus. *Violence Against Women* 2: 148–62.

Scott, J., and P. C. Jobes (2007). Policing of rural Australia. In *Crime in Rural Australia*, edited by E. Barclay, J. F. Donnermeyer, J. Scott, and R. Hogg, 127–37. Annandale, NSW, Australia: Federation Press.

Scully, D. (1990). *Understanding Sexual Violence*. Boston: Unwin Hyman.

Sernau, S. (2001). *Worlds Apart: Social Inequalities in a New Century*. Thousand Oaks, Calif.: Pine Forge Press.

—— (2006). *Global Problems: The Search for Equity, Peace, and Sustainability*. Boston: Pearson.

Sev'er, A. (1997). Recent or imminent separation and intimate violence against women: A conceptual overview and some Canadian examples. *Violence Against Women* 3: 566–89.

—— (2001). *An Ode to Survivors of Abuse*. Toronto: Department of Sociology, University of Toronto.

—— (2002). *Fleeing the House of Horrors: Women Who Have Left Abusive Partners*. Toronto: University of Toronto Press.

Shalansky, C., J. Ericksen, and A. D. Henderson (1999). Abused women and child custody: The ongoing exposure to abusive ex-partners. *Journal of Advanced Nursing* 29: 416–26.

Sharps, P. W., J. C. Campbell, D. W. Campbell, F. Gary, and D. Webster (2003). Risky mix: Drinking, drug use, and homicide. *NIJ Journal* 250: 8–13.

Sherman, J. (2005). *Men without Sawmills: Masculinity, Rural Poverty, and Family Stability*. Columbia, Mo.: Rural Poverty Research Center.

Shope, J. H. (2004). When words are not enough: The search for the effect of pornography on abused women. *Violence Against Women* 10: 56–72.

Siegel, L., and C. McCormick (2012). *Criminology in Canada: Theories, Patterns, and Typologies.* 5th ed. Toronto: Nelson.

Silberg, J., and S. Dallam (2014). *What Can We Learn from Turned-Around Cases?* Webinar for the Battered Women's Justice Project. www.bwjp.org/resource-center/resource-results/what-can-we-learn-from-turned-around-cases.html.

Sillito, C. L., and S. Salari (2011). Child outcomes and risk factors in U.S. homicide-suicide cases, 1999–2004. *Journal of Family Violence* 26: 285–97.

Silverstein, J. (2015). Texas judge returned children to Houston killer David Conley in 2013 case: Report. *New York Daily News*, Aug. 23. www.nydailynews.com/news/national/judge-returned-kids-houston-killer-david-conley-2013-article-1.2324564.

——— (2016). Virginia Tech students worked together on elaborate plot to kill teen girl: Prosecutors. *New York Daily News*, Feb. 4. www.nydailynews.com/news/national/virginia-tech-student-charged-teen-death-denied-bail-article-1.2520217.

Sinclair, D. (2004). *Overcoming the Backlash: Telling the Truth about Power, Privilege, and Oppression.* London: Centre for Research and Education on Violence Against Women and Children.

Skjørten, K. (2013). Children's voices in Norwegian custody cases. *International Journal of Law, Policy and the Family* 27, no. 3: 289–309.

Slote, K. Y., C. Cuthbert, C. J. Mesh, M. G. Driggers, L. Bancroft, and J. G. Silverman (2005). Battered mothers speak out: Participatory human rights documentation as a model for research and activism in the United States. *Violence Against Women* 11: 1367–95.

Sluser, R., and M. Kaufman (1992). The white ribbon campaign: Mobilizing men to take action. Paper presented at the 17th National Conference on Men and Masculinity, Chicago, July.

Smart, C. (2013). *The Ties That Bind: Law, Marriage and the Reproduction of Patriarchal Relations.* London: Routledge.

Smit, P. R., R. R. de Jong, and C. J. H. Bijleveld (2013). Homicide data in Europe: Definitions, sources, and statistics. In *Handbook of European Homicide Research: Patterns, Explanations, and Country Studies,* edited by M. C. A. Liem and W. A. Pridemore, 5–23. New York: Springer.

Smith, M. D. (1987). The incidence and prevalence of woman abuse in Toronto. *Violence and Victims* 2: 173–87.

——— (1990). Patriarchal ideology and wife beating: A test of a feminist hypothesis. *Violence and Victims* 5: 257–73.

—— (1994). Enhancing the quality of survey data on woman abuse: A feminist approach. *Gender and Society* 8: 109–27.

Snell, J. E., R. J. Rosenwald, and A. Robey (1964). The wife beater's wife: A study of family interaction. *Archives of General Psychiatry* 11: 107–13.

Snider, M. (2015). Game not over: Harassment online persists, women say. *USA Today*, Aug. 18, p. 4B.

Southworth, C., J. Finn, S. Dawson, C. Fraser, and S. Tucker (2007). Intimate partner violence, technology and stalking. *Violence Against Women* 13: 842–56.

Squires, P. (2014). *Gun Crime in Global Contexts*. London: Routledge.

Stark, E. (2007). *Coercive Control: How Men Entrap Women in Personal Life*. New York: Oxford University Press.

Stebnar, B. (2013). "I'm tired of hiding": Revenge-porn victim speaks out over her abuse after she claims ex posted explicit photos of her online. *New York Daily News*, May 3. www.nydailynews.com/news/national/revenge-porn-victim-speaks-article-1.1334147.

Stedman, B. (1917). Right of husband to chastise wife. *Virginia Law Register* 3 (Aug.): 214–48.

Straus, M. A. (2014). Addressing violence by female partners is vital to stop violence against women: Evidence from the multisite batterer intervention evaluation. *Violence Against Women* 20: 889–99.

Straus, M. A., R. J. Gelles, and S. Steinmetz (1981). *Behind Closed Doors: Violence in the American Family*. Garden City, N.J.: Anchor Press/Doubleday.

Stroud, M., and J. Mattise (2014). Jody Hunt was angry, agitated before rampage: Stepson. *Huffington Post*, Dec. 3. www.huffingtonpost.com/2014/12/03/jody-hunt_n_6260678.html.

Stryker, S., and A. S. Macke (1978). Status inconsistency and role conflict. *Annual Review of Sociology* 4: 57–90.

Tanha, M., C. J. A. Beck, A. J. Figueredo, and C. Raghavan (2010). Sex differences in intimate partner violence and the use of coercive control as a motivational factor for intimate partner violence. *Journal of Interpersonal Violence* 25: 1836–54.

Thorne-Finch, R. (1992). *Ending the Silence: The Origins and Treatment of Male Violence against Men*. Toronto: University of Toronto Press.

Toews, J. C. (2010). The disappearing family farm. *Real Truth*, June 10. http://realtruth.org/articles/100607-006-family.html.

Toews, M. L., P. C. McKenry, and B. S. Catlett (2003). Male-initiated partner abuse during marital separation prior to divorce. *Violence and Victims* 18, no. 4: 387–402.

Tolman, R. M., and J. L. Edleson (2011). Intervening with men for violence prevention. In *Sourcebook on Violence against Women*, edited by C. M. Renzetti,

J. L. Edleson, and R. Kennedy Bergen, 2d ed., 351–68. Thousand Oaks, Calif.: Sage.

Truman, J. L., and R. E. Morgan (2014). *Special Report: Nonfatal Domestic Violence, 2003-2012*. Washington, D.C.: U.S. Department of Justice, Bureau of Justice Statistics.

United Nations General Assembly (2006). *In-depth Study of All Forms of Violence Against Women: Report of the Secretary General*. July 6. http://daccess-dds-ny.un.org/doc/UNDOC/GEN/N06/419/74/PDF/N0641974.pdf?OpenElement.

United Nations Office on Drugs and Crime (2011). *2011 Global Study on Homicide: Trends, Contexts, Data*. Vienna: UnODC Statistics and Surveys Section.

University of Kentucky Violence Intervention and Prevention Center (2012). *Green Dots for Men*. www.uky.edu/StudentAffairs/VIPCenter/learn_greendot.php.

Ursel, E. (1986). The state and maintenance of patriarchy: A case study of family and welfare legislation. In *Family, Economy and State*, edited by J. Dickinsin and B. Russell, 150–91. Toronto: Garamond.

Vallee, B. (2007). *The War on Women*. Toronto: Key Porter.

Varcoe, C., and L. G. Irwin (2004). "If I killed you, I'd get the kids": Women's survival and protection work with child custody and access in the context of woman abuse. *Qualitative Sociology* 27: 77–99.

Vargas Martin, M., M. A. Garcia-Ruiz, and A. Edwards (2011). Preface. In *Technology for Facilitating Humanity and Combating Social Deviations: Interdisciplinary Perspectives*, edited by M. Vargas Martin, M. A. Garcia Ruiz, and A. Edwards, xxii–xxvii. Hershey, Pa.: Information Science Reference.

Ver Steegh, N., and C. Dalton (2008). Report from the Wingspread Conference on domestic violence and family courts. *Family Court Review* 46, no. 3: 454–75.

Ver Steegh, N., and G. Davis (2015). Calculating safety: Reckoning with domestic violence in the context of child support parenting time initiatives. *Family Court Review* 53: 279–91.

Violence Policy Center (2015). *More than 1,600 women murdered by men in one year, new study finds*. Washington, D.C.: VPC. www.vpc.org/press/more-than-1600-women-murdered-by-men-in-one-year-new-study-finds.

Volant, A. M., J. A. Johnson, E. Gullone, and G. J. Coleman (2008). The relationship between domestic violence and animal abuse: An Australian study. *Journal of Interpersonal Violence* 23: 1277–95.

Wakefield, S., and C. Wildeman (2014). *Children of the Prison Boom: Mass Incarceration and the Future of American Inequality*. New York: Oxford University Press.

Walker, L. (1979). *The Battered Woman*. New York: Harper and Row.

Walker, R., T. K. Logan, C. E. Jordan, and J. C. Campbell (2004). An integrative review of separation in the context of victimization: Consequences and implications for women. *Trauma, Violence, and Abuse* 5: 143–93.

Warshaw, R. (1988). *I Never Called It Rape*. New York: Harper and Row.

Wastler, S. (2010). The harm in sexting? Analyzing the constitutionality of child pornography statutes that prohibit the voluntary production, possession, and dissemination of sexually explicit images by teenagers. *Harvard Journal of Law and Gender* 33: 687–702.

Websdale, N. (1998). *Rural Woman Battering and the Justice System: An Ethnography*. Thousand Oaks, Calif.: Sage.

—— (1999). *Understanding Domestic Homicide*. Thousand Oaks, Calif.: Sage.

—— (2003). Reviewing domestic violence deaths. *NIJ Journal* 250: 26–31.

Websdale, N., M. Town, and B. Johnson (1999). Domestic violence fatality reviews: From a culture of blame to a culture of safety. *Juvenile and Family Court Journal* (spring): 61–74.

Weins, W. J. (2014). Concepts and context. In *Sexting and Youth*, edited by T. Heistand and W. J. Weins, 63–76. Durham, N.C.: Carolina Academic Press.

Weisheit, R. A., D. N. Falcone, and L. E. Wells (2006). *Crime and Policing in Rural and Small-town America*. 3d ed. Prospect Heights, Ill.: Waveland Press.

Wells, L. E., and D. N. Falcone (2008). Rural crime and policing in American Indian communities. *Southern Rural Criminology* 23: 199–225.

Wendt, S. (2009). *Domestic Violence in Rural Australia*. Annandale, NSW, Australia: Federation Press.

Wilkinson, S. (1998). Focus groups in feminist research: Power, interaction, and the co-construction of meaning. *Women's Studies International Forum* 21: 111–25.

Williams, S. L., and I. H. Frieze (2005). Courtship behaviors, relationship violence, and breakup persistence in college men and women. *Psychology of Women Quarterly* 29: 248–57.

Wilson, J. S., and N. Websdale (2006). Domestic violence fatality review teams: An interprofessional model to reduce deaths. *Journal of Interprofessional Care* 20: 535–44. http://doi.org/10.1080/13561820600959253.

Wilson, M., and M. Daly (1992). Till death do us part. In *Femicide: The Politics of Women Killing*, edited by J. Radford and D. E. H. Russell, 83–98. New York: Twayne.

—— (1993). Spousal homicide risk and estrangement. *Violence and Victims* 8: 3–16.

—— (1998). Lethal and nonlethal violence against wives and the evolutionary psychology of male proprietariness. In *Rethinking Violence against Women*, edited by R. E. Dobash and R. P. Dobash, 224–30. Thousand Oaks, Calif.: Sage.

Wilson, M., M. Daly, and A. Daniele (1995). Familicide: The killing of spouse and children. *Aggressive Behavior* 21: 275–91.

Wilson, W. J. (1987). *The Truly Disadvantaged: The Inner-city, the Underclass and Public Policy*. Chicago: University of Chicago Press.

—— (1996). *When Work Disappears: The World of the New Urban Poor*. New York: Knopf.

Wilson, W. J., and R. P. Taub (2006). *There Goes the Neighborhood: Racial, Ethnic, and Class Tensions in Four Chicago Neighborhoods and Their Meaning for America*. New York: Knopf.

Wolcott, I., and J. Hughes (1999). *Towards Understanding the Reasons for Divorce*. Working Paper 20. Melbourne: Australian Institute of Family Studies. https://aifs.gov.au/publications/towards-understanding-reasons-divorce.

Wolfe, D. A., C. V. Crooks, V. Lee, A. McIntyre-Smith, and P. G. Jaffe (2003). The effects of children's exposure to domestic violence: A meta-analysis and critique. *Clinical Child and Family Psychology Review* 6: 171–87.

Women's Aid (2015). *Women's Aid Welcomes Coercive Control Law*. Bristol, Engl.: Women's Aid. www.womensaid.org.uk/womens-aid-welcomes-coercive-control-law.

Wood, K. (2005). Contextualizing group rape in post-apartheid South Africa. *Culture, Health, and Sexuality* 7: 303–17.

Working to Halt Online Abuse (2013). *Online harassment/cyberstalking statistics*. www.haltabuse.org/resources/stats.

World Bank (2013). *Rural population (% of total population) in Canada*. www.tradingeconomic.con/canada/rural-population-wb-data.html.

World Health Organization (2012). *Estimating Global Homicide Rates*. Geneva, Switzerland: WHO. www.who.int/violence_injury_prevention/violence/status_report/2014/report/Estimating_global_homicide_deaths.pdf.

Wuest, J., and M. Merritt-Gray (1999). Not going back: Sustaining the separation in the process of leaving abusive relationships. *Violence Against Women* 5: 110–33.

Xie, M., K. Heimer, and J. L. Lauritsen (2012). Violence against women in U.S. metropolitan areas: Changes in women's status and risk, 1980–2004. *Criminology* 50: 105–44.

Young, J. (2013). *The Criminological Imagination*. Malden, Mass.: Polity.

Yu, T., G. S. Pettit, J. E. Lansford, K. A. Dodge, and J. E. Bates (2010). The interactive effects of marital conflict and divorce on parent–adult children's relationships. *Journal of Marriage and Family* 72: 282–92.

Zabala, L., and R. Stickney (2015). "Revenge porn" defendant sentenced to 18 years. www.nbcnewyork.com/news/national-international/Kevin-Bollaert-Revenge-Porn-Sentencing-San-Diego-298603981.html.

Zeoli, A. M., E. A. Rivera, C. M. Sullivan, and S. Kubiak (2013). Post-separation abuse of women and their children: Boundary-setting and family court utilization among victimized mothers. *Journal of Family Violence* 28: 547–60.

Zorza, J. (2007). The "friendly parent" concept: Another gender biased legacy from Richard Gardner. *Domestic Violence Report* 12: 65–78.

abuse, 5, 9, 18, 28, 32, 72, 74, 128, 129, 170; alcohol, 43; drug, 43; economic, 146; economical, 17; emotional, 12, 16, 146; male-to-female, 11; mental, 132; paper, 118; physical, 12, 17, 25, 132, 146; psychological, 13, 15, 17, 38, 146; sexual, 9, 17, 25; spiritual, 17; substance, 39; verbal, 17. *See also* child abuse *and* image-based sexual abuse *and* Partner Abuse *and* separation/divorce abuse *and* woman abuse

Acker, S. E., 170, 172

Adams, D., 94, 114

African American, 51; men, 44; women, 43, 60

aggrieved entitlement, 21

alcohol abuse. *See* abuse

Aldarondo, E., 56

Alvi, S., 109, 110

Amato, P. R., 131, 132

America, 53, 76, 87, 103, 110, 121, 144; rural, 57, 63

Anderson, D. K., 56

angry white men, 21, 23, 24, 25, 26, 27

antifeminist: backlash, 21, 25; men and women, 26; researchers, 20

Arendell, T. J., 113

assault, 55, 96; lethal, 8; lethal and nonlethal, 7; nonlethal physical, 38, 54, 62; physical, 25; separation, 10.

See also attack *and* pornography *and* separation/divorce assault *and* sexual assault

attack, 8, 17. *See also* assault

Australia, 12, 36, 39, 41, 58, 73, 79, 117, 118, 119, 120, 127, 132, 133, 134, 137, 153, 164, 167, 169, 171

Bachman, R., 59

back talk, 51

backlash. *See* antifeminist backlash

Ball, M, 11

Ball, R. A., 87

Bancroft, L., 76

batterer(s), 15, 43, 56, 93, 96, 98, 117, 118, 125, 126, 131, 139, 140, 142, 143, 160; programs, 146, 148, 165; sporadic, 95, 97

Bergen, R. K., 88, 102

Berkshire, Sharon Kay, 1, 4

Best Interest of the Child, 133

Biroscak, B. K., 42

bitcoins, 78

Black Twitter, 71, 173. *See also* social media

Black, D., 121

Block, C. R., 11, 114

Bonds-Raacke, J., 72

Bonistall, E., 97

Bourgois, P., 112

Bowker, L. H., 44, 46, 92, 95, 96
Boyd, S. B., 128–29
Brinig, M. F., 127, 139
Brown, J. D., 82
Brownridge, 4, 8, 10, 57, 59, 114,
Brownstein, H. H., 111,
bullying, 74, 75
Burgess, J., 120
Burleigh, N., 24
Butts, J. D., 43
Bybee, D. I., 55

Campbell, H., 108
Campbell, J. C., 42, 55, 56
Canada, 12, 18, 27, 39, 41, 49, 58, 127, 133,
    149, 167, 169; and filicide, 113, public
    housing in, 110–11
Canadian national survey, 9, 25–26
Cao, L., 32
Carrington, K., 101, 107
challenge thesis, 91, 100,
Charan case, 40–41
Chereb, S., 123, 124
child abuse, 27, 116, 120, 121, 127, 131, 157,
    158; syndrome, 30. See also abuse
child custody, 135, 139, 140, 157, 178n2;
    evaluation, 137, 138
child support, 2, 117; definition of, 3–10
children, 18, 19, 27, 41, 115, 119, 122, 123,
    124, 126, 128, 129, 130, 131, 133, 134,
    135, 138, 140, 151, 160, 161, 162, 174;
    suicide attempts, 123
coercive control, 15–17, 93, 158; crimi-
    nalizing, 153–54
coercive entrapment, 17
cohabitation, 9, 76
common-law: partner, 9, union, 10
Community Accountability Wheel, 142,
    149
conflict resolution, 99–100, 149
Conflict Tactics Scale, 20
Conley, David, 34, 151, 152
contextual factors, 161
co-parenting, 118, 125, 127, 129. See also
    parenting
Corsianos, M., 168
Cratty, A., 72

crime control, 24
criminology: orthodox, 87, 108
Crisafi, D. N., 72
Crofts, T. 156
Cullen, F. T., 87.
Currie, E., 111
Cusimano, A.M., 130
cyberstalking, 67–70, 74, 75; separation/
    divorce, 69. See also stalking

Daly, M., 36, 42, 87, 91, 100, 103, 114,
    118. See also male proprietariness
    thesis
Daniele, A., 118
Davis, G., 129
Davis, K. E., 125
De Graaf, P.M., 132–33
DeKeseredy, W. S., 7, 10, 11, 13, 17, 18, 21,
    24, 25, 27, 44, 45, 48, 49, 50, 51, 53,
    58, 59, 60, 61, 62, 63, 77, 88, 66, 91,
    92, 93, 94, 95, 96, 97, 98, 99, 100,
    101, 103, 104, 105, 109, 110, 114,
    146, 168
Dempster, J. M., 109
DePrince, A. P., 161
Dines, G., 50
divorce, 3, 4, 10, 15, 29, 90, 96, 99, 112,
    113, 116, 120, 124, 125, 126, 128, 129,
    130, 131, 132, 133, 134, 157, 158;
    mediation, 99–100
Dobash, R. E., 35, 48, 91, 98
Dobash, R. P., 35, 48, 91, 98
domestic violence, 19, 21, 25, 36, 41, 85,
    98, 119, 123, 127, 132, 137, 139, 146,
    149, 153; homicides, 122; on children,
    121
domestic violence fatality review teams,
    40
Dragiewicz, M., 27, 59, 119, 120,
Drozd, L. M., 127, 139
Duluth Model. See Pence, Ellen
DVFRT, 40

economic exclusion/male peer support
    model, 110. See also male peer
    support model
Elam, P., 72–73

Ellis, D., 7, 30, 44, 91, 92, 93, 94, 95, 96, 97, 98, 99, 100, 103, 114
emotional separation, 4
employment, 61,
End Revenge Porn, 97, 81
Ericksen, J., 125
Eth, S., 122
exit, 6, 103; female emotional, 5; interventions invoked by, 91, 92, 94, 98, 99, 100; via shelters, 98, 99; women-initiated, 10, 88

Fabricius, A., 24
Facebook, 23, 24, 26, 70, 72, 170. *See also* social media
Faller, K. C., 139
familicide, 118, 160
family law, 27, 43, 116, 124, 125, 126, 127, 129, 130, 131, 132, 133, 134, 137, 138, 140, 146, 157, 158, 160
femicide, 32, 33, 36, 37, 38, 39, 40, 41, 44, 54, 69, 93, 94, 96, 99, 112, 121, 122, 126, 160; separation/divorce, 43, 44, 91, 94, 100
feminist, 23, 25, 31, 73, 86, 166, 167, 169; research, 147; scholar, 32, 101, 146; theory, 107, 140
filicide, 118, 120; retaliating, 18; separation/divorce, 119
Finkelhor, D., 9, 101
First Amendment, 155, 156,
Fisher, E. R., 93, 94, 95, 97
Fleury, R. E., 55, 57
Flickr, 71. *See also* social media
Fontes, L., 15, 17, 38
Franklin, C. A., 107
Frederick, L. M., 127, 139
Friendly parent, 19, 129, 134, 135
Funk, R. E., 167, 168
Funnell, N., 84

Gallup-Black, A., 49
Gardner, R., 135
gender, 85, 106, 108, 148, 149; structure, 103
Global Study on Homicide, 39
Godenzi, A., 167

Goetting, A., 92, 160
Goldenberg, M. J., 32, 148
Gondolf, E. W., 93, 94, 95, 97
gonzo, 50
Goodmark, L., 85
Google+, 71
Greenberg, M. A., 167
Greeson, M. L., 19
Grisso, J. A., 56
gun control, 149, 151

Hall, S., 86
Hall-Sanchez, A., 24, 47, 48, 49, 51, 53, 60, 104, 105, 106, 107
Hamby, S., 97, 100
handgun control, 153
Hardesty, J. L., 56, 123, 139
Haselschwerdt, M. L., 92
Hayes, B. E., 115
Henderson, A. D., 125
Henry, N., 78, 79
Henson, B., 85
heteronormativity, 11
Hinduja, S., 74
Hispanic women, 43, 60
Hogg, R., 107
Holland, K. M., 120, 127
Holt, T. J., 85
Holzman, H. R., 109
homicide, 27, 35, 36, 39, 41, 42, 43, 94, 118, 119, 122, 150, 151, 153; same-sex intimate partner, 39; separation/divorce, 40; spousal, 87; -suicide, 118, 120, 122. *See also* familicide *and* femicide *and* filicide *and* intimate femicide *and* murder
Hotaling, G., 114
Huessy, J., 111
Hughes, J., 132
Hunt, J. L., 1, 2, 4, 35, 92
Hyatt, R. A., 109

image-based sexual abuse, 78, 79, 155, 157. *See also* abuse *and* revenge pornography
Iniguez, N., 155–56
Instagram, 71. *See also* social media

Internet, 21, 22, 23, 34, 52, 65, 70, 71, 72, 74, 76, 77, 78, 82, 83, 150, 173
intimate femicide, 1, 2, 35, 36, 37, 39, 41, 43, 48, 49, 91, 95, 97, 99, 100, 114, 151, 153. *See also* familicide *and* femicide *and* filicide *and* homicide *and* intimate femicide *and* murder
intimate partner, 2, 21, 35, 37, 38, 40, 41, 48, 58, 59, 79, 88, 91, 92, 94, 150, 157, 166; female, 115; homicide, 39, 40, 42, 49; relationship, 18, 25; violence, 11, 12, 19, 21, 40, 135, 175n9
intimate relationship, 10, 23
intimate violence, 20,
Irwin, C.G., 120
Isreal, 39

Jackson, V., 151
Jacobs, H., 79, 81
Jacobson, N.S., 56
Jeltsen, M., 150
Jensen, R., 76
Jewkes, R., 46

Kalmijn, M., 132–33
Kaplan, T., 121
Katz, J., 166, 167, 170
Keller, S., 82
Kempe, H., 30
keylogging. *See* spyware
Kik, 71. *See also* social media
Kimmel, M., 21
Kirkwood, C., 12, 16
Kirkwood, D., 120
Klein, R., 174

LaCapria, K., 73
Laing, M., 134
Lampard, R., 132
Lamphere, R.D., 78
legal separation, 4; lethal and nonlethal, 2
Leighton, P., 153
Lewandowski, L.A., 122, 126
Lilly, J.R., 87
Loftin, C., 153
Logan, T.K., 163

Lovell, N., 72
loyalty/love: interventions invoked by, 91, 92, 94, 95, 96
Luke's Place, xii, 18, 19, 179n1
Lyndon, A., 72

MacDonald, G.S., 130–31, 138, 159
MacLeod, L., 92, 164
Maier, S.L., 109
male dominance, 44
male peer support, 44, 46, 47, 48, 101, 104, 109, 110, 113; and separation/ divorce assault, 63; groups, 74; model of separation and divorce sexual assault, 101; rural, 49. *See also* assault
male proprietariness, 99, 103, 104, 112, 113; thesis, 87. *See also* proprietariness
marital status, ix, 54, 112, 114, 122
masculinity, 45, 102, 104, 107, 108, 163. *See also* rural
mass shootings, 35, 149, 150, 151, 152, 169
Matlow, R.B., 161
McFarlane, J.M., 38, 39
McGlynn, C., 78, 80–81
McIntosh, J.A., 131
McNair, B., 50
media, 2, 27, 36, 160, 167; mass, 21, 50. *See also* social media
mediation, 125
Menaker, T.A., 107
Messinger, A.M., 11
Messner, M.A., 167
Miller, S.L., 97
minor aggression, 10
misogynist(s), 23, 25, 26, 73, 143
Moloney, L., 116
Montreal Massacre, 169
Moracco, K.E., 43
Mulcahy, J.M., 111
murder, 2, 119, 121, 149, 153; and children, 123. *See also* familicide *and* femicide *and* homicide

National Crime Victimization Survey, ix, 59, 60, 62

National Rifle Association, 152
Navarro, J. N., 67, 69
NCVS, ix, 59, 60, 62
New York Times, 22, 84,
NiCarthy, G., 12,
North America, 20, 60, 76, 87, 101, 103,
    109, 110, 144, 154, 164; shelters, 14

O'Brien, J. E., 29, 30
O'Hagan, K., 120,
Obama, B., 149, 150
Ontario Women's Directorate, 168

Parental Alienation Syndrome, 135, 136,
    137
parenting, 19, 43, 113, 125, 128, 129, 133,
    139, 140; post-divorce, 56, 126;
    post-separation, 128. See also
    co-parenting
Partner Abuse, 148
PAS, 135, 136, 137
Patchin, J. W., 74
patriarchal, 23, 158, 174; culture, 85;
    dominance and control, 28, 44, 47,
    103, 167; family norms, 128; society,
    90
patriarchy, 26, 27, 102, 103, 107, 112, 114,
    128, 139, 167; familial, 107, 114, 128,
    177n10; societal, 103
Peek-Asa and colleagues, 60
Pence, E., 138, 142, 144
Peretz, T., 167
pet(s), 13, 14, 18, 36, 37, 39, 63, 115, 145
Peterson del Mar, D., 15, 90, 112
physical abuse, 12, 17, 25, 132, 146. See
    also abuse
Pikciunas, K. T., 78
pornography, 50, 52, 53, 54, 75–78,
    176n8; child, 156; involuntary, 78;
    revenge, 80–81, 105, 155, 156, 167,
    168. See also image based sexual
    assault
Porter, T., 166
positivism, 86, 147
Post, L. A., 42
Powell, A., 79
Power and Control Wheel, 142, 144

pregnancy, 62, 82
Previti, 132
proprietariness, 88, 89, 92, 93, 99; and
    separation/divorce assault, 90–91.
    See also male proprietariness
psychological, 13, 15, 17, 38, 146. See also
    abuse
Ptacek, J., 36
public housing, 109, 110, 111, 112
Pynoos, R. S., 122

QNLS, 109, 111, 112
Quality of Neighborhood Life Survey,
    109, 111, 112

Rackley, E., 78, 80–81
rape, 8, 21, 25, 6, 27, 32, 46, 59, 60, 62,
    64, 73, 76, 84, 88, 90, 104, 108;
    culture, 24; gang, 22, 46, 50; marital,
    9, 101, 102
rape-supportive cultures, 76–77, 85
Raphael, J., 22, 109,
Reiman, J., 153
Rennison, C. M., 59, 60, 61, 62
Rentschler, C. A., 23
Renzetti, C. M., 109
Return of Kings, 73, 74. See also
    Valizadeh, D.
revenge porn. See image-based sexual
    abuse and pornography
Reyns, B. W., 85
Rice, R., 20,
Riggio, H. R., 130
Riggs, S. A., 130
Rockell, B. A., 58
Rodger, E., 23, 25, 149, 169
Rogness, M., 101, 103, 105
Roof, D., 21, 151
Runyan, C. W., 43
rural, 6, 18; criminology, 108; mascu
    linity, 107; masculinity crisis/male
    peer support model, 105; Ohio, 47,
    48, 51, 59, 146, 162; women, 45
Russell, D. E. H., 102

Saini, M. A., 135
Salter, M., 156

Saltzman, L., 59
Sampson, R. J., 148
saturation model, 111
Saunders, D. G., 139
Schillings, L., xii, 18, 19, 179n1
Schulman, M. A., 30
Schwartz, M. D., ix, 7, 10, 13, 17, 18, 21,
    44, 45, 48, 49, 50, 51, 58, 59, 60, 62,
    63, 77, 88, 92, 101, 103, 104, 105, 109,
    110, 121, 146
screenlogging. *See* spyware
Scully, D., 64
separation, 3, 7, 8, 10, 29, 90, 94, 98,
    104, 115, 122, 125, 152, 157; and
    children's risk, 42; and divorce, 4,
    8, 10, 36, 37, 47, 48, 140; definition
    of, 8; emotional, 5, 99; killings, 41;
    marital, 87; physical, 5, 17; proximal
    phase of, 7; separation/divorce, 27,
    37, 69, 98, 144
separation/divorce abuse, 33, 141. *See also*
    abuse
separation/divorce assault, 6, 7, 8, 10, 11,
    13, 17, 28, 29, 30, 33, 44, 46, 49, 51,
    54, 55, 58, 61, 105, 108, 162, 163;
    and pornography, 50; in rural
    communities, 101, 103, 104; lethal,
    63; nonlethal, 63, 114; physical, 31;
    risk factors, 48; sexual, 31. *See also*
    assault
separation/divorce violence against
    women, 1, 3, 17, 67, 72, 86, 113, 141,
    153, 161; and new technologies, 65;
    definition of, 17-18
separation/divorce woman abuse, 36,
    113; and homicide, 41-42. *See also*
    abuse; woman abuse
Serious Crime Act, 154
Sernau, S., 105, 110
Sev'er, A., 14, 92
sex, 13, 17, 50, 52, 53, 88
sexting, 81, 82, 83. *See also* image-based
    sexual abuse
sexual abuse, 9, 17, 25. *See also* abuse
sexual assault, 5, 22, 24, 25, 31, 47, 54, 59,
    77, 93, 104, 109; and pornography,
    52; marital, 103; separation/divorce,

13, 47, 53, 113; research, 31; rural,
    104. *See also* assault
Shalansky, C. J., 125
shelter(s), 4, 55-56, 58, 97, 162. *See also*
    exit
Sherman, J., 108
Shin, M., 164
Smart, C., 128
Smith, C., 7, 44, 91, 128
Smith, M. D., 63, 105
Smith, P. K., 42
Snapchat, 71. *See also* social media
Sobolewski, J. M., 131
social media, 23, 24, 26, 71, 84, 85, 170.
    See also Black Twitter; Facebook;
    Flikr; Instagram; Kik; Snapchat;
    Tumblr; Twitter; WhatsApp
Soekin, K. L., 56
South Africa, 39, 46
Southern Poverty Law Center (SPLC), 26
spyware, 68
stalking, 5, 10, 15, 38, 43, 60, 62, 63, 67,
    69, 74, 85, 93, 119, 155; and abuse, 67.
    See also cyberstalking
Stark, E., 7, 27, 102, 153, 154
Stern, S., 82
"stitch rule," 14
streamlining, 46
Stuckless, N., 7, 44, 91, 99
suburban, 48, 49, 53, 58, 59, 60, 61,
    62, 63
Sugarman, D., 114
suicide, 40, 43, 74, 75, 94, 153
Sullivan, C. M., 55
Supplementary Homicide Reports, 35,
    40, 42

technologies: new 83, 170, 171, 173
technology, 66, 67, 84, 85
theory; collective efficacy, 32, 108;
    evolutionary psychological, 87;
    parental alienation, 135, 136-37,
    138, 159; routine activities, 32; social
    disorganization, 108. *See also* Lilly
Thorne-Finch, R., 168
Tolman, R. M., 139
Tomaszewski, E. A., 109

Tumblr, 23, 26, 71. *See also* social media
Twitter, 20, 23, 24, 26, 71, 170, 173

underreporting, 9, 86
unemployment, 3, 108, 111, 112
United States, 12, 24, 25, 26, 30, 35, 39, 40, 42, 43, 48, 49, 58, 60, 63, 83, 110, 118, 127, 133, 137, 150, 151, 152, 153, 156, 160, 165, 167, 169
University of Kentucky Violence Intervention and Prevention Center, 168
urban areas, 6, 48

Valizadeh, D., 73
Varcoe, C., 120
Ver Steegh, N., 129
victimization, 10; female, 8
violence, 3, 5, 11, 12, 18, 19, 20, 32, 56, 57, 61, 93, 95, 99, 100, 125, 129, 142, 146, 157, 158, 165; against wives, 29; after separation, 56; and abuse, 43; economic, 5, 9; emotional, 9, 14; fatal, 36, 43; female, 5, 12; female-on-male, 20; intimate, 2, 20; lethal, 5, 100; male, 5, 24, 43, 93, 108, 112, 128, 166; male-to-female, 7, 12, 24, 36, 49, 64; nonlethal, 36; nonsexual, 103; physical, 5, 12, 14, 56, 60, 89, 90, 125, 126; psychological, 5, 12; post-separation, 4; separation/ divorce violence, 54, 57, 87, 111, 149, 163; sexual, 56, 90; spiritual, 12; verbal, 12
violence against women, 1, 3, 4, 11, 12, 15, 19, 20, 27, 30, 32, 39, 60, 61, 63, 64, 77, 88, 120, 124, 128, 131, 135, 140, 165, 169, 171; male, 21
Violence Against Women Act, 151

Virginia Tech, 72
voice, interventions invoked by, 91, 92, 94, 96, 97, 98

Warshaw, R., 168
Washington, 41, 70
Washington, D.C., 6, 153, 162
Wastler, S., 82
weapon, 43, 48, 49, 60
Websdale, N., 48, 58
Wendt, S., 60
WhatsApp, 71. *See also* social media
White Ribbon Campaign, 166, 169
Wilson, M., 36, 42, 87, 91, 100, 103, 114, 118. *See also* male proprietariness thesis *and* evolutionary psycho logical theory
Winlow, S., 86
Wolcott, I., 132
woman abuse, 12, 18, 19, 20, 30, 32, 33, 36, 37, 40, 59, 61, 66, 89, 97, 101, 103, 104, 109, 110, 114, 116, 118, 120, 121, 124, 126, 140, 142, 147, 148, 166, 167, 170; data, 53; intimate, 111; nonlethal, 42, 149. *See also* abuse *and* pornography
women: Native American, 43, 60; battered, 12, 27, 41, 43, 98, 139, 174
Women Against Feminism (WAF), 23, 24, 25, 26
Women's Aid, 154
women's dangerous exits, 18
World Health Organization, 35
Wright, L., 30

Yik Yak, 83, 84. *See also* social media
Yllo, K., 9, 101
Young, J., 86, 87
YouTube, 24. *See also* social media